Mastering Web Application Development with AngularJS

Build single-page web applications using the power of AngularJS

Pawel Kozlowski

Peter Bacon Darwin

PUBLISHING

BIRMINGHAM - MUMBAI

Mastering Web Application Development with AngularJS

First published: August 2013

Production Reference: 1170813

Published by Packt Publishing Ltd.
Livery Place
35 Livery Street
Birmingham B3 2PB, UK..

ISBN 978-1-78216-182-0

www.packtpub.com

Cover Image by Abhishek Pandey (abhishek.pandey1210@gmail.com)

Credits

Authors

Pawel Kozlowski

Peter Bacon Darwin

Reviewers

Stephane Bisson

Miško Hevery

Lee Howard

Acquisition Editors

Rukhsana Khambatta

Pramila Balan

Lead Technical Editor

Dayan Hyames

Technical Editors

Shashank Desai

Krishnaveni Haridas

Saumya Kunder

Project Coordinators

Arshad Sopariwala

Priyanka Goel

Proofreaders

Judith Bill

Bernadette Watkins

Indexer

Monica Ajmera Mehta

Graphics

Ronak Dhruv

Abhinash Sahu

Production Coordinator

Aditi Gajjar

Cover Work

Aditi Gajjar

About the Authors

Pawel Kozlowski has over 15 years of professional experience in web development and was fortunate enough to work with variety of web technologies, languages, and platforms. He is not afraid of hacking both at client side and server side and always searches for the most productive tools and processes.

Pawel strongly believes in free, open source software. He has been very committed in the AngularJS project and also is very active in the AngularJS community. He also contributes to Angular UI – the companion suite to the AngularJS framework, where he focuses on the Twitter's Bootstrap directives for AngularJS.

When not coding, Pawel spreads a good word about AngularJS at various conferences and meetups.

Acknowledgments

Reflecting on the last few months I can't believe how fortunate I was to work on this book with so many great people. This text wouldn't have been possible without all the help and hard work of you all. Thank you.

Firstly I would like to say a "Thank you" to all the members of the AngularJS team at Google. You are the dream team working on an amazing framework. Keep up the great work! My special thanks go to Brad Green, Miško Hevery, Igor Minar, and Vojta Jína. Brad, thank you for putting Peter and me in contact with the publisher and encouraging us to write this book. Miško, thank you for reviewing our book and bearing with us when we had naive questions about AngularJS. Igor, for your constant support and an endless stream of good hints, which made this book much better. It was a lot of fun to work with all of you guys.

I would like to extend my gratitude to the entire AngularJS community, especially to people with whom I've interacted on the mailing list and other forums. I can't name you all, but your insightful questions were great inspiration for this book. A vibrant, supportive community behind AngularJS is one more reason why this framework is so great.

Thanks are due to all the people at Packt Publishing: Rukhsana Khambatta, Dayan Hyames, and Arshad Sopariwala. You've made the entire writing and publishing process very smooth and straightforward. Thank you.

I would like to thank my co-workers at Amadeus, where I've learned what it takes to be a client-side programmer. Firstly, my managers Bertrand Laporte and Bruno Chabrier. Bertrand, thank you for introducing me to the world of client-side development and encouraging me to write this book. Bruno, thank you for letting me work part time and focus on this project. Thank you both for your generosity. Thanks to Julian Descottes and Corinne Krych, who reviewed an earlier draft of the book and provided valuable feedback.

Very, very special thanks to Peter who agreed to co-author this book with me. Peter, I've throughly enjoyed every minute of working with you on this project. I could hardly dream of a better co-author.

Lastly, but most importantly, I would like to thank my wonderful soon-to-be wife Ania. Without your unconditional support and patience I wouldn't have even thought of starting work on this book.

About the Authors

Peter Bacon Darwin has been programming for over two decades. He worked with .NET from before it was released; he contributed to the development of IronRuby and was an IT consultant for Avanade and IMGROUP before quitting to share his time between freelance development and looking after his kids.

Peter is a notable figure in the AngularJS community. He has recently joined the AngularJS team at Google as an external contractor and is a founder member of the AngularUI project. He has spoken about AngularJS at Devoxx UK and numerous London meetups. He also runs training courses in AngularJS. His consultancy practice is now primarily focused on helping businesses make best use of AngularJS.

I would like to thank the team at Google for giving us AngularJS, in particular the ones who got it all going: Miško Hevery, Igor Minar, Brad Green, and Vojta Jína. They are a constant inspiration. My co-author, Pawel, is the driving force behind this book. He conceived the structure, wrote most of the content, and is a great guy to work with. We have all benefited from the awesome active community that has built up around AngularJS in such a short time, especially the folks in the AngularUI project. Finally, I couldn't have completed the book without the love and support of my wife, Kelyn, and kids, Lily and Zachary.

About the Reviewers

Stephane Bisson has been a developer at ThoughtWorks, a global IT consultancy. He is currently based in Toronto, Canada. He has also worked on several rich web applications for medical, financial, and manufacturing industries.

Miško Hevery has been working as an Agile Coach at Google where he is responsible for coaching Googlers to maintain the high level of automated testing culture. This allows Google to do frequent releases of its web applications with consistent high quality. Previously he worked at Adobe, Sun Microsystems, Intel, and Xerox, where he became an expert in building web applications using web-related technologies such as Java, JavaScript, Flex, and ActionScript. He is very involved in open source community and is an author of several open source projects, most notable of which is AngularJS (`http://angularjs.org`).

Lee Howard has a Computer Science degree from Appalachian State University and is currently the lead programmer analyst for the Northwest Area Health Education Center at Wake Forest Baptist Health Medical Center in Winston-Salem, NC. He has developed a variety of web applications to facilitate the creation, registration, delivery, and completion of live and the online continuing medical education courses for the Northwest AHEC. He has also developed Northwest AHEC's CreditTrakr mobile app for IOS devices, which allows physicians and other medical professionals to track their CME credits with their IOS devices.

www.PacktPub.com

Support files, eBooks, discount offers and more

You might want to visit www.PacktPub.com for support files and downloads related to your book.

Did you know that Packt offers eBook versions of every book published, with PDF and ePub files available? You can upgrade to the eBook version at www.PacktPub.com and as a print book customer, you are entitled to a discount on the eBook copy. Get in touch with us at service@packtpub.com for more details.

At www.PacktPub.com, you can also read a collection of free technical articles, sign up for a range of free newsletters and receive exclusive discounts and offers on Packt books and eBooks.

http://PacktLib.PacktPub.com

Do you need instant solutions to your IT questions? PacktLib is Packt's online digital book library. Here, you can access, read and search across Packt's entire library of books.

Why Subscribe?

- Fully searchable across every book published by Packt
- Copy and paste, print and bookmark content
- On demand and accessible via web browser

Free Access for Packt account holders

If you have an account with Packt at www.PacktPub.com, you can use this to access PacktLib today and view nine entirely free books. Simply use your login credentials for immediate access.

Table of Contents

Preface

AngularJS is a relatively new JavaScript MVC framework but it is the real game changer. It has a novel approach to templating and bi-directional data binding which makes the framework very powerful and easy to use. People constantly report a dramatic reduction in the number of lines of code needed in applications using AngularJS as compared to other approaches.

AngularJS is an outstanding piece of engineering. With its strong emphasis on testing and code quality it promotes good practices for the entire JavaScript ecosystem. Given the quality and novelty of the technology, it is not surprising to see that many people are attracted to the framework, creating a very vibrant and supportive community around AngularJS, which contributes to its growing popularity.

As AngularJS becomes more and more popular, people will start to use it in complex projects. But you will soon face problems that are not solved in the standard documentation or in the simple examples found on the Web. AngularJS, as any other technology, has its own set of idioms, patterns, and best practices that have been uncovered by the community, based on their collective experiences.

This is where this book comes in – it aims to show how to write non-trivial AngularJS applications in a canonical way. Instead of describing how the framework works, this book focuses on how to use AngularJS to write a complex web application. It provides real answers to real questions being asked by the AngularJS community.

In short, this is a book written for application developers, by application developers, and based on real developers questions. In this book you will learn:

- How to build a complete, robust application using existing AngularJS services and directives.

- How to extend AngularJS (directives, services, filters) when there is no out-of-the-box solution
- How to set up a high quality AngularJS development project (code organization, build, testing, performance tuning)

What this book covers

Chapter 1, Angular Zen, serves as an introduction to AngularJS framework and the project. The first chapter outlines project's philosophy, its main concepts, and basic building blocks.

Chapter 2, Building and Testing, lays a foundation for a sample application used in this book. It introduces problem domain and covers topics such as testing and building best practices for the system.

Chapter 3, Communicating with a Back-end Server, teaches us how to fetch data from a remote back-end and feed those data effectively to the UI powered by AngularJS. This chapter has extensive coverage of the promise API.

Chapter 4, Displaying and Formatting Data, assumes that data to be displayed were already fetched from back-end and shows how to render those data in the UI. This chapter discusses the usage of AngularJS directives for UI rendering and filters for data formatting.

Chapter 5, Creating Advanced Forms, illustrates how to allow users to manipulate data through forms and various types of input fields. It covers various input types supported by AngularJS and contains deep dive into forms validation.

Chapter 6, Organizing Navigation, shows how to organize individual screens into an easy-to-navigate application. It starts by explaining role of URLs in single-page web applications and familiarizes a reader with key AngularJS services for managing URLs and navigation.

Chapter 7, Securing Your Application, goes into the details of securing single-page web applications written using AngularJS. It covers the concepts and techniques behind authenticating and authorizing users.

Chapter 8, Building Your Own Directives, serves as an introduction to one of the most exciting parts of the AngularJS: directives. It will guide the reader through a structure of sample directives as well as demonstrate testing approaches.

Chapter 9, Building Advanced Directives, is based on *Chapter 8, Building Your Own Directives* and covers more advanced topics. It is filled with a real-life directive examples clearly illustrating complex techniques.

Chapter 10, Building AngularJS Web Applications for an International Audience, deals with internationalization of AngularJS applications. Covered topics include approaches to translating templates as well as managing locale-dependent settings.

Chapter 11, Writing Robust AngularJS Web Applications focuses on non-functional, performance requirements for web applications. It peeks under the hood of AngularJS to familiarize readers with its performance characteristics. A good understanding of AngularJS internals will allow us to avoid common performance-related pitfalls.

Chapter 12, Packaging and Deploying AngularJS Web Applications will guide you through a process of preparing a finished application for production deployment. It illustrates how to optimize application load with a special focus on the landing page.

What you need for this book

To experiment with AngularJS examples all you need is a web browser and a text editor (or your favorite IDE). But in order to take full advantage of this book we would recommend installing `node.js` (`http://nodejs.org/`) and its `npm` package manager with the following modules:

- Grunt (`http://gruntjs.com/`)
- Karma runner (`http://karma-runner.github.io`)

Code examples illustrating interactions with a back-end are making use of a cloud-hosted MongoDB database (MongoLab) so a working internet connection is needed to run many examples from this book.

Who this book is for

This book will be mostly useful to developers who are evaluating or have decided to use AngularJS for a real-life project. You should have some prior exposure to AngularJS, at least through basic examples. We assume that you've got working knowledge of HTML, CSS, and JavaScript.

Conventions

In this book, you will find a number of styles of text that distinguish between different kinds of information. Here are some examples of these styles, and an explanation of their meaning.

Code words in text are shown as follows: "We can include other contexts through the use of the `include` directive."

A block of code is set as follows:

```
angular.module('filterCustomization', [])
  .config(function ($provide) {
varcustomFormats = {
    'fr-ca': {
      'fullDate': 'y'
    }
  };
```

When we wish to draw your attention to a particular part of a code block, the relevant lines or items are set in bold:

```
<head>
<meta charset="utf-8">
<script src="/lib/angular/angular.js"></script>
<script src="/lib/angular/angular-locale_<%= locale %>.js"></script>
<base href="/<%= locale %>/">
```

New terms and **important words** are shown in bold. Words that you see on the screen, in menus or dialog boxes for example, appear in the text like this: "clicking the **Next** button moves you to the next screen".

Warnings or important notes appear in a box like this.

Tips and tricks appear like this.

Reader feedback

Feedback from our readers is always welcome. Let us know what you think about this book—what you liked or may have disliked. Reader feedback is important for us to develop titles that you really get the most out of.

To send us general feedback, simply send an e-mail to feedback@packtpub.com, and mention the book title via the subject of your message.

If there is a topic that you have expertise in and you are interested in either writing or contributing to a book, see our author guide on www.packtpub.com/authors.

Customer support

Now that you are the proud owner of a Packt book, we have a number of things to help you to get the most from your purchase.

Downloading the example code

You can download the example code files for all Packt books you have purchased from your account at http://www.packtpub.com. If you purchased this book elsewhere, you can visit http://www.packtpub.com/support and register to have the files e-mailed directly to you.

Errata

Although we have taken every care to ensure the accuracy of our content, mistakes do happen. If you find a mistake in one of our books—maybe a mistake in the text or the code—we would be grateful if you would report this to us. By doing so, you can save other readers from frustration and help us improve subsequent versions of this book. If you find any errata, please report them by visiting http://www.packtpub.com/submit errata, selecting your book, clicking on the errata submission form link, and entering the details of your errata. Once your errata are verified, your submission will be accepted and the errata will be uploaded on our website, or added to any list of existing errata, under the Errata section of that title. Any existing errata can be viewed by selecting your title from http://www.packtpub.com/support.

Piracy

Piracy of copyright material on the Internet is an ongoing problem across all media. At Packt, we take the protection of our copyright and licenses very seriously. If you come across any illegal copies of our works, in any form, on the Internet, please provide us with the location address or website name immediately so that we can pursue a remedy.

Please contact us at copyright@packtpub.com with a link to the suspected pirated material.

We appreciate your help in protecting our authors, and our ability to bring you valuable content.

Questions

You can contact us at questions@packtpub.com if you are having a problem with any aspect of the book, and we will do our best to address it.

1
Angular Zen

This chapter serves as an introduction to AngularJS, both the framework and the project behind it. Firstly we are going to take a brief look at the project itself: who drives it, where to find the source code and the documentation, how to ask for help, and so on.

Most of this chapter is filled with introduction to the AngularJS framework, its core concepts, and coding patterns. There is a lot of material to cover, so to make the learning process fast and painless, there are plenty of code examples.

AngularJS is a unique framework that without doubt will shape the web development space in the years to come. This is why the last part of this chapter explains what makes AngularJS so special, how it compares to other existing frameworks, and what we can expect from it in the future.

In this chapter we will cover the following topics:

- How to write a simple Hello World application in AngularJS. In the process of doing so, you will come to know where to find framework source code, its documentation, and community.

- To get familiar with the basic building blocks of any AngularJS application: templates with directives, scopes, and controllers.

- To become aware of the AngularJS sophisticated dependency injection system with all its nuances.

- To understand how AngularJS compares to other frameworks and libraries (especially jQuery) and what makes it so special.

Meet AngularJS

AngularJS is a client-side MVC framework written in JavaScript. It runs in a web browser and greatly helps us (developers) to write modern, single-page, AJAX-style web applications. It is a general purpose framework, but it shines when used to write CRUD (Create Read Update Delete) type web applications.

Getting familiar with the framework

AngularJS is a recent addition to the client-side MVC frameworks list, yet it has managed to attract a lot of attention, mostly due to its innovative templating system, ease of development, and very solid engineering practices. Indeed, its templating system is unique in many respects:

- It uses HTML as the templating language
- It doesn't require an explicit DOM refresh, as AngularJS is capable of tracking user actions, browser events, and model changes to figure out when and which templates to refresh
- It has a very interesting and extensible components subsystem, and it is possible to teach a browser how to interpret new HTML tags and attributes

The templating subsystem might be the most visible part of AngularJS, but don't be mistaken that AngularJS is a complete framework packed with several utilities and services typically needed in single-page web applications.

AngularJS also has some hidden treasures, **dependency injection (DI)** and strong focus on testability. The built-in support for DI makes it easy to assemble a web application from smaller, thoroughly tested services. The design of the framework and the tooling around it promote testing practices at each stage of the development process.

Finding your way in the project

AngularJS is a relatively new actor on the client-side MVC frameworks scene; its 1.0 version was released only in June 2012. In reality, the work on this framework started in 2009 as a personal project of Miško Hevery, a Google employee. The initial idea turned out to be so good that, at the time of writing, the project was officially backed by Google Inc., and there is a whole team at Google working full-time on the framework.

AngularJS is an open source project hosted on GitHub (`https://github.com/angular/angular.js`) and licensed by Google, Inc. under the terms of the MIT license.

The community

At the end of the day, no project would survive without people standing behind it. Fortunately, AngularJS has a great, supportive community. The following are some of the communication channels where one can discuss design issues and request help:

- `angular@googlegroups.com` mailing list (Google group)
- Google + community at `https://plus.google.com/u/0/communities/115368820700870330756`
- #angularjs IRC channel
- [angularjs] tag at `http://stackoverflow.com`

AngularJS teams stay in touch with the community by maintaining a blog (`http://blog.angularjs.org/`) and being present in the social media, Google + (+ AngularJS), and Twitter (`@angularjs`). There are also community meet ups being organized around the world; if one happens to be hosted near a place you live, it is definitely worth attending!

Online learning resources

AngularJS has its own dedicated website (`http://www.angularjs.org`) where we can find everything that one would expect from a respectable framework: conceptual overview, tutorials, developer's guide, API reference, and so on. Source code for all released AngularJS versions can be downloaded from `http://code.angularjs.org`.

People looking for code examples won't be disappointed, as AngularJS documentation itself has plenty of code snippets. On top of this, we can browse a gallery of applications built with AngularJS (`http://builtwith.angularjs.org`). A dedicated YouTube channel (`http://www.youtube.com/user/angularjs`) has recordings from many past events as well as some very useful video tutorials.

Libraries and extensions

While AngularJS core is packed with functionality, the active community keeps adding new extensions almost every day. Many of those are listed on a dedicated website: `http://ngmodules.org`.

Tools

AngularJS is built on top of HTML and JavaScript, two technologies that we've been using in web development for years. Thanks to this, we can continue using our favorite editors and IDEs, browser extensions, and so on without any issues. Additionally, the AngularJS community has contributed several interesting additions to the existing HTML/JavaScript toolbox.

Batarang

Batarang is a Chrome developer tool extension for inspecting the AngularJS web applications. Batarang is very handy for visualizing and examining the runtime characteristics of AngularJS applications. We are going to use it extensively in this book to peek under the hood of a running application. Batarang can be installed from the Chrome's Web Store (*AngularJS Batarang*) as any other Chrome extension.

Plunker and jsFiddle

Both Plunker (`http://plnkr.co`) and jsFiddle (`http://jsfiddle.net`) make it very easy to share live-code snippets (JavaScript, CSS, and HTML). While those tools are not strictly reserved for usage with AngularJS, they were quickly adopted by the AngularJS community to share the small-code examples, scenarios to reproduce bugs, and so on. Plunker deserves special mentioning as it was written in AngularJS, and is a very popular tool in the community.

IDE extensions and plugins

Each one of us has a favorite IDE or an editor. The good news is that there are existing plugins/extensions for several popular IDEs such as Sublime Text 2 (`https://github.com/angular-ui/AngularJS-sublime-package`), Jet Brains' products (`http://plugins.jetbrains.com/plugin?pr=idea&pluginId=6971`), and so on.

AngularJS crash course

Now that we know where to find the library sources and their accompanying documentation, we can start writing code to actually see AngularJS in action. This section of the book lays the foundation for the subsequent chapters by covering AngularJS templates, modularity, and dependency injection. Those are the basic building blocks of any AngularJS web application.

Hello World – the AngularJS example

Let's have a look at the typical "Hello, World!" example written in AngularJS to get the first impression of the framework and the syntax it employs.

```
<html>
<head>
    <script src="http://ajax.googleapis.com/ajax/libs/angularjs/1.0.7/
angular.js"></script>
</head>
```

```
<body ng-app ng-init="name = 'World'">
    <h1>Hello, {{name}}!</h1>
</body>
</html>
```

First of all, we need to include the AngularJS library to make our sample run correctly in a web browser. It is very easy as AngularJS, in its simplest form, is packaged as a single JavaScript file.

 AngularJS library is a relatively small one: a minified and gzipped version has a size of around 30 KB. A minified version without gzip compression has a size of around 80 KB. It doesn't require any third-party dependencies.

For the short examples in this book we are going to use an un-minified, developer-friendly version hosted on Google's **content delivery network (CDN)**. Source code for all versions of AngularJS can be also downloaded from http://code.angularjs.org.

Including the AngularJS library is not enough to have a running example. We need to bootstrap our mini application. The easiest way of doing so is by using the custom ng-app HTML attribute.

Closer inspection of the <body> tag reveals another non-standard HTML attribute: ng-init. We can use ng-init to initialize model before a template gets rendered. The last bit to cover is the {{name}} expression which simply renders model value.

Even this very first, simple example brings to light some important characteristics of the AngularJS templating system, which are as follows:

- Custom HTML tags and attributes are used to add dynamic behavior to an otherwise static HTML document
- Double curly braces ({{expression}}) are used as a delimiter for expressions outputting model values

In the AngularJS, all the special HTML tags and attributes that the framework can understand and interpret are referred to as directives.

Two-way data binding

Rendering a template is straightforward with AngularJS; the framework shines when used to build dynamic web applications. In order to appreciate the real power of AngularJS, let's extend our "Hello World" example with an input field, as shown in the following code:

```
<body ng-app ng-init="name = 'World'">
    Say hello to: <input type="text" ng-model="name">
    <h1>Hello, {{name}}!</h1>
</body>
```

There is almost nothing special about the `<input>` HTML tag apart from the additional `ng-model` attribute. The real magic happens as soon as we begin to type text into the `<input>` field. All of a sudden the screen gets repainted after each keystroke, to reflect the provided name! There is no need to write any code that would refresh a template, and we are not obliged to use any framework API calls to update the model. AngularJS is smart enough to detect model changes and update the DOM accordingly.

Most of the traditional templating system renders templates in a linear, one-way process: a model (variables) and a template are combined together to produce a resulting markup. Any change to the model requires re-evaluation of a template. AngularJS is different because any view changes triggered by a user are immediately reflected in the model, and any changes in the model are instantly propagated to a template.

The MVC pattern in AngularJS

Most existing web applications are based on some form of the well-known **model-view-controller (MVC)** pattern. But the problem with the MVC is that it is not a very precise pattern, but rather a high-level, architectural one. Worse yet, there are many existing variations and derivatives of the original pattern (MVP and MVVM seem to be the most popular ones). To add to the confusion, different frameworks and developers tend to interpret the mentioned patterns differently. This results in situations where the same MVC name is used to describe different architectures and coding approaches. *Martin Fowler* summarizes this nicely in his excellent article on GUI architectures (`http://martinfowler.com/eaaDev/uiArchs.html`):

> *Take Model-View-Controller as an example. It's often referred to as a pattern, but I don't find it terribly useful to think of it as a pattern because it contains quite a few different ideas. Different people reading about MVC in different places take different ideas from it and describe these as 'MVC'. If this doesn't cause enough confusion you then get the effect of misunderstandings of MVC that develop through a system of Chinese whispers.*

The AngularJS team takes a very pragmatic approach to the whole family of MVC patterns, and declares that the framework is based on the MVW (model-view-whatever) pattern. Basically one needs to see it in action to get the feeling of it.

Bird's eye view

All the "Hello World" examples we've seen so far didn't employ any explicit layering strategy: data initialization, logic, and view were all mixed together in one file. In any real-world application, though, we need to pay more attention to a set of responsibilities assigned to each layer. Fortunately, AngularJS provides different architectural constructs that allows us to properly build more complex applications.

 All the subsequent examples throughout the book omit the AngularJS initialization code (scripts inclusion, ng-app attribute, and so on) for readability.

Let's have a look at the slightly modified "Hello World" example:

```
<div ng-controller="HelloCtrl">
    Say hello to: <input type="text" ng-model="name"><br>
    <h1>Hello, {{name}}!</h1>
</div>
```

The ng-init attribute was removed, and instead we can see a new ng-controller directive with a corresponding JavaScript function. The HelloCtrl accepts a rather mysterious $scope argument as follows:

```
var HelloCtrl = function ($scope) {
    $scope.name = 'World';
}
```

Scope

A $scope object in AngularJS is here to expose the domain model to a view (template). By assigning properties to scope instances, we can make new values available to a template for rendering.

Scopes can be augmented with both data and functionality specific to a given view. We can expose UI-specific logic to templates by defining functions on a scope instance.

For example, one could create a getter function for the `name` variable, as given in the following code:

```
var HelloCtrl = function ($scope) {
    $scope.getName = function() {
        return $scope.name;
    };
}
```

And then use it in a template as given in the following code:

```
<h1>Hello, {{getName()}}!</h1>
```

The `$scope` object allows us to control precisely which part of the domain model and which operations are available to the view layer. Conceptually, AngularJS scopes are very close to the ViewModel from the MVVM pattern.

Controller

The primary responsibility of a controller is to initialize scope objects. In practice, the initialization logic consists of the following responsibilities:

- Providing initial model values
- Augmenting `$scope` with UI-specific behavior (functions)

Controllers are regular JavaScript functions. They don't have to extend any framework-specific classes nor call any particular AngularJS APIs to correctly perform their job.

 Please note that a controller does the same job as the `ng-init` directive, when it comes to setting up initial model values. Controllers make it possible to express this initialization logic in JavaScript, without cluttering HTML templates with code.

Model

AngularJS models are plain, old JavaScript objects. We are not obliged to extend any of the framework's base classes nor construct model objects in any special way.

It is possible to take any existing, pure JavaScript classes or objects and use them in the same way as in the model layer. We are not limited to model properties being represented by primitive values (any valid JavaScript object or an array can be used). To expose a model to AngularJS you simply assign it to a `$scope`.

AngularJS is not intrusive and lets us keep model objects free from any framework-specific code.

Scopes in depth

Each `$scope` is an instance of the `Scope` class. The `Scope` class has methods that control the scope's lifecycle, provide event-propagation facility, and support the template rendering process.

Hierarchy of scopes

Let's have another look at the simple `HelloCtrl` example, which we've examined already:

```
var HelloCtrl = function ($scope) {
    $scope.name = 'World';
}
```

The `HelloCtrl` looks similar to a regular JavaScript constructor function, there is absolutely nothing special about it apart from the `$scope` argument. Where might this argument might be coming from?

A new scope was created by the `ng-controller` directive using the `Scope.$new()` method call. Wait a moment; it looks like we need to have at least one instance of a scope to create a new scope! Indeed, AngularJS has a notation of the `$rootScope` (a scope that is a parent of all the other scopes). The `$rootScope` instance gets created when a new application is bootstrapped.

The `ng-controller` directive is an example of a scope-creating directive. AngularJS will create a new instance of the `Scope` class whenever it encounters a scope-creating directive in the DOM tree. A newly-created scope will point to its parent scope using the `$parent` property. There can be many scope-creating directives in the DOM tree and as a result many scopes will be created.

Scopes form a parent-child, tree-like relationship rooted at the `$rootScope` instance. As scopes' creation is driven by the DOM tree, it is not surprising that scopes' tree will mimic the DOM structure.

Now that we know that some directives create new child scopes you might be wondering why all this complexity is needed. To understand this, let's have a look at the example that makes use of a `ng-repeat` repeater directive.

The controller is as follows:

```
var WorldCtrl = function ($scope) {
$scope.population = 7000;
$scope.countries = [
        {name: 'France', population: 63.1},
        {name: 'United Kingdom', population: 61.8},
];
};
```

And the markup fragment looks in the following manner:

```
<ul ng-controller="WorldCtrl">
    <li ng-repeat="country in countries">
        {{country.name}} has population of {{country.population}}
    </li>
    <hr>
    World's population: {{population}} millions
</ul>
```

The `ng-repeat` directive allows us to iterate over a collection of countries and create new DOM elements for each item in a collection. The syntax of the `ng-repeat` directive should be easy to follow; a new variable `country` is created for each item and exposed on a `$scope` to be rendered by a view.

But there is a problem here, that is, a new variable needs to be exposed on a `$scope` for each `country` and we can't simply override previously exposed values. AngularJS solves this problem by creating a new scope for each element in a collection. Newly created scopes will form a hierarchy closely matching the DOM tree structure, and we can visualize this by using the excellent Batarang extension for Chrome as shown in the following screenshot:

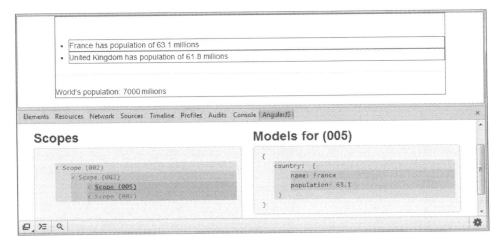

As we can see in the screenshot, each scope (boundaries marked with a rectangle) holds its own set of model values. It's possible to define the same variable on different scopes without creating name collisions (different DOM elements will simply point to different scopes and use variables from a corresponding scope to render a template). This way each item has its own namespace, in the previous example every `<li>` element gets its own scope where the country variable can be defined.

Scopes hierarchy and inheritance

Properties defined on one scope are visible to all child scopes, provided that a child scope doesn't redefine a property using the same name! This is very useful in practice, since we don't need to redefine over and over again properties that should be available throughout a scope hierarchy.

Building on our previous example, let's assume that we want to display the percentage of the world's population that lives in a given country. To do so, we can define the worldsPercentage function on a scope managed by the WorldCtrl as given in the following code:

```
$scope.worldsPercentage = function (countryPopulation) {
    return (countryPopulation / $scope.population)*100;
}
```

And then call this function from each scope instance created by the ng-repeat directive as follows:

```
<li ng-repeat="country in countries">
    {{country.name}} has population of {{country.population}},
    {{worldsPercentage(country.population)}} % of the World's
population
</li>
```

Scope's inheritance in AngularJS follows the same rules as prototypical inheritance in JavaScript (when we try to read a property, the inheritance tree will be traversed upwards till a property is found).

Perils of the inheritance through the scopes hierarchy

Inheritance through the scopes hierarchy is rather intuitive and easy to understand when it comes to the read access. When it comes to the write access, however, things become a little bit complicated.

Let's see what happens if we define a variable on one scope and omit if from a child scope. The JavaScript code is as follows:

```
var HelloCtrl = function ($scope) {
};
```

And the view code is as follows:

```
<body ng-app ng-init="name='World'">
<h1>Hello, {{name}}</h1>
<div ng-controller="HelloCtrl">
    Say hello to: <input type="text" ng-model="name">
    <h2>Hello, {{name}}!</h2>
</div>
</body>
```

If you try to run this code, you will observe that the name variable is visible across the whole application; even if it was defined on the top-most scope only! This illustrates that variables are inherited down the scope hierarchy. In other words, variables defined on a parent scope are accessible in child scopes.

Now, let's observe what will happen if we start to type text into the <input> box, as shown in the following screenshot:

You might be a bit surprised to see that a new variable was created in the scope initialized by the HelloCtrl controller, instead of changing a value set up on the $rootScope instance. This behavior becomes less surprising when we realize that scopes prototypically inherit from each other. All the rules that apply to the prototypical inheritance of objects in JavaScript apply equally to scopes prototypical inheritance. Scopes are just JavaScript objects after all.

There are several ways of influencing properties defined on a parent scope from a child scope. Firstly, we could explicitly reference a parent scope using the $parent property. A modified template would look as follows:

```
<input type="text" ng-model="$parent.name">
```

While it is possible to solve an issue using this example by directly referencing a parent scope, we need to realize that this is a very fragile solution. The trouble is that an expression used by the ng-model directive makes strong assumptions about the overall DOM structure. It is enough to insert another scope-creating directive somewhere above the <input> tag and $parent will be pointing to a completely different scope.

As a rule of thumb, try to avoid using the $parent property as it strongly links AngularJS expressions to the DOM structure created by your templates. An application might easily break as a result of simple changes in its HTML structure.

Another solution involves binding to a property of an object and not directly to a scope's property. The code for this solution is as follows:

```
<body ng-app ng-init="thing = {name : 'World'}">
<h1>Hello, {{thing.name}}</h1>
<div ng-controller="HelloCtrl">
    Say hello to: <input type="text" ng-model="thing.name">
    <h2>Hello, {{thing.name}}!</h2>
</div>
</body>
```

This approach is much better as it doesn't assume anything about the DOM tree structure.

Avoid direct bindings to scope's properties. Two-way data binding to object's properties (exposed on a scope) is a preferred approach.

As a rule of thumb, you should have a dot in an expression provided to the ng-model directive (for example, ng-model="thing.name").

Hierarchy of scopes and the eventing system

Scopes organized in a hierarchy can be used as an event bus. AngularJS allows us to propagate named events with a payload through the scopes' hierarchy. An event can be dispatched starting from any scope and travel either upwards ($emit) or downwards ($broadcast).

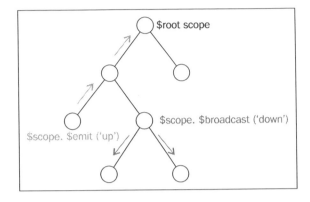

AngularJS core services and directives make use of this event bus to signal important changes in the application's state. For example, we can listen to the $locationChangeSuccess event (broadcasted from the $rootScope instance) to be notified whenever a location (URL in a browser) changes, as given in the following code:

```
$scope.$on('$locationChangeSuccess', function(event, newUrl, oldUrl){

//react on the location change here
//for example, update breadcrumbs based on the newUrl

});
```

The $on method available on each scope instance can be invoked to register a scope-event handler. A function acting as a handler will be invoked with a dispatched event object as its first argument. Subsequent arguments will correspond to the event's payload and are event-type dependent.

Similar to the DOM events, we can call the preventDefault() and stopPropagation() methods on event object. The stopPropagation() method call will prevent an event from bubbling up the scopes' hierarchy, and is available only for events dispatched upwards in the hierarchy ($emit).

> While AngularJS event system is modeled after the DOM one, both event propagation systems are totally independent and have got no common parts.

While events propagated through the scopes' hierarchy are very elegant solutions to several problems (especially when it comes to notifications related to global, asynchronous state changes), those should be used sparingly. Usually we can rely on the two-way data binding to end up with a cleaner solution. In the entire AngularJS framework, there are only three events being emitted ($includeContentRequested, $includeContentLoaded, $viewContentLoaded), and seven events being broadcasted ($locationChangeStart, $locationChangeSuccess, $routeUpdate, $routeChangeStart, $routeChangeSuccess, $routeChangeError, $destroy). As you can see, scope events are used very sparingly and we should evaluate other options (mostly the two-way data binding) before sending custom events.

> Don't try to mimic the DOM event-based programming model in AngularJS. Most of the time there are better ways of structuring your application, and you can go very far with the two-way data binding.

Scopes lifecycle

Scopes are necessary to provide isolated namespaces and avoid variable name collisions. Scopes which are smaller and organized in a hierarchy help in managing memory usage. When one of the scopes is no longer needed, it can be destroyed. As a result, model and functionality exposed on this scope will be eligible for garbage collection.

New scopes are usually brought to life and destroyed by the scope-creating directives. It is also possible to manually create and destroy scopes by calling the $new() and $destroy() methods, respectively (both methods are defined on the Scope type).

View

We've seen enough examples of AngularJS templates to realize that it is not yet another templating language, but quite a different beast. Not only does the framework rely on the HTML for its template syntax and allow us to extend the HTML vocabulary, but it has the unique ability to refresh parts of the screen without any manual intervention!

In reality, AngularJS has even more intimate connections to HTML and the DOM as it depends on a browser to parse the template's text (as a browser would do with any other HTML document). After a browser is done transforming the markup's text to the DOM tree, AngularJS kicks in and traverses the parsed DOM structure. Each time it encounters a directive, AngularJS executes its logic to turn directives into dynamic parts of the screen.

> Since AngularJS depends on a browser to parse templates, we need to ensure that the markup represents valid HTML. Pay special attention to close the HTML tags properly (failing to do so won't produce any error messages, but the view won't be rendered correctly). AngularJS works using the live, valid DOM tree!

AngularJS makes it possible to enrich HTML's vocabulary (we can add new attributes or HTML elements and teach a browser how to interpret them). It is almost similar to creating a new **domain-specific language (DSL)** on top of HTML and instructing a browser on how to make sense of the new instructions. You can often hear that AngularJS "teaches browsers new tricks".

Declarative template view – the imperative controller logic

There are many handy directives shipped with AngularJS, and we are going to cover most of the existing ones in the following chapters. What is probably more important, however, is not the syntax and functionality of individual directives but rather the underlying AngularJS philosophy of building UIs.

AngularJS promotes a declarative approach to UI construction. What it means in practice is that templates are focused on describing a desired effect rather than on ways of achieving it. It all might sound a bit confusing, so an example might come in handy here.

Let's imagine that we were asked to create a form where a user can type in a short message, and then send it by clicking on a button. There are some additional **user-experience (UX)** requirements such as message size should be limited to 100 characters, and the **Send** button should be disabled if this limit is exceeded. A user should know how many characters are left as they type. If the number of remaining characters is less than ten, the displayed number should change the display style to warn users. It should be possible to clear text of a provided message as well. A finished form looks similar to the following screenshot:

Remaining: 74

orem ipsum dolor sit amet,

Send   Clear

The preceding requirements are not particularly challenging and describe a fairly standard text form. Nevertheless, there are many UI elements to coordinate here such as we need to make sure that the button's `disabled` state is managed correctly, the number of remaining characters is accurate and displayed with an appropriate style, and so on. The very first implementation attempt looks as follows:

```
<div class="container" ng-controller="TextAreaWithLimitCtrl">
        <div class="row">
            <textarea ng-model="message">{{message}}</textarea>
        </div>
        <div class="row">
          <button ng-click="send()">Send</button>
          <button ng-click="clear()">Clear</button>
        </div>
</div>
```

Let's use the preceding code as a starting point and build on top of it. Firstly, we need to display the number of remaining characters, which is easy enough, as given in the following code:

```
<span>Remaining: {{remaining()}}</span>
```

The `remaining()` function is defined in the `TextAreaWithLimitCtrl` controller on the `$scope` as follows:

```
$scope.remaining = function () {
    return MAX_LEN - $scope.message.length;
};
```

Next, we need to disable the **Send** button if a message doesn't comply with the required length constraints. This can be easily done with a little help from the `ng-disabled` directive as follows:

```
<button ng-disabled="!hasValidLength()"...>Send</button>
```

We can see a recurring pattern here. To manipulate UI, we only need to touch a small part of a template and describe a desired outcome (display number of remaining characters, disable a button, and so on) in terms of the model's state (size of a message in this case). The interesting part here is that we don't need to keep any references to DOM elements in the JavaScript code and we are not obliged to manipulate DOM elements explicitly. Instead we can simply focus on model mutations and let AngularJS do the heavy lifting. All we need to do is to provide some hints in the form of directives.

Coming back to our example, we still need to make sure that the number of remaining characters changes style when there are only a few characters left. This is a good occasion to see one more example of the declarative UI in action, as given in the following code:

```
<span ng-class="{'text-warning' : shouldWarn()}">
Remaining: {{remaining()}}
</span>
```

where the `shouldWarn()` method is implemented as follows:

```
$scope.shouldWarn = function () {
return $scope.remaining() < WARN_THRESHOLD;
};
```

The CSS class change is driven by the model mutation, but there is no explicit DOM manipulation logic anywhere in the JavaScript code! UI gets repainted based on a declaratively expressed "wish". What we are saying using the `ng-class` directive is this: "the `text-warning` CSS class should be added to the `<span>` element, every time a user should be warned about exceeded character limit". This is different from saying that "when a new character is entered and the number of characters exceeds the limit, I want to find a `<span>` element and change the `text-warning` CSS class of this element".

What we are discussing here might sound like a subtle difference, but in fact declarative and imperative approaches are quite opposite. The imperative style of programming focuses on describing individual steps leading to a desired outcome. With the declarative approach, focus is shifted to a desired result. The individual little steps taken to reach to this result are taken care of by a supporting framework. It is like saying "Dear AngularJS, here is how I want my UI to look when the model ends up in a certain state. Now please go and figure out when and how to repaint the UI".

The declarative style of programming is usually more expressive as it frees developers from giving very precise, low-level instructions. The resulting code is often very concise and easy to read. But for the declarative approach to work, there must be machinery that can correctly interpret higher-level orders. Our programs start to depend on these machinery decisions and we need to give up some of the low-level control. With the imperative approach, we are in full control and can fine tune each and every single operation. We've got more control, but the price to pay for "being in charge" is a lot of lower-level, repetitive code to be written.

People familiar with SQL language will find all this sounding familiar (SQL is a very expressive, declarative language for adhoc data querying). We can simply describe the desired result (data to be fetched) and let a (relational) database figure out how to go about retrieving specified data. Most of the time, this process works flawlessly and we quickly get what we have asked for. Still there are cases where it is necessary to provide additional hints (indexes, query planner hints, and so on) or take control over data-retrieval process to fine tune performance.

Directives in AngularJS templates declaratively express the desired effect, so we are freed from providing step-by-step instructions on how to change individual properties of DOM elements (as is often the case in applications based on jQuery). AngularJS heavily promotes declarative style of programming for templates and imperative one for the JavaScript code (controllers and business logic). With AngularJS , we rarely apply low-level, imperative instructions to the DOM manipulation (the only exception being code in directives).

> As a rule of thumb, one should never manipulate the DOM elements in AngularJS controllers. Getting a reference to a DOM element in a controller and manipulating element's properties indicates imperative approach to UI - something that goes against AngularJS way of building UIs.

Declarative UI templates written using AngularJS directives allow us to describe quickly complex, interactive UIs. AngularJS will take all the low-level decisions on when and how to manipulate parts of the DOM tree. Most of the time AngularJS does "the right thing" and updates the UI as expected (and in a timely fashion). Still, it is important to understand the inner workings of AngularJS, so that we can provide appropriate hints to the framework if needed. Using the SQL analogy once again here, most of the time we don't need to worry about the work done by a query planner. But when we start to hit performance problems, it is good to know how query planner arrived at its decisions so that we can provide additional hints. The same applies to UIs managed by AngularJS: we need to understand the underlying machinery to effectively use templates and directives.

Modules and dependency injection

Vigilant readers have probably noticed that all the examples presented so far were using global constructor functions to define controllers. But global state is evil, it hurts application structure, makes code hard to maintain, test, and read. By no means is AngularJS suggesting usage of global state. On the contrary, it comes with a set of APIs that make it very easy to define modules and register objects in those modules.

Modules in AngularJS

Let's see how to turn an ugly, globally-defined controller definition into its modular equivalent, before a controller is declared as follows:

```
var HelloCtrl = function ($scope) {
    $scope.name = 'World';
}
```

And when using modules it looks as follows:

```
angular.module('hello', [])
  .controller('HelloCtrl', function($scope){
    $scope.name = 'World';
  });
```

AngularJS itself defines the global `angular` namespace. There are various utility and convenience functions exposed in this namespace, and `module` is one of those functions. A `module` acts as a container for other AngularJS managed objects (controllers, services, and so on). As we are going to see shortly, there is much more to learn about modules than simple namespacing and code organization.

To define a new module we need to provide its name as the very first argument to the `module` function call. The second argument makes it possible to express a dependency on other modules (in the preceding module we don't depend on any other modules).

A call to the `angular.module` function returns an instance of a newly created module. As soon as we've got access to this instance, we can start defining new controllers. This is as easy as invoking the `controller` function with the following arguments:

- Controller's name (as string)
- Controller's constructor function

Globally-defined controller's constructor functions are only good for quick-code examples and fast prototyping. Never use globally-defined controller functions in larger, real life applications.

A module is defined now, but we need to inform AngularJS about its existence. This is done by providing a value to the ng-app attribute as follows:

```
<body ng-app="hello">
```

Forgetting to specify a module's name in the ng-app attribute is a frequent mistake and a common source of confusion. Omitting a module name in the ng-app attribute will result in an error indicating that a controller is undefined.

Collaborating objects

As we can see, AngularJS provides a way to organize objects into modules. A module can be used not only to register objects that are directly invoked by the framework (controllers, filters, and so on) but any objects defined by applications' developers.

Module pattern is extremely useful to organize our code, but AngularJS goes one step further. In addition to registering objects in a namespace, it is also possible to declaratively describe dependencies among those objects.

Dependency injection

We could already see that the $scope object was being mysteriously injected into controllers' instances. AngularJS is somehow able to figure out that a new scope instance is needed for a controller, and then creates a new scope instance and injects it. The only thing that controllers had to do was to express the fact that it depends on a $scope instance (no need to indicate how a new $scope object should be instantiated, should this $scope instance be a newly created one or reused from previous calls). The whole dependency management boils down to saying something along those lines: "To function correctly I need a dependency (collaborating object): I don't know from where it should be coming or how it should be created. I just know that I need one, so please provide it".

AngularJS has the dependency injection (DI) engine built in. It can perform the following activities:

- Understand a need for a collaborator expressed by objects
- Find a needed collaborator
- Wire up objects together into a fully-functional application

The idea of being able to declaratively express dependencies is a very powerful one; it frees objects from having to worry about collaborating objects' lifecycles. Even better, all of a sudden it is possible to swap collaborators at will, and then create different applications by simply replacing certain services. This is also a key element in being able to unit test components effectively.

Benefits of dependency injection

To see the full potential of a system integrated using dependency injection, let's consider an example of a simple notification service to which we can push messages and retrieve those messages later on. To somewhat complicate the scenario, let's say that we want to have an archiving service. It should cooperate with our `notifications` service in the following way, as soon as the number of notifications exceeds a certain threshold the oldest notifications should be pushed to an archive. The additional trouble is that we want to be able to use different archiving services in different application. Sometimes dumping old messages to a browser's console is all that is needed; other times we would like to send expired notifications to a server using XHR calls.

The code for the notifications service could look as follows:

```
var NotificationsService = function () {
  this.MAX_LEN = 10;
  this.notificationsArchive = new NotificationsArchive();
  this.notifications = [];
};


NotificationsService.prototype.push = function (notification) {

  var newLen, notificationToArchive;

  newLen = this.notifications.unshift(notification);
  if (newLen > this.MAX_LEN) {
    notificationToArchive = this.notifications.pop();
    this.notificationsArchive.archive(notificationToArchive);
  }
};


NotificationsService.prototype.getCurrent = function () {
  return this.notifications;
};
```

The preceding code is tightly coupled to one implementation of an archive (NotificationsArchive), since this particular implementation is instantiated using the new keyword. This is unfortunate since the only contract to which both classes need to adhere to is the archive method (accepting a notification message to be archived).

The ability to swap collaborators is extremely important for testability. It is hard to imagine testing objects in isolation without the ability to substitute real implementations with fake doubles (mocks). On the following pages of this chapter, we are going to see how to refactor this tightly-coupled cluster of objects into a flexible and testable set of services working together. In the process of doing so, we are going to take full advantage of the AngularJS dependency injection subsystem.

Registering services

AngularJS is only capable of wiring up objects it is aware of. As a consequence, the very first step for plugging into DI machinery is to register an object with an AngularJS module. We are not registering the object's instance directly, rather we are throwing object-creation recipes into the AngularJS dependency injection system. AngularJS then interprets those recipes to instantiate objects, and then connects them accordingly. The end effect is a set of instantiated, wired-up objects forming a running application.

In AngularJS there is a dedicated $provide service that allows us to register different recipes for objects creation. Registered recipes are then interpreted by the $injector service to provide fully-baked, ready-to-be-used object instances (with all the dependencies resolved and injected).

Objects that were created by the $injector service are referred to as services. AngularJS will interpret a given recipe only once during the application's lifecycle, and as a result will create only a single instance of an object.

 Services created by $injector are singletons. There will be only one or instance of a given service per instance of a running application.

At the end of the day, AngularJS module just holds a set of object instances but we can control how those objects are created.

Values

The easiest way of having AngularJS to manage an object is to register a pre-instantiated one as follows:

```
var myMod = angular.module('myMod', []);
myMod.value('notificationsArchive', new NotificationsArchive());
```

Any service managed by AngularJS' DI mechanism needs to have a unique name (for example, `notificationsArchive` in the preceding example). What follows is a recipe for creating new instances.

Value objects are not particularly interesting, since object registered via this method can't depend on other objects. This is not much of the problem for the `NotificationArchive` instance, since it doesn't have any dependencies. In practice, this method of registration only works for very simple objects (usually expressed as instances of built-in objects or object literals).

Services

We can't register the `NotificationsService` service as a value object, since we need to express a dependency on an archive service. The simplest way of registering a recipe for objects, depending on other objects, is to register a constructor function. We can do this using the `service` method as follows:

```
myMod.service('notificationsService', NotificationsService);
```

where the `NotificationsService` constructor function can now be written as follows:

```
var NotificationsService = function (notificationsArchive) {

    this.notificationsArchive = notificationsArchive;

};
```

By using AngularJS dependency injection we could eliminate the `new` keyword from the `NoficiationsService` constructor function. Now this service is not concerned with dependencies instantiation and can accept any archiving service. Our simple application is much more flexible now!

 A service is one of those overloaded words that might mean many different things. In AngularJS the word service can refer to either the method of registering constructor functions (as shown in the previous example) or any singleton object that is created and managed by AngularJS DI system, regardless of the method of registering used (this is what most people mean by using the word service in the context of AngularJS modules).

In practice the `service` method is not commonly used but might come in handy for registering pre-existing constructor functions, and thus make AngularJS manage objects created by those constructors.

Factories

The `factory` method is another way of registering recipes for objects creation. It is more flexible as compared to the `service` method, since we can register any arbitrary object-creating function. An example is shown in the following code

```
myMod.factory('notificationsService',function(notificationsArchive){

    var MAX_LEN = 10;
    var notifications = [];

    return {
      push:function (notification) {
        var notificationToArchive;
        var newLen = notifications.unshift(notification);

        //push method can rely on the closure scope now!
        if (newLen > MAX_LEN) {
          notificationToArchive = this.notifications.pop();
          notificationsArchive.archive(notificationToArchive);
        }
      },
      // other methods of the NotificationsService
    };
```

AngularJS will use a supplied `factory` function to register an object returned. It can be any valid JavaScript object, including `function` objects!

The `factory` method is the most common way of getting objects into AngularJS dependency injection system. It is very flexible and can contain sophisticated creation logic. Since factories are regular functions, we can also take advantage of a new lexical scope to simulate "private" variables. This is very useful as we can hide implementation details of a given service. Indeed, in the preceding example we can keep the `notificationToArchive` service, all the configuration parameters (`MAX_LEN`) and internal state (`notifications`) as "private".

Constants

Our `NotificationsService` is getting better and better, it is decoupled from its collaborators and hides its private state. Unfortunately, it still has a hard-coded configuration `MAX_LEN` constant. AngularJS has a remedy for this, that is, constants can be defined on a module level and injected as any other collaborating object.

Ideally, we would like to have our NotificationsService service to be provided with a configuration value in the following manner:

```
myMod.factory('notificationsService',

function (notificationsArchive, MAX_LEN) {
  ...
  //creation logic doesn't change
});
```

And then supply configuration values outside of NotificationsService, on a module level as shown in the following code:

```
myMod.constant('MAX_LEN', 10);
```

Constants are very useful for creating services that can be re-used across many different applications (as clients of a service can configure it at their will). There is only one disadvantage of using constants, that is, as soon as a service expresses a dependency on a constant, a value for this constant must be supplied. Sometimes it would be good to have default configuration values and allow clients to change them only when needed.

Providers

All the registration methods described so far are just special cases of the most generic, ultimate version of all of them, provider. Here is the example of registering the notificationsService service as a provider:

```
myMod.provider('notificationsService', function () {

  var config = {
    maxLen : 10
  };
  var notifications = [];

  return {
    setMaxLen : function(maxLen) {
      config.maxLen = maxLen || config.maxLen;
    },

    $get : function(notificationsArchive) {
      return {
        push:function (notification) {
          ...
          if (newLen > config.maxLen) {
            ...
          }
```

```
        },
        // other methods go here
      };
    }
  };
});
```

Firstly a `provider` is a function that must return an object containing the `$get` property. The mentioned `$get` property is a factory function, that when invoked should return a `service` instance. We can think of providers as objects that embed factory functions in their `$get` property.

Next, an object returned from a `provider` function can have additional methods and properties. Those are exposed, so it is possible to set configuration options before the `$get` (factory) method gets invoked. Indeed, we can still set the `maxLen` configuration property, but we are no longer obliged to do so. Furthermore, it is possible to have more complex configuration logic, as our services can expose configuration methods and not only simple configuration values.

Modules lifecycle

In the previous paragraphs, we could see that AngularJS supports various recipes for object's creation. A `provider` is a special kind of recipe, since it can be further configured before it produces any object instances. To effectively support providers, AngularJS splits module's lifecycle into two phases, which are as follows:

- **The configuration phase**: It is the phase where all the recipes are collected and configured

- **The run phase**: It is the phase where we can execute any post-instantiation logic

The configuration phase

Providers can be configured only during the configuration (first) phase. Surely, it doesn't make sense to change a recipe after objects are baked, right? Providers can be configured as shown in the following code:

```
myMod.config(function(notificationsServiceProvider){
    notificationsServiceProvider.setMaxLen(5);
});
```

The important thing to notice here is a dependency on the `notificationsServiceProvider` objects with the `Provider` suffix representing the recipes that are ready to be executed. The configuration phase allows us to do the last-moment tweaks to the objects' creation formula.

The run phase

The run phase allows us to register any work that should be executed upon the application's bootstrap. One could think of the run phase as an equivalent of the main method in other programming languages. The biggest difference is that AngularJS modules can have multiple configure and run blocks. In this sense, there is not even a single entry point (a running application is truly a collection of collaborating objects).

To illustrate how the run phase could be useful, let's imagine that we need to display application's start time (or uptime) to the users. To support this requirement, we could set application's start time as a property of the $rootScope instance as follows:

```
angular.module('upTimeApp', []).run(function($rootScope) {
    $rootScope.appStarted = new Date();
});
```

And then retrieve it any template, as given in the following code:

```
Application started at: {{appStarted}}
```

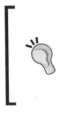 In the example showing the run block in action we are setting properties directly on the $rootScope instance. It is important to realize that the $rootScope instance is a global variable and it suffers from all the problems of a global state. The $rootScope instance should be used to define new properties only sparingly and only for properties that need to be accessible in many templates.

Different phases and different registration methods

Let's summarize different methods of creating objects and how those methods correspond to module's lifecycle phases:

	What gets registered?	Injectable during the configuration phase?	Injectable during the run phase?
Constant	Constant's value	Yes	Yes
Variable	Variable's value	-	Yes
Service	A new object created by a constructor function	-	Yes
Factory	A new object returned from a factory function	-	Yes
Provider	A new object created by the $get factory function	Yes	-

Modules depending on other modules

Not only does AngularJS do the excellent job of managing object dependencies, but in addition it takes care of inter-module dependencies. We can easily group related services into one module, and thus create (potentially re-usable) service libraries.

As an example, we could move both the notifications and archiving services into their own modules (named `notifications` and `archive`, respectively) as follows:

```
angular.module('application', ['notifications', 'archive'])
```

This way each service (or a group of related services) can be combined into a re-usable entity (a module). Then the top-most (application-level) module can declare dependencies on all the modules needed for proper functioning of a given application.

The ability to depend on other modules is not reserved for the top-most modules. Each module can express dependencies on its child modules. In this way, modules can form a hierarchy. So, when dealing with AngularJS modules we need to think about two distinct, but related, hierarchies: modules hierarchy and services hierarchy (as services can express dependencies on other services, values, and constants).

AngularJS modules can depend on each other and every module can contain several services. But individual services can also depend on other services. This raises several interesting questions, which are as follows:

- Can a service defined in one AngularJS module depend on services in another module?
- Can services defined in a child module depend on a service in a parent module, or only on services defined in child modules?
- Can we have module-private services visible only in a certain module?
- Can we have several services with the same name defined in different modules?

Services and their visibility across modules

As one might expect services defined in child modules are available for injection into services in parent modules the following code example should make it clear:

```
angular.module('app', ['engines'])

  .factory('car', function ($log, dieselEngine) {
    return {
      start: function() {
        $log.info('Starting ' + dieselEngine.type);
      };
```

```
    }
  });

angular.module('engines', [])
  .factory('dieselEngine', function () {
    return {
      type: 'diesel'
    };
  });
```

Here the car service is defined in the app module. The app module declares a dependency on the engines module, where the dieselEngine service is defined. Not surprisingly a car can be injected with an instance of an engine.

Perhaps more surprisingly, services defined on sibling modules are also visible to each other. We could move a car service into a separate module, and then change module dependencies, so that an application depends on both the engines and cars modules as follows:

```
angular.module('app', ['engines', 'cars'])

angular.module('cars', [])
  .factory('car', function ($log, dieselEngine) {
    return {
      start: function() {
        $log.info('Starting ' + dieselEngine.type);
      }
    };
  });

angular.module('engines', [])
  .factory('dieselEngine', function () {
    return {
      type: 'diesel'
    };
  });
```

In the preceding case an engine can still be injected into a car without any problem.

A service defined in one of the application's modules is visible to all the other modules. In other words, hierarchy of modules doesn't influence services' visibility to other modules. When AngularJS bootstraps an application, it combines all the services defined across all the modules into one application, that is, global namespace.

Since AngularJS combines all the services from all the modules into one big, application-level set of services there can be one and only one service with a given name. We can use this to our advantage in cases where we want to depend on a module, but at the same time override some of the services from this module. To illustrate this, we can redefine the dieselEngine service directly in the cars module in the following manner:

```
angular.module('app', ['engines', 'cars'])
  .controller('AppCtrl', function ($scope, car) {
    car.start();
  });

angular.module('cars', [])
  .factory('car', function ($log, dieselEngine) {
    return {
      start: function() {
        $log.info('Starting ' + dieselEngine.type);
      };
    }
  })

  .factory('dieselEngine', function () {
    return {
      type: 'custom diesel'
    };
  });
```

In this case, the car service will be injected with the dieselEngine service defined in the same module as that of the car service. The car module level, dieselEngine, will override (shadow) the dieselEngine service defined under the engines module.

There can be one and only one service with a given name in an AngularJS application. Services defined in the modules closer to the root of modules hierarchy will override those defined in child modules.

In the current version of AngularJS, all the services defined on one module are visible to all the other modules. There is no way of restricting service's visibility to one module or a subset of modules.

At the time of writing, there is no support provided for module-private services.

Why use AngularJS modules

The fact that AngularJS combines all the services from all the modules into one application-level namespace might come as a surprise, and you might wonder why to use modules. At the end of the day, all the services are ending up in one big bag, so what is the point of laboriously dividing services into individual modules?

AngularJS modules can help us organize multiple JavaScript files in an application. There are many strategies for dividing an application into modules, and we are going to spend a big portion of *Chapter 2, Building and Testing* discussing different approaches, their pros, and cons. Also, small and focused modules help facilitate unit testing as we can load a well-identified set of services under test. Once again, *Chapter 2, Building and Testing,* has more details.

AngularJS and the rest of the world

Choosing a perfect framework for your next project is not easy. Some frameworks might be a better fit for certain types of applications and team's experience, personal preferences, as well as many other factors can dictate the ultimate choice.

AngularJS will be inevitably be compared to other popular JavaScript MV* frameworks. Different comparisons will most probably yield different results, and different points of view will fuel many passionate discussions. Instead of offering hard-and-fast rules or feature-by-future comparisons, we would like to summarize how AngularJS is different compared to other frameworks.

 If you would like to see how code written with AngularJS compares to code written with other frameworks, the *TodoMVC* (`http://addyosmani.github.com/todomvc`) is the place to go. This is a project where one can see the same sample application (TODO list) reimplemented using different JavaScript MV* frameworks. This is a unique opportunity to compare architectural approaches and code syntax, its size, and readability.

There are many things about AngularJS that make it stand out from the crowd. We saw already that its approach to UI templates is quite novel, as mentioned in the following features:

- Automatic refresh and the two-way data binding frees developers from the tedious work of explicitly triggering UI repaints

- Live DOM generated from HTML syntax is used as a templating language. More importantly, it is possible to extend an existing HTML vocabulary (by creating new directives), and then build UIs using a new HTML-based DSL

- Declarative approach to the UI results in a very concise and expressive way
- The excellent UI templating machinery doesn't put any constraints on the JavaScript code (for example, models and controllers can be created using plain, old JavaScript without the AngularJS APIs called all over the place)

AngularJS is breaking new ground by bringing solid testing practices into the JavaScript world. The framework itself is thoroughly tested (practice what you preach!), but the whole testability story doesn't stop here, the whole framework and the ecosystem around it were built with the testability in mind. It continues as follows:

- The dependency injection engine enables testability, since the whole application can be composed from smaller, well tested services.
- Most of the code examples in the AngularJS documentation have got an accompanying test, it is the best proof that code written for AngularJS is indeed testable!
- The AngularJS team created an excellent JavaScript test runner called Testacular (spectacular test runner!). Testacular turns an overall testing workflow into a joyful experience, which is useful, fast, and reliable. Testing is not always easy, so it is important to have tools that assist us instead of getting in a way

Above all, AngularJS makes the web development fun again! It takes care of so many low-level details that the application's code is extremely concise of. It is not uncommon to hear that rewriting an application in AngularJS reduces the overall code base by a factor of five or even more. Of course everything depends on an application and a team, but AngularJS lets us move fast and produce results in the blink of an eye.

jQuery and AngularJS

AngularJS and jQuery form an interesting relationship that needs special mentioning. To start with, AngularJS embeds, as part of its sources, a simplified version of jQuery, that is, jqLite. This is really a tiny subset of the complete jQuery functionality that focuses on the DOM manipulation routines.

 By embedding jqLite, AngularJS can work with no dependency on any external library.

But AngularJS is a good citizen of the JavaScript community and can work hand in hand with jQuery. Upon detecting jQuery, AngularJS will use its DOM manipulation functionality instead of relying on jqLite.

> If you plan to use jQuery with AngularJS you need to include it before AngularJS script.

Things get more complicated if one tries to reuse any of the UI components from the jQuery UI suite. Some of them will work just fine, but most of the time there will be some friction. It is just that the underlying philosophy of two libraries is so different that we can hardly expect any seamless integration. *Chapter 8, Building Your Own Directives* looks closely into integrating and creating UI widgets that can correctly work in AngularJS applications.

Apples and oranges

jQuery and AngularJS can cooperate, but comparing the two is a tricky business. First of all, jQuery was born as a library that simplifies DOM manipulation, and as such focuses on document traversing, event handling, animating, and Ajax interactions.

AngularJS, on the other hand, is a complete framework that tries to address all the aspects of the modern web 2.0 applications development.

The most important thing is that AngularJS takes a completely different approach for building UI, where the declaratively specified view is driven by model changes. Using jQuery too often involves writing DOM-centric code that can go out of hand as a project grows (both in terms of size and interactivity).

> AngularJS' model-centric and jQuery's DOM-centric paradigms are radically different. Seasoned jQuery developers new to AngularJS might fall into a trap of using AngularJS with the jQuery paradigms in mind. This results in code that "fights AngularJS" rather than unleashing its full potential. This is why we recommend that you skip jQuery dependency, while learning AngularJS (just not to be tempted to fall back to the old habits and learn the AngularJS way of solving problems).

AngularJS takes a holistic approach to modern web application development, and tries to make a browser a better development platform.

A sneak peek into the future

AngularJS has a truly novel approach to many aspects of web development, and it might shape the way we write code for the future browsers. At the time of writing, there are two interesting specifications in the works that are based on ideas similar to the ones implemented in AngularJS.

The `Object.observe` (`http://wiki.ecmascript.org/doku. php?id=harmony:observe`) specification aims at building into a browser the ability to track JavaScript object changes. AngularJS relies on the object's state comparison (dirty checking) to trigger UI repaints. Having a native in a browser—the mechanism to detect model changes could greatly improve performance of many JavaScript MVC frameworks, including AngularJS. In fact, the AngularJS team did some experiments using the `Object.observe` specification and saw as much as 20 percent to 30 percent performance improvements.

Web components (`http://dvcs.w3.org/hg/webcomponents/raw-file/tip/ explaincr/index.html`) specification tries to define widgets with a level of visual richness (which is not possible with CSS alone), and ease of composition and reuse (which is not possible with script libraries today).

This is not an easy goal, but AngularJS directives show that it is possible to define well-encapsulated and re-usable widgets.

AngularJS is not only an innovative framework by today's standards, but it also influences the web development space of tomorrow. The AngularJS team works closely with the authors of the mentioned specifications, so there is a chance that many ideas promoted by AngularJS will make it into the browser's internals! We can expect that time spent learning and playing with AngularJS will pay off in the future.

Summary

We've covered a lot in this chapter. Our journey started by getting familiar with the AngularJS project and the people behind it. We've learned where to find the library's sources and documentation, so that we could write our first "Hello World" application. It is a pleasant surprise that AngularJS is very light-weight and easy to start with.

Most of this chapter, though was about building solid foundations for the rest of this booke saw how to work with the AngularJS controllers, scopes and views, and how those elements play together. A big chunk of this chapter was devoted to the way AngularJS services can be created in AngularJS modules and wired up using dependency injection.

Finally, we saw how AngularJS compares to other JavaScript frameworks and what is so special about it. Hopefully, now you are convinced that time spent in learning AngularJS is the time well invested.

AngularJS views, controllers, and services are the basic ingredients of any AngularJS application, so it was necessary to gain an in-depth understanding of those topics. Luckily, now we know how to start creating both the service layer and the view, so we are ready to tackle real projects. In the next chapter we will prepare a structure of a non-trivial application, starting from code organization and then covering topics such as building and testing.

2
Building and Testing

The previous chapter served as an introduction to AngularJS and covered nuts and bolts of the framework project itself, people behind it, and basic usage scenarios. Now, we are well primed to build a complete, more elaborate web application. The rest of this book is constructed around a sample application that presents how to use AngularJS in real-life projects.

In the following chapters, we are going to build a simplified project management tool supporting SCRUM agile software development methodology. This sample application will help us to demonstrate AngularJS APIs and idioms as well as cover typical scenarios, such as communicating with a back-end, organizing navigation, security, internationalization, and so on. This chapter introduces the sample application, its problem domain and the technical stack used.

Each project starts with some initial decisions regarding files organization strategy, a build system, and basic workflows employed. Our sample application is no different and we are going to discuss build system and project-layout related topics in this chapter.

Automated testing is a solid engineering practice that is promoted by AngularJS and the whole ecosystem around it. We strongly believe that automated testing is mandatory for any but the most trivial projects. This is why the last part of this chapter is fully devoted to testing: different types of it, mechanics and workflows, best practices, and tooling.

In this chapter, we are going to learn more about:

- The sample application used in this book, its problem domain, and the technical stack used.
- The recommended build system for the AngularJS web applications as well as associated tools and workflows.

- Suggested organization of files, folders and modules.

- Automated testing practices, different types of tests and their place in a project. You will get familiar with testing libraries and tools typically used in AngularJS web applications.

Introducing the sample application

This section gives more details on the sample application that will serve as a case study throughout this book.

 The source code for the sample application is publicly available in the git repository hosted on GitHub at `https://github.com/angular-app/angular-app`. This repository contains complete source code, detailed installation instructions and the whole project history.

Getting familiar with the problem domain

To showcase AngularJS in its most advantageous environment we are going to build a project management tool supporting teams using the **SCRUM** methodology.

AngularJS shines when used as a framework for constructing CRUD-like applications; ones that consist of many screens filled with dynamic forms, list and tables.

SCRUM is a popular agile method for running projects, so hopefully many readers are already familiar with it. Those new to SCRUM should not worry, since the basics of SCRUM are easy to grasp. There are many excellent books and articles covering SCRUM in depth but to gain basic understanding it is probably enough to go over the introductory Wikipedia article on the topic at `http://en.wikipedia.org/wiki/Scrum_(development)`.

The aim of our sample application is to assist teams in managing SCRUM artifacts: projects and their backlog, sprints and their backlog, tasks, progress charts, and so on. The application also has a fully functional administration module to manage users and projects being worked on.

 Our sample application doesn't strive for full and strict adherence to all the SCRUM principles. When necessary we took several shortcuts to clearly illustrate AngularJS usage at the expense of building a real SCRUM project management tool.

The application, when finished will look as shown on the following screenshot:

Looking at the screenshot we can immediately see that what we are going to build is a fairly typical CRUD web application covering:

- Retrieving, displaying and editing data from a persistent store.
- Authentication and authorization.
- Rather complex navigation schema with all the supporting UI elements, such as menus, breadcrumbs and, so on.

Technical stack

This book is focused on AngularJS but to build any nontrivial web application we need more than a JavaScript library running in a browser. As a bare minimum a persistence store and a back-end are required. This book doesn't prescribe any stack, and we do realize that people are going to use AngularJS in connection with different back-ends, server-side frameworks and persistent stores. Still, we had to make choices to illustrate how AngularJS fits into a bigger picture.

First and foremost, we have chosen to use JavaScript-friendly technologies whenever possible. There are many excellent back-ends, platforms and persistence stores out there but we would like to make our examples easy to follow for JavaScript developers. Additionally, we were trying to use technologies that are considered as mainstream in the JavaScript ecosystem.

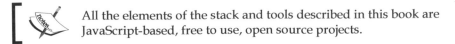 All the elements of the stack and tools described in this book are JavaScript-based, free to use, open source projects.

Persistence store

When it comes to data storage there are many options to choose from and the recent NoSQL movement only multiplied a number of alternatives. For the purpose of this book we are going to use the document-oriented MongoDB database as it fits well into the JavaScript-oriented environment:

- Documents are stored using the JSON-style data format (Binary JSON - BSON in short).
- Querying and manipulating data can be done using JavaScript and the familiar JSON syntax.
- It is possible to expose data as REST endpoints serving and consuming data in the JSON format.

No prior knowledge of MongoDB is needed to follow the examples in this book, and we will try to explain tricky bits while discussing code snippets. By no means are we suggesting that MongoDB or document-oriented, NoSQL databases are a better fit for AngularJS applications. AngularJS is back-end and storage-agnostic.

MongoLab

MongoDB is relatively easy to start with, and most of JavaScript developers will feel at home while working with this document-oriented database. To makes things even easier our sample application relies on the hosted version of the MongoDB. As a result, no software installation is necessary to run examples from this book.

There are multiple cloud-based hosting options available for MongoDB, but we've found that MongoLab (`https://mongolab.com`) is reliable, easy to start with and offers free hosting for databases of size below 0.5 GB. The free storage space offered by MongoLab is more than enough to play with the examples from this book.

MongoLab has one more, non-negligible advantage; it exposes hosted databases through a very well-designed REST interface. We are going to rely on this interface to demonstrate how AngularJS can talk to REST endpoints.

The online registration is necessary to start using MongoLab, but it is a fairly painless process that boils down to filling in a short, electronic form. As soon as this is done, we can enjoy access to a hosted MongoDB database, the REST interface speaking JSON, and the online administration console.

Server-side environment

Databases hosted by MongoLab could be accessed directly from AngularJS applications through the REST interface. While talking to MongoLab directly from a browser might be a good approach for very simple projects; it is not an option one would choose for any real-life, public-facing application. There is simply not enough security built in into the MongoLab offering.

In practice most of the UIs written in AngularJS will communicate with some kind of back-end to retrieve data. A middleware will typically provide security services (authentication) and will verify access rights (authorization) as well. Our sample application is no different and needs a back-end. Once again, we are going to bet on JavaScript-based solution; node.js.

The node.js binaries are available for all popular operating systems, and can be obtained from http://nodejs.org/. You need to download and install node.js runtime in order to be able to run examples from this book on your local machine.

Introducing node.js is well beyond the scope of this book. Fortunately only very basic knowledge of node.js and its package manager (node.js package manager – npm) is needed to run the examples from this book. Developers familiar with node.js will find it easier to understand what is happening on the server-side end of the sample application, but node.js knowledge is not mandatory to follow and understand AngularJS examples from this book.

Apart from the node.js itself we are going to use the following node.js libraries to build server-side components of the sample application:

- Express (http://expressjs.com/) as the server-side web application framework that can provide routing, serve data and static resources.
- Passport (http://passportjs.org/) as a security middleware for node.js.
- Restler (https://github.com/danwrong/restler) as an HTTP client library for node.js.

While familiarity with node.js and the mentioned libraries might be helpful it is not necessary to effectively learn AngularJS. You might want to dive into node.js and the listed libraries, if you want to gain deeper understanding of the server-side part of examples we've prepared for this book. If, on the other hand, your work involves using different back-end you may safely ignore most of the node.js related details.

Third-party JavaScript libraries

AngularJS can be used alone as a single library to write fairly complex applications. At the same time, it doesn't try to reinvent the wheel and reimplement popular libraries.

The sample application tries to keep dependencies on external, third parties' libraries to the absolute minimum so we can focus on what AngularJS can do for us. Still, many projects will use well-known libraries like jQuery, `underscore.js` and so on. To demonstrate how AngularJS can coexist with other libraries the latest compatible version of jQuery made it into the project.

Bootstrap CSS

AngularJS doesn't force or prescribe any particular CSS usage so anyone is free to style their application as needed. To make our SCRUM application look pretty we will use the popular Twitter Bootstrap (`http://twitter.github.com/bootstrap/`) CSS.

The sample application includes LESS templates of the Bootstrap's to illustrate how LESS compilation can be included in the build chain.

Build system

There were times when JavaScript was used as a toy language, those days are long over. In recent years, JavaScript has become a mainstream language. New, large and complex applications are being written and deployed every day. Rising complexity means more code being written. These days it is not uncommon to see projects consisting of tens of thousands of lines of JavaScript code.

It is no longer practical to have one JavaScript file that can be simply included in an HTML document; we need a build system. Our JavaScript and CSS files will undergo many checks and transformations before being deployed on productions servers. Some examples of those transformations include:

- JavaScript source code must be checked for compliance with coding standards using tools like jslint (`http://www.jslint.com/`), jshint (`http://www.jshint.com/`) or similar.

- Test suites should be executed as often as possible; at least as part of each and every build. As such testing tools and processes must be tightly integrated with the build system.

- Some files might need to be generated (for example CSS files from templates like LESS).

- Files need to be merged together and minified to optimize in-browser performance.

In addition to the steps, which are listed previously, there are usually other tasks that must be executed before an application can be deployed to production servers, such as files must be copied to a final destination, documentation updated, and so on. In a non-trivial project there are always many laborious tasks that we should try to automate.

Build system principles

Developers love writing code but in reality only a fraction of our time is spent in front of a text editor. In addition to the fun part (designing, talking with peers, coding and bug fixing) there are tons of fatiguing tasks that must be executed often; sometimes very often. Building an application is one of those tasks that must be run again and again so it should be as fast and painless as possible. Here, we discuss some principles governing the design of our build system.

Automate everything

The authors of this book are really bad at executing manual, repetitive tasks over and over again. We are slow, make mistakes, and to be frank, get bored easily by the chore of building. If you are anything like us you will easily understand why we strongly believe in automating every possible step of the build process.

Computers are good at doing repetitive work for us; they don't take false steps, don't need a coffee break and don't get distracted. Our machines won't complain if we offload the majority of the recurring tasks on them! Time invested in automating every possible step of the build process will pay off quickly, since we will be saving time every day!

Fail fast, fail clean

A typical build process will consist of several distinct steps. Some of those steps will execute just fine most of the time, while others will be failing from time to time. Tasks that are more probable to fail should be executed early in the process, and break the build as soon as an abnormality is detected. This assures that more time-consuming steps are not executed until basics are covered.

We learned the hard way how important this rule is. Initially, the build system for the sample application was executing automated tests before `jshint`. We often found ourselves waiting for all the automated tests to execute; just to find that the build was broken due to invalid JavaScript. The solution was to move the `jshint` task to the very beginning of the build pipeline and break the build as early as possible.

It is important to include clear error messages that are printed out when the build breaks. With unambiguous error messages in place, we should be able to identify the root cause of the failure in a matter of seconds. There is nothing worse than staring at a cryptic error message wondering what is going on when we should be already going live with our project.

Different workflows, different commands

As developers we are responsible for different tasks. One day we might be busy adding new code (with tests!), and spend time integrating newly developed features a day after. Our build system should reflect this reality by providing different commands for different types of workflows. In our experience a build system should have three different build tasks:

1. Fast to run and critical for asserting code correctness: In a JavaScript project it might mean running `jslint` / `jshint` and executing unit tests. This command should be really fast so it can be executed very frequently. This build task is very useful for developing code using the **Test Driven Development (TDD)** approach.

2. A command to deploy a fully functional application for testing purposes: After executing this build task we should be able to run an application in a browser. In order to do so, we need to do more processing here, such as generating CSS files and so on. This build task is focused on a UI-related development workflow.

3. Production-deployment build task should run all the verifications listed in the previous step as well as prepare an application for the final deployment, such as merge and minify files, execute integration tests, and so on.

Build scripts are code too

Build scripts are a part of project's artifacts, and we should treat them with the same care as any other deliverables. Build scripts will have to be read, understood and maintained - just like any other source code. Badly written build scripts can significantly slow down your progress and guarantee some frustrating debugging sessions.

Tools

The build-system design principles outlined in the previous section can be applied to any project and any tool set. Our selected tool-chain is operating system (OS) agnostic, so you should be able to run sample applications or any popular OS.

While we've selected the build tools that in our opinion are the best for the purpose of the sample project, we do realize that different projects will use different tools. The rest of this book and the recommendations from this chapter should still be relevant and easily adaptable to different build systems.

Grunt.js

The build system of the sample SCRUM application is powered by Grunt (http://gruntjs.com/). The grunt.js is advertised as:

> *"A task-based command line build tool for JavaScript projects."*

What is important for us is that grunt.js build scripts are written in JavaScript and executed on the node.js platform. This is very good news as it means that we can use the same platform and the same programming language for both building and running the sample application.

The Grunt belongs to the same category of task-oriented build tools as Gradle (scripts written in Groovy) or Rake (scripts written in Ruby), so people familiar with those tools should feel at home.

Testing libraries and tools

AngularJS uses, promotes and encourages automated testing practices. The AngularJS team takes testability very seriously, and they made sure that code written using AngularJS is easy to test. But the whole testability story doesn't stop here, as the AngularJS team written or extended tools in order to make testing easy in practice.

Jasmine

The tests for the AngularJS code base were written using **Jasmine** (http://pivotal. github.com/jasmine/). Jasmine is a framework for testing JavaScript code and has its roots in the Behavior Driven Development (BDD) movement which has influence on its syntax.

All the examples in the original AngularJS documentation are using Jasmine's syntax so this testing framework is a natural choice for our sample application. Moreover, AngularJS have written various mock objects and Jasmine extensions to provide a nicely integrated, practical day-to-day testing experience.

Karma runner

Karma runner (`http://karma-runner.github.io`) is enabled to easily execute JavaScript tests. Karma runner was born to replace another popular test runner JS TestDriver with a stable, pure JavaScript, `node.js` based solution.

The Karma runner is able to dispatch source and test code to a running instance of a browser (or start a new one if needed!), trigger execution of tests, collect individual tests outcomes and report the final result. It uses real browsers to execute tests. This is a big deal in the JavaScript world, since we can simultaneously execute tests in several browsers making sure that our code will operate correctly in the wild.

 The Karma runner is a remarkable tool when it comes to stability and speed. It is used in the AngularJS project to execute tests as part of the continuous integration build. On each build Karma runner executes around 2000 unit tests on multiple browsers. In total around 14,000 tests are being executed in about 20 seconds. Those numbers should raise our confidence in Karma runner as a tool, and AngularJS as a framework.

Testing is such a central theme in AngularJS that we are going to have deeper look into Jasmine tests and Karma runner later in this chapter.

Organizing files and folders

So far we've made some pretty important decisions regarding the technical stack and tools to be used, while constructing the sample SCRUM application. Now, we need to answer one more crucial question; how to organize different files in meaningful folders structure.

There are multiple ways of organizing files in any given project. Sometimes choices are made for us, since some of the existing tools and frameworks force a prescribed layout. But neither `grunt.js` nor AngularJS impose any particular directory structure so we are free to make our choices. In the following paragraphs you can find one proposal for organizing files and rationales behind this proposal. You might choose to use the described structure as is in your future projects or tweak it to suit your particular needs.

Root folders

While designing folders layout we would like to end up with a directory structure that makes it easy to navigate in the code base. At the same time we need to keep build complexity at a reasonable level.

Here are some basic assumptions leading us to the high-level directory structure:

- Source code for the application and the accompanying tests should be clearly separated. This is to keep the build system easy to maintain, as there are usually different sets of build tasks to be executed for tests and for the source code.

- Third-party code for any external libraries should be clearly isolated from our internal code base. External libraries will be changing at the different pace as compared to our deliverables. We want to make it easy to upgrade external dependencies at any time. Mixing our sources with external libraries would make such upgrades harder and time consuming.

- Build-related scripts should reside in their own dedicated folders and not be scattered through the code base.

- Build results should be outputted to a separate folder. The content and structure of the build output should closely match the one mandated by the production deployment requirements. It should be very easy to just grab the output of the build and deploy it in its final destination.

Taking all of the above assumptions into consideration we ended up with the following set of top level directories in the project.

- `src`: It contains application's source code

- `test`: It contains accompanying automated tests

- `vendor`: It contains third party dependencies

- `build`: It contains build scripts

- `dist`: It contains build results, ready to be deployed in a target environment

Finally, here is the top-level folders structure visualized:

Name	Type	Size
build	File folder	
dist	File folder	
src	File folder	
test	File folder	
vendor	File folder	
.gitignore	Text Document	1 KB
grunt.js	JScript Script File	4 KB
LICENSE	File	2 KB
package.json	JSON File	1 KB

In addition to the described folders we can notice several top level files. Just for reference those files are:

- `.gitignore`: The git SCM related includes rules to indicate which files should not be tracked in a git repository

- `LICENSE`: It contains terms of the MIT license

- `Gruntfile.js`: It is the entry point to the `grunt.js` build

- `package.json`: It contains the package description for the `node.js` applications

Inside the source folder

With the basics addressed we are now ready to dive into the structure of the **src** folder. Let's have a look at its visualization first:

Name	Type	Size
app	File folder	
assets	File folder	
common	File folder	
less	File folder	
index.html	Chrome HTML Do...	1 KB

The `index.html` file is the entry point to the sample application. Then, there are four folders, two of them holding AngularJS-specific code (`app` and `common`) and two others contain AngularJS-agnostic presentation artifacts (`assets` and `less`).

It is easy to decipher the purpose of the `assets` and the `less` folders; the first one holds images and icons while the second one, LESS variables. Please note that the LESS templates for Twitter's Bootstrap CSS are located in the `vendor` folder, here we just keep variable values.

AngularJS specific files

AngularJS applications consist of two different file types, namely, scripts and HTML templates. Any non-trivial project will produce many files of each type and we need to find a way to organize this mass of files. Ideally we would like to group related files together and keep the unrelated ones further apart. The trouble is that files can relate to each other in many different ways and we've got only one directory tree to express those relations.

Common strategies of solving this problem involve grouping files by a feature (package by feature), by an architectural layer (package by layer), or by a file type. What we would like to propose here is a hybrid approach:

- Most of the application files should be organized by feature. Scripts and partials that are functionally related to each other should go together. Such an arrangement is very convenient while working on vertical slices of an application since all the files changing together are grouped together.

- Files encapsulating cross-cutting concerns (persistence store access, localization, common directives, and so on) should be grouped together. The rationale here is that infrastructure-like scripts don't change at the same pace as the strictly functional code. In a typical life-cycle of an application some technical infrastructure is written early on and the focus is shifted to the functional code as the application matures. Files in the common, infrastructure level area are best organized by an architectural layer.

We can directly translate the above recommendations to the following directory structure of the sample application:

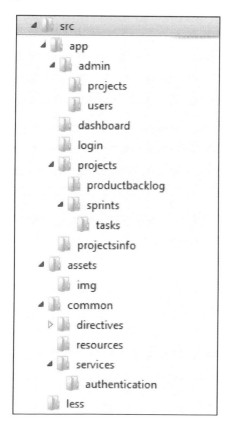

 The directory structure described here is different from the one recommended by the AngularJS seed project (`https://github.com/angular/angular-seed`). The directory layout from the angular-seed project works well for a simple project, but the general consensus in the AngularJS community is that larger projects are better organized by feature.

Start simple

Looking at the folder structure you will notice that some of the folders containing functional code have a deep hierarchy. Those folders closely match hierarchical navigation in the application itself. This is desirable since looking at the UI of the application we can quickly understand where the corresponding code might be stored.

It is good idea to start a project with a very simple structure, and take small steps toward the final directories' layout. For example, the sample application didn't have any subfolders in the admin section at the beginning and contained all the functionality for managing SCRUM projects and users in one directory. As the code base evolved and files were growing bigger (and more numerous) new subfolders were added. The folder structure can be refactored and evolved in several iterations, exactly like source code.

Controllers and partials evolve together

It is rather common to see projects where files are organized into folders based on their type. In AngularJS context JavaScript scripts and templates often get separated into different directory structures. This separation sounds like a good idea but in practice templates and the corresponding controllers tend to evolve at the same pace. This is why in the sample SCRUM application templates and controllers are kept together. Each functional area will have its own folder and both templates and controllers will reside in one folder.

As an example here is the content of the folder related to the users' administration functionality:

Name	Date modified	Type	Size
admin-users.js	2012-11-20 17:59	JScript Script File	1 KB
admin-users-edit.js	2012-11-27 21:25	JScript Script File	3 KB
users-edit.tpl.html	2012-11-26 19:29	Chrome HTML Document	2 KB
users-list.tpl.html	2012-11-20 17:59	Chrome HTML Document	1 KB

Inside the test folder

Automated tests are written to assert whether an application is operating properly, and the test code is closely related to the functional code. As such, it shouldn't be surprising that the structure of the `test` folder closely mimics the one of the `src/app`:

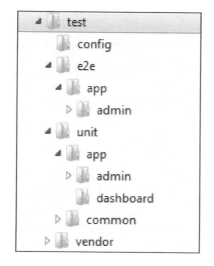

It is easy to see that the content of the test folder almost mirrors the root source folder. All the tests libraries are located in their dedicated `vendor` folder and the Karma runner's test configuration has its home too (`config`).

File-naming conventions

It is important to establish some file naming conventions to make navigation in the code base easier. Here are a set of conventions often followed in the AngularJS community and adopted in the book:

- All the JavaScript files are named with the standard `.js` extension.
- Partials get the `.tpl.html` suffix so we can easily distinguish them from other HTML files.
- Test files get the same name as a file being tested and the suffix dependent on the test type. Unit tests would get the `.spec.js` suffix.

AngularJS modules and files

Now that our application is nicely organized into folders and files we can start looking into content of the individual files. Here we are going to focus on JavaScript files, their content and relation to AngularJS modules.

One file, one module

In *Chapter 1, Angular Zen,* we've seen that AngularJS modules can depend on each other. This means that in the AngularJS application we need to deal with both directories hierarchy and modules hierarchy. Now we are going to dig more into those topics in order to come up with pragmatic recommendations for organizing AngularJS modules and their content.

There are basically three approaches we could take to relate individual files and AngularJS modules:

- Allow multiple AngularJS modules in one JavaScript file
- Have AngularJS modules spanning multiple JavaScript files
- Define exactly one AngularJS module per JavaScript file

Defining multiple modules in one file is not extremely harmful but it might result in big files with hundreds of lines of code. On top of this it is harder to find a particular module in the code base as we need to locate both a file in a file system, and a module within a file. While having multiple modules in one file might work for very simple projects it is not optimal for larger code bases.

Having one module spanning over multiple files is something that should be probably avoided. As soon as the code for one module is spread across multiple files we need to start thinking about load order of those files: module declaration need to come before providers are registered. Additionally, such modules tend to be bigger and as such harder to maintain. Big modules can be particularly undesirable for unit testing, where we want to load and exercise units of code as small as practically possible.

Out of the three proposals having exactly one AngularJS module per file seems to be the most sensible approach.

Stick to the one file equals one AngularJS module principle. This will allow you to maintain relatively small, focused files and modules. Additionally you won't be concerned with the load order of those files. Also it will be possible to load individual modules under unit tests.

Inside a module

As soon as a module is declared it can be used to register recipes for the object's creation. As a reminder, those recipes are called providers in AngularJS terminology. Each provider, when executed, will produce exactly one run-time service instance. While recipes for services creation can be expressed using multitude of forms (factories, services, providers and variables) the net effect is always the same; a configured instance of a service.

Different syntax for registering providers

To register a new provider we need to get a hand on a module's instance first. It is easy as a module instance will be always returned from a call to the `angular. module` method.

We could save a reference to the returned module instance and reuse it to register multiple providers. For example, to register two controllers on the module responsible for managing projects we could write:

```
var adminProjects = angular.module('admin-projects', []);

adminProjects.controller('ProjectsListCtrl', function($scope) {
  //controller's code go here
});

adminProjects.controller('ProjectsEditCtrl', function($scope) {
  //controller's code go here
});
```

While this approach certainly works it has one drawback; we are obliged to declare an intermediate variable (`adminProjects` in this case) just to be able to declare multiple providers on a module. Worse yet, the intermediate variable could end up in the global namespace if we don't take additional precautions (wrapping module declaration into a closure, creating a namespace, and so on.). Ideally, we would like to be able to somehow retrieve an instance of an already declared module. It turns out that we can do this as shown in the next example:

```
angular.module('admin-projects', []);

angular.module('admin-projects').controller('ProjectsListCtrl',
function($scope) {
  //controller's code goes here
});
```

```
angular.module('admin-projects').controller('ProjectsEditCtrl',
function($scope) {
  //controller's code goes here
});
```

We've managed to eliminate the extra variable but our code didn't get any better. Can you notice how the `angular.module('admin-projects')` is repeated all over the place All code duplication is evil and this one can hit us hard, if we decide to rename a module one day. On top of this the syntax to declare a new module and to retrieve an existing one can be easily mistaken leading, to very confusing results. Just compare the `angular.module('myModule')` with `angular.module('myModule', [])`. It is easy to overlook the difference, isn't it?

 It is better to avoid retrieving AngularJS modules using the `angular.module('myModule')` construct. The syntax is verbose and results in code duplication. Worse yet, module's declaration can be easily confused with accessing instances of an existing module.

Luckily there is one more approach that addresses all the problems described so far. Let's have a look at the code first:

```
angular.module('admin-projects', [])

  .controller('ProjectsListCtrl', function($scope) {
    //controller's code go here
  })

  .controller('ProjectsEditCtrl', function($scope) {
    //controller's code go here
  });
```

We can see that it is possible to chain calls to the controller's registration logic. Each call to the `controller` method will return an instance of a module on which the method was invoked. Other provider-registering methods (`factory`, `service`, `value`, and so on) are returning a module's instance, as well so it is possible to register different providers using the same pattern.

In our sample SCRUM application we are going to use the chaining syntax just described to register all the providers. This way of registering providers eliminates the risk of creating superfluous (potentially global!) variables and avoids code duplication. It is also very readable provided that some effort is put into code formatting.

Syntax for declaring the configure and run blocks

As described in *Chapter 1*, *Angular Zen* the process of bootstrapping an AngularJS application is divided in two distinct phases, the `configure` phase and the `run` phase. Each module can have multiple configure and run blocks. We are not restricted to a single one.

It turns out that AngularJS supports two different ways of registering functions that should be executed in the configuration phase. We saw already that it is possible to specify a configuration function as the third argument to the `angular.module` function:

```
angular.module('admin-projects', [], function() {
  //configuration logic goes here
});
```

The preceding method allows us to register one and only one configure block. On top of this module declaration becomes quite verbose (especially, if a module specifies dependencies on other modules). An alternative exists is the form of the `angular.config` method:

```
angular.module('admin-projects', [])
  .config(function() {
    //configuration block 1
  })

  .config(function() {
    //configuration block 2
  });
```

As you can see, the alternative method makes it possible to register several configuration blocks. This might come handy to split big configuration functions (especially ones with multiple dependencies) into smaller, focused functions. Small, cohesive functions are easier to read, maintain and test.

In the SCRUM sample application we are going to use the later form of registering configuration and run functions as we find it more readable.

Downloading the example code

You can download the example code files for all Packt books you have purchased from your account at http://www.packtpub.com. If you purchased this book elsewhere, you can visit http://www.packtpub.com/supportand register to have the files e-mailed directly to you.

Automated testing

Software development is hard. As developers, we need to juggle customer requirements and pressure of deadlines, work effectively with other team members, and all this while being proficient with multitude of software development tools and programing languages. As the complexity of software rises so is the number of bugs. We are all human and we will make mistakes, tons of them. Lower-level, programming errors are only one type of defect that we need to constantly fight. Installation, configuration and integration issues will also plague any non-trivial project.

Since, it is so easy to introduce different types of bugs in a project we need effective tools and techniques to battle those errors. The software development industry as the whole realizes more and more that only rigorously applied automated testing can guarantee quality, on-time deliverables.

Automated testing practices were firstly popularized by the agile development methodologies (eXtreme Programming, XP). But, what was new and revolutionary several years ago (and to a certain point controversial) is now a widely accepted, standard practice. These days, there is really no excuse for not having a comprehensive, automated test battery.

Unit tests are our first defense line in the battle against programming bugs. Those tests as the name implies are focused on small units of code, usually individual classes or clusters of closely collaborating objects. Unit tests are a tool for a developer. They help us assert that we got the lower-level constructs right, and that our functions produce expected results. But unit tests bring much more benefits beyond simple, one-off code verification:

- They help us find problems early in the development process when the debugging and fixing is the least costly.
- A well-written set of tests can be executed on each and every build providing a non-regression test suite. This gives us peace of mind and allows us to introduce code changes with great confidence.
- There is arguably no better and more lightweight development environment than just an editor and a test runner. We can move quickly without building, deploying and clicking through the application to verify that our change is correct.

- Writing code test-first using the Test Drive Development (**TDD**) approach helps us design classes and their interfaces. Tests serve as yet another client invoking our code and as such helps us design flexible, loosely coupled classes and interfaces.

- Last but not least existing tests can serve as documentation. We can always open a test to see how a given method should be invoked, what is a set of accepted arguments. What's more, this documentation is executable and always up to date.

Unit tests are of great help but they can't catch all the possible problems. In particular all the configuration and integration issues won't be detected by unit tests. To thoroughly cover our applications with automated tests we need to execute higher-level, end-to-end (integration) tests as well. The goal of integration tests is to exercise an assembled application and make sure that all the individual units play nicely together to form a fully functional application.

Writing and maintaining automated tests is a skill apart that as any other skill needs to be learned and honed. At the beginning of your testing journey you might feel like testing practices are slowing you down and are not worth it. But as you get more proficient with testing techniques you will appreciate how much time we can actually gain by rigorously testing the code.

> There is a quote saying that writing code without a version control system (VCS) is like skydiving without a parachute. Today one would hardly consider running a project without using a VCS. Same applies to the automated testing and we could say: "Writing software without an automated test suite is like climbing without a rope or skydiving without a parachute". You can try but the results will be almost for sure disastrous.

AngularJS team fully recognizes the importance of the automated testing and strictly applies testing practices while working on the framework. What is fantastic, though, is that AngularJS comes with a set of tools, libraries and recommendations that make our application easy to test.

Unit tests

AngularJS adopted Jasmine as its testing framework: unit tests for the framework itself are written using Jasmine and all the examples in the documentation are using Jasmine syntax as well. Moreover AngularJS extended the original Jasmine library with few useful add-ons that make testing even easier.

Anatomy of a Jasmine test

Jasmine announces itself as the "behavior-driven development framework for testing JavaScript code". The behavior-driven testing roots are reflected in the syntax employed by the library tests specifications that are supposed to read as English sentences. Let's examine a simple test exercising a standard JavaScript class to see how it works in practice:

```
describe('hello World test', function () {

  var greeter;
  beforeEach(function () {
    greeter = new Greeter();
  });

  it('should say hello to the World', function () {
    expect(greeter.say('World')).toEqual('Hello, World!');
  });
});
```

There are several constructs in the above tests that need a word of explanation:

- The describe function, describes a feature of an application. It acts as an aggregating container for individual tests. If you are familiar with other testing frameworks you can think of the describe blocks as of test suites. The describe blocks can be nested inside each other.

- The test itself is located inside the it function. The idea is to exercise one particular aspect of a feature in one test. A test has a name and a body. Usually the first section of the test's body calls methods on an object under test while the later one verifies expected results.

- Code contained in the beforeEach block will get executed before each individual test. This is a perfect place for any initialization logic that has to be executed before each test.

- The last things to mention are the expect and the toEqual functions. Using those two constructs we can compare actual results with the expected ones. Jasmine, as many other popular testing frameworks, comes with a rich set of matchers, toBeTruthy, toBeDefined, toContain are just few examples of what is available.

Testing AngularJS objects

Testing AngularJS objects is not much different from testing any other, regular JavaScript class. Specific to AngularJS is its dependency injection system and the way it can be leveraged in unit tests. To learn how to write tests leveraging the DI machinery we are going to focus on testing services and controllers.

 All the tests-related extensions and mock objects are distributed in a separate AngularJS file named `angular-mocks.js`. Don't forget to include this script in your test runner. At the same time it is important not to include this script in the deployed version of an application.

Testing services

Writing tests for objects registered in AngularJS modules is easy but requires a bit of initial setup. More specifically, we need to ensure that a proper AngularJS module is initialized and the whole DI machinery brought to life. Fortunately AngularJS provides a set of methods that make Jasmine tests and the dependency injection system play together really nicely.

Let's break down a simple test for the notificationsArchive introduced in *Chapter 1, Angular Zen* to see how to test AngularJS services. As a reminder here is the code for the service itself:

```
angular.module('archive', [])
  .factory('notificationsArchive', function () {

    var archivedNotifications = [];
    return {
      archive:function (notification) {
        archivedNotifications.push(notification);
      },
      getArchived:function () {
        return archivedNotifications;
      }};
  });
```

Here is the corresponding test:

```
describe('notifications archive tests', function () {

  var notificationsArchive;
  beforeEach(module('archive'));
```

```
  beforeEach(inject(function (_notificationsArchive_) {
    notificationsArchive = _notificationsArchive_;
  }));

  it('should give access to the archived items', function () {
    var notification = {msg: 'Old message.'};
    notificationsArchive.archive(notification);

    expect(notificationsArchive.getArchived())
      .toContain(notification);
  });
});
```

At this point you should be able to recognize the familiar structure of the Jasmine test plus spot some new function calls: module and inject.

The module function is used in Jasmine tests to indicate that services from a given module should be prepared for the test. The role of this method is similar to the one played by the ng-app directive. It indicated that AngularJS $injector should be created for a given module (and all the dependent modules).

> Don't confuse the module function used in the test with the angular.module method. While both have the same name their roles are quite different. The angular.module method is used to declare new modules while the module function allows us to specify modules to be used in a test.

In reality it is possible to have multiple module function calls in one test. In this case all the services, values and constants from the specified modules will be available through the $injector.

The inject function has one simple responsibility, that is it injects the services into our tests.

The last part that might be confusing is the presence of the mysterious underscores in the inject function call:

```
var notificationsArchive;
beforeEach(inject(function (_notificationsArchive_) {
  notificationsArchive = _notificationsArchive_;
}));
```

What is happening here is that $injector will strip any a pair leading and trailing underscores when inspecting the function's arguments to retrieve dependencies. This is a useful trick since we can save variable names without underscores for the test itself.

Testing controllers

A test for a controller follows similar a pattern to the one for a service. Let's have a look at the fragment of the `ProjectsEditCtrl` controller from the sample application. This controller in question is responsible for the editing projects in the administration part of the application. Here we are going to test methods of the controller responsible for adding and removing project's team members:

```
angular.module('admin-projects', [])
    .controller('ProjectsEditCtrl', function($scope, project) {

    $scope.project = project;

    $scope.removeTeamMember = function(teamMember) {
      var idx = $scope.project.teamMembers.indexOf(teamMember);
      if(idx >= 0) {
        $scope.project.teamMembers.splice(idx, 1);
      }
    };

    //other methods of the controller
});
```

The logic of the presented controllers is not complex and will let us to focus on the test itself:

```
describe('ProjectsEditCtrl tests', function () {

  var $scope;
  beforeEach(module('admin-projects'));
  beforeEach(inject(function ($rootScope) {
    $scope = $rootScope.$new();
  }));

  it('should remove an existing team member', inject(function
($controller) {

    var teamMember = {};
    $controller('ProjectsEditCtrl', {
      $scope: $scope,
      project: {
        teamMembers: [teamMember]
      }
    });

    //verify the initial setup
    expect($scope.project.teamMembers).toEqual([teamMember]);
```

```
    //execute and verify results
    $scope.removeTeamMember(teamMember);
    expect($scope.project.teamMembers).toEqual([]);
  }));
});
```

The `removeTeamMember` method that we want to test here will be defined on a `$scope` and it is the `ProjectsEditCtrl` controller that defines this method. To effectively test the `removeTeamMember` method we need to create a new scope, a new instance of the `ProjectsEditCtrl` controller and link the two together. Essentially we need to manually do the job of the `ng-controller` directive.

Let's turn our attention to the `beforeEach` section for one more moment, as there are interesting things going on in there. Firstly we are getting access to the `$rootScope` service and creating a new `$scope` instance (`$scope.$new()`). We do so to simulate what would happen in a running application, where the `ng-controller` directive would create a new scope.

To create an instance of the controller we can use the `$controller` service (please notice how the `inject` function can be placed on the `beforeEach` section as well as on the `it` level).

 Look how easy it is to specify controller's constructor arguments while invoking the `$controller` service. This is dependency injection at its best; we can provide both a fake scope and test data to exercise controller's implementation in complete isolation.

Mock objects and asynchronous code testing

We can see how AngularJS provides a very nice integration of its dependency injection system with the Jasmine testing framework. But the good testability story continues as AngularJS provides some excellent mock objects as well.

Asynchronous programming is the bread and butter of JavaScript. Unfortunately asynchronous code tends to be hard to test. Asynchronous events are not very predictable, and can fire in any order and trigger actions after an unknown period of time. The good news is that the AngularJS team provides excellent mock objects that make testing asynchronous code really easy and what is important is that they are fast and predictable. How can this be? Let's have a look at the example test exercising the code using the `$timeout` service. First at the code itself:

```
angular.module('async', [])
  .factory('asyncGreeter', function ($timeout, $log) {
    return {
```

```
    say:function (name, timeout) {
      $timeout(function(){
        $log.info("Hello, " + name + "!");
      })
    }
  };
});
```

The $timeout service is a replacement for the JavaScript setTimeout
function. Using $timeout is preferable for the purpose of deferring
actions as it is tightly integrated with the AngularJS HTML compiler
and will trigger the DOM refresh after the time is up. On top of this the
resulting code is easy to test.

Here is the test:

```
describe('Async Greeter test', function () {

  var asyncGreeter, $timeout, $log;
  beforeEach(module('async'));
  beforeEach(inject(function (_asyncGreeter_, _$timeout_, _$log_) {
    asyncGreeter = _asyncGreeter_;
    $timeout = _$timeout_;
    $log = _$log_;
  }));

  it('should greet the async World', function () {
    asyncGreeter.say('World', 999999999999999999);
    //
    $timeout.flush();
    expect($log.info.logs).toContain(['Hello, World!']);
  });
});
```

Most of this code should be easy to follow but there are two very interesting bits
that require more attention. Firstly we can see a call to the $timeout.flush()
method. This one little call on the $timeout mock simulates an asynchronous event
being triggered. The interesting part is that we've got full control over when this
event is going to be triggered. We don't need to wait for the timeout to occur, nor
are we on the mercy of external events. Please note that we've specified a very long
timeout period, yet our test will execute immediately, since we don't depend on the
JavaScript's setTimeout. Rather it is the $timeout mock that simulates the behavior
of the asynchronous environment.

Excellent, predictable mocks for the asynchronous services are one of the reasons why AngularJS tests can run blazing fast.

On many platforms there are often fundamental, global services that are rather difficult to test. Logging and exception handling code are examples of such logic that causes testing headaches. Luckily, AngularJS has a remedy here; it provides services addressing those infrastructural concerns alongside with accompanying mock objects. You've probably noticed that the test example makes use of one more mock, namely, $log. The mock for the $log service will accumulate all the logging statements and store them for further assertions. Using a mock object assures that we are not invoking real platform services; especially the ones that are potentially expensive in terms of performance and could have side-effects (for example, one could imagine that the $log service sends logs to a server over HTTP, and it would be very bad idea to perform network calls while executing tests).

End-to-end tests

AngularJS introduced its own end-to-end testing solution called **Scenario Runner**. The Scenario Runner can execute integration tests by driving actions in a real browser. It automatically executes actions (filling in forms, clicking on buttons, and links and so on) and verifies UI responses (page change, proper information displayed, and so on), thus greatly reducing the need for the manual verifications traditionally performed by the quality assurance teams.

AngularJS solution has similar functionality as other existing tools (for example, the very popular **Selenium**), but it tightly integrates with the framework. More specifically:

- The Scenario Runner is aware of asynchronous events (most importantly XHR calls). It can pause the execution of a test until the asynchronous event completes. In practice this means that the test code doesn't have to use any explicit waiting instructions. Anyone who has tried to test an Ajax-heavy web application using traditional tools will highly appreciate this feature.

- We can take advantage of binding information already available in the AngularJS templates to select DOM elements for further manipulations and verifications. Essentially it is possible to locate DOM elements and form inputs based on model to which those elements are bound. This means that we neither need to embed superfluous HTML attributes (usually IDs or CSS classes) nor rely on fragile XPath expressions so the testing framework can locate the DOM elements.

- The syntax used by the Scenario Runner makes it really easy to find DOM elements, interact with them, and assert on their properties. There is a complete **domain-specific language (DSL)** for searching and matching repeaters, inputs, and so on.

Unfortunately, as the time was passing by more and more limitations of the Scenario Runner were surfacing. Due to this, as of time of this writing, the Scenario Runner is not actively maintained. There are plans to replace it with another solution based on Selenium integration, namely, Protractor. The work in progress can be seen in the GitHub repository at `https://github.com/angular/protractor`.

 We recommend against using the existing Scenario Runner for any new project. It is not actively maintained and it won't evolve. Instead, you should keep an eye on Protractor.

Daily workflow

In order to be effective, automated testing needs to be applied rigorously. Tests should be run as often as practicably possible and failing tests should be fixed as soon as possible. A failing test should be treated as a failing build, and fixing a broken build should be a top priority for a team.

During the day we will be switching, back and forth between JavaScript code and UI templates. When focusing on the pure JavaScript code and other AngularJS artifacts (such as filters or directives), it is important to run unit tests often. In fact, due to the remarkable speed at which AngularJS test can be executed with the Karma test runner it becomes practical to run all the unit tests as often as on every file save!

While writing the sample SCRUM application, the authors of this book were working with the Karma runner set up in a way that it would monitor all the file changes (both to the source code and the test code). On each and every file save a complete suite of tests were executed providing an immediate health-check. In such a setup, the feedback loop becomes very short, and we can always know that either our code still works as expected or was broken just seconds before. If things are in order we can swiftly move on, but if tests start failing we know that it is due to one of the latest changes. With the tests running so often, we can say goodbye to long and tedious debugging sessions.

Running tests shouldn't require much effort. It is very important to have a comfortable testing environment, where the automated test suite can be executed as often as possible. If running a test involves several manual, tedious steps, we will avoid testing.

With modern tools it is possible to have extremely efficient setup. For example, here is the screenshot of the development environment used to write examples for this book. As you can see the source and test code are opened side by side so it is easy to switch between writing test and production code. Karma runner is watching the file system to execute test on every file save operation and provide the immediate feedback (in the lower pane):

> Unit testing environment described here is in fact the lightest possible development environment. We can work all the time in our IDE and focus on writing code. No need to switch context for building, deploying or clicking in a browser to verify that our code works as expected.

Karma runner tips and tricks

Practicing Test Driven Development (TDD) greatly reduces number of long debugging sessions. When writing code test, first we are usually doing small changes and running tests often so the change that causes test to fail is just few keystrokes away. But despite our best efforts there will be times when we won't be able to understand what is going on without resorting to a debugger. In times like those we need to be able to quickly isolate a failing test and focus on this one test.

Executing a subset of tests

The Jasmine version shipped with Karma runner has very useful extensions to quickly isolate a set of tests to run:

- Prefixing a test or a suite with the x character (xit, xdescribe) will disable this tests/suite during the next run.

- Prefix a test suite with the d character (ddescribe) will only run this suite, ignoring others.

- Prefixing a test with the i character (iit) will only run this test, ignoring other tests and suites.

Those little prefixes are extremely useful in practice and can be used as shown below:

```
describe('tips & tricks', function () {

  xdescribe('none of the tests here will execute', function () {

    it('won't execute - spec level', function () {
    });

    xit('won't execute - test level', function () {
    });
  });

  describe('suite with one test selected', function () {

    iit('will execute only this test', function () {
    });

    it('will be executed only after removing iit', function () {
    });
  });

});
```

Debugging

Narrowing down a failing test is half of the success. Still we need to understand what is going on, and this often involves a debugging session. But how to debug tests executed by Karma runner? It turns out that it is pretty easy; it is enough to add the debugger statement in our test or production code.

[🔆 While using the `debugger` statement don't forget to turn on your
developer tools in your favorite browser. Otherwise a browser
won't pause and you won't be able to debug tests.]

Sometimes it might be easier to just print values of some variables on a console.
AngularJS mocks come with one convenient method for such occasions `angular.`
`mock.dump(object)`. In fact the `dump` method is also exposed on the global (window)
scope so we could simply write `dump(object)`.

Summary

This chapter prepared us for writing real-life applications with AngularJS. At the
beginning we went over the details of the sample application; its problem domain and
the technical stack. The rest of this book is filled with the examples inspired by the
sample application for managing projects using the SCRUM methodology. To write
this application we are going to use a JavaScript-based (or at least JavaScript-friendly),
open source stack: hosted MongoDB as a persistence store, `node.js` as the server-side
solution and obviously AngularJS as the front-end framework.

We spent a considerable amount of time discussing build-related problematic
philosophy behind a perfect build system and its practical implementations. We've
chosen the JavaScript-based (and `node.js` powered) `grunt.js` to write sample build
scripts. Looking into the build inevitably leads us to look into the organization of
files and folders in the sample project. We've chosen a directory structure that plays
nicely with the AngularJS module system. After pondering different ways of declaring
AngularJS modules and providers, we've settled on the syntax that avoids confusion,
doesn't pollute the global namespace, and keeps our build system complexity at
reasonable levels.

The benefits of automated testing are well known and understood these days. We are
lucky since AngularJS puts strong emphasizes on testability of the code written using
the framework. We saw that AngularJS comes with the complete testing offering
tools (Karma runner), integration with the existing testing libraries (Jasmine), and the
built in dependency injection system that makes it easy to test individual objects in
isolation. We saw how to test AngularJS artifacts in practice as well testing AngularJS
services and controllers should have no secrets for you at this point. With all the
solutions in place it is easy to put in place a very nice, lightweight testing workflow.

So far we've learned AngularJS basics and saw how to structure a non-trivial
application. We can now use this foundation to add concrete, real-life elements.
Since any CRUD application needs to work with the data fetched from a persistent
store, the next chapter is devoted to the AngularJS-way of communicating with
various back-ends.

3
Communicating with a Back-end Server

More often than not web applications need to communicate with a persistent store to fetch and manipulate data. This is especially true for CRUD-like applications where data editing is the essential part.

AngularJS is well equipped to communicate with various back-ends using **XMLHttpRequest (XHR)** and **JSONP** requests. It has a general purpose `$http` service for issuing XHR and JSONP calls as well as a specialized `$resource` service to easily target **RESTful** endpoints.

In this chapter, we are going to examine different APIs and techniques to communicate with various back-ends. In particular, we are going to learn how to:

- Make basic XHR calls using the `$http` service and test code relying on `$http`
- Effectively work with asynchronous requests, using the promise API exposed by AngularJS in the `$q` service
- Easily talk to RESTful endpoints using the dedicated `$resource` factory
- Build a custom, `$resource`-like API tailored to our back-end needs

Making XHR and JSONP requests with $http

The `$http` service is a fundamental, all-purpose API for making XHR and JSONP calls. The API itself is well-crafted and easy to use, as we are going to see shortly. Before diving into the details of the `$http` API though, we need to learn a bit more about data model of our sample SCRUM application so we can follow meaningful examples.

Getting familiar with the data model and MongoLab URLs

The data model of the sample SCRUM application is rather simple and can be illustrated on the following diagram:

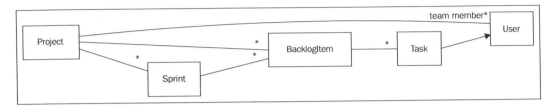

There are five different MongoDB collections holding data of users, projects and project-related artifacts. All the data are accessible through the RESTful interface exposed by MongoLab. The REST API can be invoked by targeting URLs with a well-defined pattern:

```
https://api.mongolab.com/api/1/databases/[DB name]/collections/
[collection name]/[item id]?apiKey=[secret key]
```

> All the REST API calls targeting databases hosted on MongoLab need to include a request parameter named apiKey. The apiKey parameter, with the value unique to an individual account, is necessary to authorize MongoLab REST API calls. The complete description of the REST API exposed by MongoLab can be consulted at https://support.mongolab.com/entries/20433053-rest-api-for-mongodb.

$http APIs quick tour

Doing XHR and JSONP calls using the $http service is straightforward. Let's consider an example of fetching JSON content with a GET request:

```
var futureResponse = $http.get('data.json');
futureResponse.success(function (data, status, headers, config) {
  $scope.data = data;
});
futureResponse.error(function (data, status, headers, config) {
  throw new Error('Something went wrong...');
});
```

First of all we can see that there is a dedicated method to issue XHR GET requests. There are equivalent methods for other types of XHRrequests as well:

- GET: `$http.get(url, config)`
- POST: `$http.post(url, data, config)`
- PUT: `$http.put(url, data, config)`
- DELETE: `$http.delete(url, config)`
- HEAD: `$http.head`

It is also possible to trigger a JSONP request with `$http.jsonp(url, config)`.

The parameters accepted by the `$http` methods differ slightly depending on the HTTP method used. For calls that can carry data in their body (POST and PUT) the method signature is the following one:

- `url`: the URL to be targeted with a call
- `data`: data to be sent with a request's body
- `config`: a JavaScript object containing additional configuration options influencing a request and a response

For the remaining methods (GET, DELETE, HEAD, JSONP) where there is no data to be sent with the request's body, the signature becomes simpler and is reduced to two parameters only: `url` and `config`.

The object returned from the `$http` methods allows us to register success and error callbacks.

The configuration object primer

The JavaScript configuration object can hold different options influencing the request, response and data being transmitted. The configuration object can have the following properties (among others):

- `method`: HTTP method to be issued
- `url`: URL to be targeted with a request
- `params`: parameters to be added to the URL query string
- `headers`: additional headers to be added to a request
- `timeout`: timeout (in milliseconds) after which a XHR request will be dropped
- `cache`: enables XHR GET request caching
- `transformRequest`, `transformResponse`: transformation functions that allows us to pre-process and post-process data exchanged with a back-end

You might be a bit surprised to see `method` and `url` among configuration options since those parameters can be already supplied as part of a `$http` methods' signatures. It turns out that `$http` itself is a function that can be invoked in a generic way:

```
$http(configObject);
```

The generic form might be useful for cases where AngularJS doesn't provide a "shortcut" method (for example for PATCH or OPTIONS requests). In general we find that shortcut methods result in a more concise and easier way to read code, and we would recommend using this form over the generic one whenever possible.

Request data conversion

The `$http.post` and `$http.put` methods accept any JavaScript object (or a string) value as their `data` parameter. If data is a JavaScript object it will be, by default, converted to a JSON string.

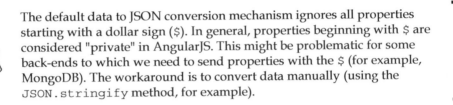

> The default data to JSON conversion mechanism ignores all properties starting with a dollar sign ($). In general, properties beginning with $ are considered "private" in AngularJS. This might be problematic for some back-ends to which we need to send properties with the $ (for example, MongoDB). The workaround is to convert data manually (using the `JSON.stringify` method, for example).

We can see the data conversion in action by issuing a POST request to create a new user in MongoLab:

```
var userToAdd = {
  name:'AngularJS Superhero',
  email:'superhero@angularjs.org'
};

$http.post('https://api.mongolab.com/api/1/databases/ascrum/collec
  tions/users',
  userToAdd, {
    params:{
      apiKey:'4fb51e55e4b02e56a67b0b66'
    }
  });
```

This example also illustrates how HTTP query string parameters (here: `apiKey`) can be added to a URL.

Dealing with HTTP responses

A request can either succeed or fail and AngularJS provides two methods to register callbacks to deal with the two outcomes: success and error. Both the methods accept a callback function that will be called with the following parameters:

- **data**: The actual response data
- **status**: The HTTP status of the response
- **headers**: A function giving access to the HTTP response headers
- **config**: The configuration object that was supplied when a request was triggered

> AngularJS will invoke success callbacks for the HTTP responses with status ranging from 200 to 299. Responses with a status outside of this range will trigger the error callback. The redirection responses (HTTP status 3xx codes) are automatically followed by a browser.

Both success and error callbacks are optional. If we don't register any callback a response will be silently ignored.

Response data conversion

As with request data conversions, the $http service will try to convert responses containing a JSON string into a JavaScript object. This conversion happens before invoking success or error callbacks. The default conversion behavior can be customized.

> In the current version of AngularJS the $http service will try to perform JSON string to JavaScript object conversion on any responses that look like JSON (that is, starts with { or [and end with] or }).

Dealing with same-origin policy restrictions

Web browsers enforce the **same-origin security policy**. This policy authorizes XHR interactions only with resources originating from the same source (defined as a combination of a protocol, host and its port) and enforces restrictions on interactions with "foreign" resources.

As web developers, we need to constantly balance security considerations with functional requirements to aggregate data from multiple sources. Indeed, it is often desirable to fetch data from third party services and present those data in our web applications. Unfortunately, XHR requests can't easily reach servers outside of the source domain unless we play some tricks.

There are several techniques for accessing data exposed by external servers: **JSON with padding (JSONP)** and **Cross-origin resource sharing (CORS)** are probably the most popular ones in the modern web. This section shows how AngularJS helps us applying those techniques in practice.

Overcoming same-origin policy restrictions with JSONP

Using JSONP is a trick that allows fetching data by passing the same-origin policy restrictions. It relies on the fact that browsers can freely pull JavaScript from foreign servers by using the `<script>` tag.

JSONP calls don't trigger XHR requests but instead generate a `<script>` tag whose source points to an external resource. As soon as a generated script tag appears in the DOM a browser performs its duty and calls the server. The server pads the response with a function invocation (thus the "padding" in the name of JSONP technique) in the context of our web application.

Let's examine a sample JSONP request and response to see how it works in practice. First of all we need to invoke a JSONP request:

```
$http
  .jsonp('http://angularjs.org/greet.php?callback=JSON_CALLBACK', {
    params:{
      name:'World'
    }
  }).success(function (data) {
    $scope.greeting = data;
  });
```

Upon invoking the `$http.jsonp` method AngularJS will dynamically create a new `<script>` DOM element like:

```
<script type="text/javascript" src="http://angularjs.org/greet.
php?callback=angular.callbacks._k&name=World"></script>
```

As soon as this script tag is attached to the DOM the browser will request the URL specified in the `src` attribute. The response, upon arrival, will have a body following a pattern like:

```
angular.callbacks._k ({"name":"World","salutation":"Hello","greeting":
"Hello World!"});
```

A JSONP response looks like a regular JavaScript function call and in fact this exactly what it is. AngularJS generated the `angular.callbacks._k` function behind the scenes. This function, when invoked, will trigger a success callback invocation. The URL supplied to the `$http.jsonp` function call must contain the `JSON_CALLBACK` request parameter. AngularJS will turn this string into a dynamically generated function name.

 JSONP callback names generated by AngularJS will have a form of `angular.callbacks._[variable]`. Make sure that your back-end can accept callback names containing dots.

JSONP limitations

JSONP is a smart and useful work-around for the same-origin policy restrictions but it has several limitations. Firstly, we should only GET HTTP requests can be issued using the JSONP technique. Error handling is also very problematic, since browsers won't expose HTTP response status from the `<script>` tag back to JavaScript. In practice it means that it is rather difficult to reliably report the HTTP status errors and invoke error callbacks.

JSONP also exposes our web application to several security threats. Apart from the well-known XSS attack, probably the biggest issue is that a server can generate any arbitrary JavaScript in the JSONP response. This JavaScript will be loaded to a browser and executed in the context of a user's session. A server configured in a malicious way could execute undesired scripts causing different damages, ranging from simply breaking a page to stealing sensitive data. As such, we should be really careful while selecting services targeted by JSONP request and only use trusted servers.

Overcoming same-origin policy restrictions with CORS

Cross-origin resource sharing (CORS) is a W3C specification that aims at solving the same problem as JSONP in a standard, reliable, and secure way. The CORS specification builds on top of the `XMLHttpRequest` object to enable the cross-domain AJAX requests in a well-defined and controlled manner.

The whole idea behind CORS is that a browser and a foreign server need to coordinate (by sending appropriate request and response headers) to conditionally allow cross-domain requests. As such, a foreign server needs to be configured properly. Browsers must be able to send appropriate requests, and headers, and interpret server responses to successfully complete cross-domain requests.

> A foreign server must be configured properly to participate in a CORS conversation. Those who need to configure servers to accept HTTP CORS can find more information in `http://www.html5rocks.com/en/tutorials/cors/`. Here we are going to focus on the browser role in the whole communication.

CORS requests are roughly divided into "simple" and "non-simple" ones. GET, POST, and HEAD requests are considered as "simple" (but only when sending a subset of allowed headers). Using other HTTP verbs or request headers outside of the allowed set will force a browser to issue a "non-simple" CORS request.

> Most of the modern browsers support CORS communication out of the box. Internet Explorer in its Version 8 and 9 enables CORS support only with the non-standard `XDomainRequest` object. Due to limitations of the IE-specific `XDomainRequest` implementation AngularJS doesn't provide support for it. As a result, the CORS requests are not supported with the `$http` service on IE 8 and 9.

With non-simple requests, the browser is obliged to send a probing (**preflight**) OPTION request and wait for the server's approval before issuing the primary request. This is often confusing, since a closer inspection of the HTTP traffic reveals mysterious OPTIONS requests. We can see those requests by trying to call the MongoLab REST API directly from a browser. As an example, let's inspect the HTTP communication while deleting a user:

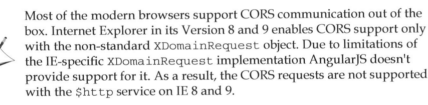

```
$http.delete('https://api.mongolab.com/api/1/databases/ascrum/
collections/users/' + userId,
  {
    params:{
      apiKey:'4fb51e55e4b02e56a67b0b66'
    }
  }
);
```

We can see two requests (**OPTIONS** and **DELETE**) targeting the same URL:

Elements	Resources	Network	Sources	Timeline	Profiles	Audits	Console	AngularJS			
Name				Method	Status		Type	Initiator		Size	Time
userid?apiKey=4fb51e55e4b02e56a67b0b66				OPTIONS	200		text/html	angular.js:9002		656 B	697 ms
userid?apiKey=4fb51e55e4b02e56a67b0b66				DELETE	200		application/j...	Other		346 B	438 ms

The response from the MongoLab server includes headers that make the final DELETE request possible:

```
▼Response Headers        view source
  Access-Control-Allow-Credentials: true
  Access-Control-Allow-Headers: accept, origin, x-requested-with, content-type
  Access-Control-Allow-Methods: DELETE
  Access-Control-Allow-Methods: OPTIONS
  Access-Control-Allow-Methods: PUT
  Access-Control-Allow-Methods: GET
  Access-Control-Allow-Origin: *
  Access-Control-Max-Age: 1728000
  Allow: PUT
  Allow: OPTIONS
  Allow: DELETE
  Allow: GET
```

The MongoLab servers are well configured to send appropriate headers in response to the CORS request. If your server is not properly configured the OPTIONS request will fail and the target request won't be executed.

 Don't be surprised upon seeing OPTIONS requests; this is just the CORS handshake mechanism at work. Failing OPTIONS requests most probably indicate that a server is not well configured.

Server-side proxies

JSONP is not an ideal technique for making cross-origin requests. The CORS specification makes the situation better, but it still requires additional configuration on the server side and a browser that supports the standard.

If you cannot use CORS or JSONP techniques, then there is always the option of avoiding cross-domain request issues altogether. We can achieve this by configuring a local server as a proxy to a foreign one. By applying a correct server configuration we can proxy cross-domain requests through our server, and thus have the browser target only our servers. This technique works on all browsers, and doesn't require pre-flight OPTIONS request. Also, it doesn't expose us to any additional security risks. The downside of this approach is that we need to configure the server accordingly.

The sample SCRUM application described in this book relies on the node.js server configured in a way that it proxies calls to the MongLab REST APIs.

The promise API with $q

JavaScript programmers are accustomed to the asynchronous programming model. Both a browser and the node.js execution environments are full of asynchronous events: XHR responses, DOM events, IO and timeouts, which can be triggered at any moment and in random order. Even if, we are all used to coping with the asynchronous nature of the execution environment the truth is that asynchronous programming might be perplexing, especially when it comes to synchronizing multiple asynchronous events.

In the synchronous world chaining function calls (invoking a function with a result of another function) and handling exceptions (with try/catch) is straightforward. In the asynchronous world, we can't simply chain function calls; we need to rely on callbacks. Callbacks are fine when dealing with just one asynchronous event, but things start to get complicated as soon as we need to coordinate multiple asynchronous events. Exceptional situation handling is particularly tough in this case.

To make asynchronous programming easier the **Promise API** was recently adopted by several popular JavaScript libraries. The concepts behind the Promise API are not new, and were proposed in the late seventies, but only recently those concepts made it into the mainstream JavaScript programming.

The main idea behind the Promise API is to bring to the asynchronous world the same ease of functions calls chaining and error handling as we can enjoy in the synchronous programming world.

AngularJS comes with the $q service a very lightweight Promise API implementation. A number of AngularJS services (most notably $http, but also $timeout and others) heavily rely on the promise-style APIs. So we need to get familiar with $q in order to use those services effectively.

The $q service was inspired by the *Kris Kowal's* Q Promise API library (https://github.com/kriskowal/q). You might want to check out this library to gain a better understanding or promise concepts and compare AngularJS lightweight implementation with the full featured Promise API library.

Working with promises and the $q service

To learn the relatively small API exposed by the $q service, we are going to use examples from real life, just to demonstrate that the Promise API can be applied to any asynchronous events, and not only to XHR calls.

Learning $q service basics

Let's imagine that we want to order a pizza over the phone and have it delivered to our home. The outcome of our pizza order can be either delivered food or a phone call indicating problems with our order. While ordering a pizza is just a matter of a short phone call, the actual delivery (order fulfillment) takes some time, and is asynchronous.

To get the feeling of the Promise API, let's have a look at the pizza order, and its successful delivery, modeled using the $q service. Firstly, we are going to define a person that can consume a pizza, or just get disappointed when an order is not delivered:

```
var Person = function (name, $log) {

this.eat = function (food) {
    $log.info(name + " is eating delicious " + food);
};
this.beHungry = function (reason) {
    $log.warn(name + " is hungry because: " + reason);
}
};
```

The Person constructor defined above can be used to produce an object containing the eat and beHungry methods. We are going to use those methods as the success and error callbacks, respectively.

Now, let's model a pizza ordering and fulfillment process written as a Jasmine test:

```
it('should illustrate basic usage of $q', function () {

  var pizzaOrderFulfillment = $q.defer();
  var pizzaDelivered = pizzaOrderFulfillment.promise;

  pizzaDelivered.then(pawel.eat, pawel.beHungry);

  pizzaOrderFulfillment.resolve('Margherita');
  $rootScope.$digest();

  expect($log.info.logs).toContain(['Pawel is eating delicious
Margherita']);
});
```

The unit test starts by the call to the $q.defer() method which returns a **deferred** object. Conceptually it represents a task that will be completed (or will fail in the future). The deferred object has two roles:

- It holds a **promise** object (in the promise property). Promises are placeholders for the future results (success or failure) of a deferred task.

- It exposes methods to trigger future task completion (resolve) or failure (reject).

There are always two players in the Promise API: one that controls future task execution (can invoke methods on the deferred object) and another one that depends on the results of the future task execution (holds onto promised results).

The deferred object represents a task that will complete or fail in the future. A promise object is a placeholder for the future results of this task completion.

An entity that controls the future task (in our example it would be a restaurant) exposes a promise object (pizzaOrderFulfillment.promise) to entities that are interested in the result of the task. In our example, Pawel is interested in the delivered order and can express his interest by registering callbacks on the promise object. To register a callback the then(successCallBack, errorCallBack) method is used. This method accepts callback functions that will be called with a future task result (in case of success callback) or a failure reason (in case of error callback). The error callback is optional and can be omitted. If the error callback is omitted and a future task fails, this failure will be silently ignored.

To signal the future task completion the resolve method should be called on the deferred object. The argument passed to the resolve method will be used as a value provided to the success callback. After a success callback is called a future task is completed and the promise is resolved (fulfilled). Similarly, the call to the reject method will trigger the error callback invocation and promise rejection.

In the test example there is a mysterious call to the $rootScope.$digest() method. In AngularJS results of promise resolution (or rejection) are propagated as part of the $digest cycle. You can refer to the *Chapter 11, Writing Well-performing AngularJS Web Applications*, to learn more about AngularJS internals and the $digest cycle.

Promises are first-class JavaScript objects

At first glance it might look like the Promise API adds unnecessary complexity. But to appreciate the real power of promises we need to see more examples. First of all we need to realize that promises are first-class JavaScript objects. We can pass them around as arguments and return them from function calls. This allows us to easily encapsulate asynchronous operations as services. For example, let's imagine a simplified restaurant service:

```
var Restaurant = function ($q, $rootScope) {

  var currentOrder;

  this.takeOrder = function (orderedItems) {
    currentOrder = {
      deferred:$q.defer(),
      items:orderedItems
    };
    return currentOrder.deferred.promise;
  };

  this.deliverOrder = function() {
    currentOrder.deferred.resolve(currentOrder.items);
    $rootScope.$digest();
  };

  this.problemWithOrder = function(reason) {
    currentOrder.deferred.reject(reason);
    $rootScope.$digest();
  };
};
```

Now the restaurant service encapsulates asynchronous tasks and only returns a promise from its `takeOrder` method. The returned promise can be then used by the restaurant customers to hold onto promised results and be notified when results are available.

As an example of this newly crafted API in action, let's write code that will illustrate rejecting promises and error callbacks being invoked:

```
it('should illustrate promise rejection', function () {

  pizzaPit = new Restaurant($q, $rootScope);
  var pizzaDelivered = pizzaPit.takeOrder('Capricciosa');
```

```
pizzaDelivered.then(pawel.eat, pawel.beHungry);

pizzaPit.problemWithOrder('no Capricciosa, only Margherita
  left');
expect($log.warn.logs).toContain(['Pawel is hungry because: no
  Capricciosa, only Margherita left']);
});
```

Aggregating callbacks

One promise object can be used to register multiple callbacks. To see this in practice let's imagine that both authors of this book are ordering a pizza and as such both are interested in the delivered order:

```
it('should allow callbacks aggregation', function () {

  var pizzaDelivered = pizzaPit.takeOrder('Margherita');
  pizzaDelivered.then(pawel.eat, pawel.beHungry);
  pizzaDelivered.then(pete.eat, pete.beHungry);

  pizzaPit.deliverOrder();
  expect($log.info.logs).toContain(['Pawel is eating delicious
    Margherita']);
  expect($log.info.logs).toContain(['Peter is eating delicious
    Margherita']);
});
```

Here multiple success callbacks are registered and all of them are invoked upon a promise resolution. Similarly, promise rejection will invoke all the registered error callbacks.

Registering callbacks and the promise lifecycle

A promise that was resolved or rejected once can't change its state. There is only one chance of providing promised results. In other words it is not possible to:

- Resolve a rejected promise
- Resolve an already resolved promise with a different result
- Reject a resolved promise
- Reject a rejected promise with a different rejection reason

Those rules are rather intuitive. For example, it wouldn't make much sense if we could be called back with the information that there are problems with our order delivery after our pizza was successfully delivered (and probably eaten!).

Any callbacks registered after a promise was resolved (or rejected) will be resolved (or rejected) with the same result (or failure reason) as the initial one.

Asynchronous action chaining

While aggregating callbacks is nice, the real power of the Promise API lies in its ability to mimic the synchronous function invocations in the asynchronous world.

Continuing our pizza example let's imagine that this time we are invited to our friends for a pizza. Our hosts will order a pizza and upon order arrival they will nicely slice and serve it. There is a chain of asynchronous events here: firstly a pizza needs to be delivered, and only then prepared for serving. There are also two promises that need to be resolved before we can enjoy a meal: a restaurant is promising a delivery and our hosts are promising that a delivered pizza will be sliced and served. Let's see the code modeling this situation:

```
it('should illustrate successful promise chaining', function () {

  var slice = function(pizza) {
    return "sliced "+pizza;
  };

  pizzaPit.takeOrder('Margherita').then(slice).then(pawel.eat);

  pizzaPit.deliverOrder();
  expect($log.info.logs).toContain(['Pawel is eating delicious sliced
    Margherita']);});
```

In the previous example, we can see a chain of promises (calls to the `then` method). This construct closely resembles synchronous code:

```
pawel.eat(slice(pizzaPit));
```

 Promise chaining is possible only because the `then` method returns a new promise. The returned promise will be resolved with the result of the return value of the callback.

What is even more impressive is how easy it is to deal with the error conditions. Let's have a look at the example of the failure propagation to a person holding onto a promise:

```
it('should illustrate promise rejection in chain', function () {

  pizzaPit.takeOrder('Capricciosa').then(slice).then(pawel.eat,
```

```
        pawel.beHungry);

    pizzaPit.problemWithOrder('no Capricciosa, only Margherita
        left');
    expect($log.warn.logs).toContain(['Pawel is hungry because: no
        Capricciosa, only Margherita left']);
});
```

Here the rejection result from the restaurant is propagated up to the person interested in the final result. This is exactly how the exception handling works in the synchronous world: a thrown exception will bubble up to a first catch block.

In the Promise API the error callbacks act as catch blocks, and as with standard catch blocks - we've got several options of handling exceptional situations. We can either:

- recover (return value from a catch block)
- propagate failure (re-throw an exception)

With the Promise API it is easy to simulate a recovery in catch block. As an example, let's assume that our hosts will take an effort of ordering another pizza if a desired one is not available:

```
it('should illustrate recovery from promise rejection', function () {

var retry = function(reason) {
    return pizzaPit.takeOrder('Margherita').then(slice);
  };

  pizzaPit.takeOrder('Capricciosa')
.then(slice, retry)
.then(pawel.eat, pawel.beHungry);

pizzaPit.problemWithOrder('no Capricciosa, only Margherita left');
pizzaPit.deliverOrder();

expect($log.info.logs).toContain(['Pawel is eating delicious sliced
    Margherita']);
});
```

We can return a new promise from an error callback. The returned promise will be part of the resolution chain, and the final consumer won't even notice that something went wrong. This is a very powerful pattern that can be applied in any scenario that requires retries. We are going to use this approach in *Chapter 7, Securing Your Application*, to implement security checks.

The other scenario that we should consider is re-throwing exceptions as it might happen that recovery won't be possible. In such a case the only option is to trigger another error and the $q service has a dedicated method ($q.reject) for this purpose:

```
it('should illustrate explicit rejection in chain', function () {

  var explain = function(reason) {
    return $q.reject('ordered pizza not available');
  };

  pizzaPit.takeOrder('Capricciosa')
.then(slice, explain)
.then(pawel.eat, pawel.beHungry);

  pizzaPit.problemWithOrder('no Capricciosa, only Margherita
    left');

  expect($log.warn.logs).toContain(['Pawel is hungry because:
    ordered pizza not available']);
});
```

The $q.reject method is an equivalent of throwing an exception in the asynchronous world. This method is returning a new promise that is rejected with a reason specified as an argument to the $q.reject method call.

More on $q

The $q service has two additional, useful methods: $q.all and $q.when.

Aggregating promises

The $q.all method makes it possible to start multiple asynchronous tasks and be notified only when all of the tasks complete. It effectively aggregates promises from several asynchronous actions, and returns a single, combined promise that can act as a join point.

To illustrate usefulness of the $q.all method, let's consider an example of ordering food from multiple restaurants. We would like to wait for both orders to arrive before the whole meal is served:

```
it('should illustrate promise aggregation', function () {

  var ordersDelivered = $q.all([
    pizzaPit.takeOrder('Pepperoni'),
    saladBar.takeOrder('Fresh salad')
```

```
    ]);

    ordersDelivered.then(pawel.eat);

    pizzaPit.deliverOrder();
    saladBar.deliverOrder();
    expect($log.info.logs).toContain(['Pawel is eating delicious
Pepperoni,Fresh salad']);
  });
```

The $q.all method accepts an array of promises as its argument, and returns an aggregated promise. The aggregated promise will be resolved only after all the individual promises are resolved. If, on the other hand, one of the individual actions fail the aggregated promise will be rejected as well:

```
it('should illustrate promise aggregation when one of the promises
  fail', function () {

  var ordersDelivered = $q.all([
    pizzaPit.takeOrder('Pepperoni'),
    saladBar.takeOrder('Fresh salad')
  ]);

  ordersDelivered.then(pawel.eat, pawel.beHungry);

  pizzaPit.deliverOrder();
  saladBar.problemWithOrder('no fresh lettuce');
  expect($log.warn.logs).toContain(['Pawel is hungry because: no fresh
lettuce']);
});
```

The aggregated promise gets rejected with the same reason as the individual promise that was rejected.

Wrapping values as promises

Sometimes we might find ourselves in a situation where the same API needs to work with results obtained from asynchronous and synchronous actions. In this case it is often easier to treat all the results as asynchronous.

The $q.when method makes it possible to wrap a JavaScript object as a promise.

Continuing our "pizza and salad" example, we could imagine that a salad is ready (synchronous action) but a pizza needs to be ordered and delivered (asynchronous action). Still we want to serve both dishes at the same time. Here is an example illustrating how to use the $q.when and the $q.all methods to achieve this in a very elegant way:

```
it('should illustrate promise aggregation with $q.when', function () {

  var ordersDelivered = $q.all([
    pizzaPit.takeOrder('Pepperoni'),
    $q.when('home made salad')
  ]);

  ordersDelivered.then(pawel.eat, pawel.beHungry);

  pizzaPit.deliverOrder();
  expect($log.info.logs).toContain(['Pawel is eating delicious
Pepperoni,home made salad']);
});
```

The $q.when method returns a promise that is resolved with a value supplied as an argument to the when method call.

$q integration in AngularJS

The $q service is not only a quite capable (yet lightweight!) Promise API implementation, but also it is tightly integrated with the AngularJS rendering machinery.

Firstly, promises can be directly exposed on a scope and rendered automatically as soon as a promise is resolved. This enables us to treat promises as model values. For example, given the following template:

```
<h1>Hello, {{name}}!</h1>
```

And the code in a controller:

```
$scope.name = $timeout(function () {
    return "World";
}, 2000);
```

The famous "Hello, World!" text will be rendered after two seconds without any manual programmer's intervention.

The $timeout service returns a promise that will be resolved with a value returned from a timeout callback.

As convenient as it might be this pattern results in code that is not very readable. Things can get even more confusing when we realize that promises returned from a function call are not rendered automatically! The template markup is as follows:

```
<h1>Hello, {{getName()}}!</h1>
```

And the following code in a controller:

```
$scope.getName = function () {
      return $timeout(function () {
        return "World";
      }, 2000);
};
```

This code won't yield the expected text in a template.

 We advise against exposing promises directly on a $scope and relying on the automatic rendering of resolved values. We find this approach is rather confusing, especially taking into account inconsistent behavior for promises returned from a function call.

The promise API with $http

Now that we've covered promises we can demystify the response object being returned from the $http method calls. If you recall a simple example from the beginning of this chapter you will remember that $http calls return an object on which the success and error callbacks can be registered. In reality the returned object is a fully fledged promise with two additional, convenience methods: success and error. As any promise, the one returned from a $http call has also the then method which allows us to rewrite the callback registration code in the following form:

```
var responsePromise = $http.get('data.json');
responsePromise.then(function (response) {
  $scope.data = response.data;
},function (response) {
  throw new Error('Something went wrong...');
});
```

Promises returned from the $http services are resolved with the response object which has the following properties: data, status, headers and config.

Calls to the $http service methods return promises with two additional methods (success and error) for easy callback registration.

Since the $http service returns promises from its methods' calls we can enjoy the full power of the Promise API while interacting with a back-end. We can easily aggregate callbacks, chain and join requests as well as take advantage of sophisticated error handling in the asynchronous world.

Communicating with RESTful endpoints

The **Representational State Transfer (REST)** is a popular architectural choice for exposing services over a network. The interface provided by $http allows us to easily interact with RESTful endpoints from any AngularJS-based web application. But AngularJS goes one step further, and provides a dedicated $resource service to make interactions with RESTful endpoints even easier.

The $resource service

RESTful endpoints often expose CRUD operations that are accessible by calling different HTTP methods on a set of similar URLs. The code that interacts witch such endpoints is usually straightforward but tedious to write. The $resource service allows us to eliminate the repetitive code. We can also start to operate on a higher abstraction level and think of data manipulation in terms of objects (resources) and method calls instead of low-level HTTP calls.

The $resource service is distributed in a separate file (angular-resource.js), and resides in a dedicated module (ngResource). To take advantage of the $resource service we need to include the angular-resource.js file and declare dependency on the ngResource module from our application's module.

To see how easy is to interact with the RESTful endpoint using the $resource service we are going to construct an abstraction over the collection of users exposed as a RESTfulservice by the MongoLab:

```
angular.module('resource', ['ngResource'])

  .factory('Users', function ($resource) {

return
$resource('https://api.mongolab.com/api/1/databases/ascrum/
  collections/users/:id', {
```

```
        apiKey:'4fb51e55e4b02e56a67b0b66',
        id:'@_id.$oid'
    });
})
```

We start by registering a recipe (a factory) for the User constructor function. But notice that we don't need to write any code for this constructor function. It is the $resource service that will prepare implementation for us.

The $resource service will generate a set of methods that make it easy to interact with a RESTFul endpoint. For example, querying for all the users in the persistence store is as simple as writing:

```
.controller('ResourceCtrl', function($scope, Users){
    $scope.users = Users.query();
});
```

What will happen upon the call to the User.query() method is that $resource generated code is going to prepare and issue an $http call. When a response is ready the incoming JSON string will get converted to a JavaScript array where each element of this array is of type Users.

 Calls to the $resource service return a generated constructor function augmented with methods to interact with a RESTful endpoint: query, get, save and delete.

AngularJS requires very little information to generate a fully functional resource. Let's examine the parameters of the $resource method to see what input is required and what can be customized:

```
$resource('https://api.mongolab.com/api/1/databases/ascrum/
collections/users/:id', {
        apiKey:'4fb51e55e4b02e56a67b0b66',
        id:'@_id.$oid'
    });
```

The first argument is a URL or rather a URL pattern. The URL pattern can contain named placeholders starting with the colon character. We can specify only one URL pattern which means that all HTTP verbs should use very similar URLs.

 If your back-end uses a port number as part of the URL, the port number needs to be escaped while supplying the URL pattern to the $resource call (For example, http://example.com\\:3000/api). This is required since a colon has a special meaning in the $resource's URL pattern.

The second argument to the `$resource` function allows us to define default parameters that should be sent with each request. Please note that here by "parameters" we mean both placeholders in a URL template, and standard request parameters sent as a query string. AngularJS will try first to "fill holes" in the URL template, and then will add remaining parameters to the URL's query string.

The default parameters can be either static (specified in a factory) or dynamic, taken from a resource object. Dynamic parameter values are prefixed with a @ character.

Constructor-level and instance-level methods

The `$resource` service automatically generates two sets of convenience methods. One set of methods will be generated on the constructor-level (class-level) for a given resource. The aim of those methods is to operate on collections of resources or cater for the situation where we don't have any resource instance created. The other set of methods will be available on an instance of a particular resource. Those instance-level methods are responsible for interacting with one resource (one record in a data store).

Constructor-level methods

The constructor function generated by the `$resource` has a set of methods corresponding to different HTTP verbs:

- `Users.query(params, successcb, errorcb)`: It issues an HTTP GET request and expects an array in the JSON response. It is used to retrieve a collection of items.

- `Users.get(params, successcb, errorcb)`: It issues an HTTP GET request and expects an object in the JSON response. It is used to retrieve a single item.

- `Users.save(params, payloadData, successcb, errorcb)`: It issues an HTTP POST request with request body generated from the payload.

- `Users.delete(params, successcb, errorcb)` (and its alias: `Users.remove`): It issues an HTTP DELETE request.

For all the methods listed earlier the `successcb` and `errorcb` denote a success and error callback functions, respectively. The `params` argument allows us to specify per-action parameters that are going to end up either as part of the URL or as a parameter in a query string. Lastly, the `payloadData` argument allows us to specify the HTTP request body where appropriate (POST and PUT requests).

Instance level methods

The $resource service will not only generate a constructor function, but also will add prototype (instance) level methods. The instance level methods are equivalents of their class-level counterparts but operate of a single instance. For example, a user can be deleted either by calling:

```
Users.delete({}, user);
```

Or by invoking a method on the user's instance like:

```
user.$delete();
```

Instance-level methods are very convenient, and allow us write concise code-manipulating resources. Let's see another example of saving a new user:

```
var user = new Users({
  name:'Superhero'
});
user.$save();
```

This could be re-written using the class-level save method:

```
var user = {
  name:'Superhero'
};
Users.save(user);
```

> The $resource factory generates both class-level and instance level methods. The instance level-methods are prefixed with the $ character. Both the methods have the equivalent functionality so it is up to you to choose the more convenient form depending on your use-case.

Custom methods

By default the $resource factory generates a set of methods that is sufficient for typical use-cases. If a back-end uses different HTTP verbs for certain operations (For example, PUT or PATCH) it is relatively easy to add custom methods on a resource level.

> By default the $resource factory doesn't generate any method corresponding to HTTP PUT requests. If your back-end maps any operations to HTTP PUT requests you will have to add those methods manually.

For example, the MongoLab REST API is using the HTTP POST method to create new items but the PUT method must be used to update existing entries. Let's see how to define a custom update method (both the class-level update and the instance-level $update):

```
.factory('Users', function ($resource) {
  return $resource('https://api.mongolab.com/api/1/databases/ascrum/
collections/users/:id', {
    apiKey:'4fb51e55e4b02e56a67b0b66',
    id:'@_id.$oid'
  }, {
    update: {method:'PUT'}
  });
})
```

As you can see defining a new method is as simple as supplying a third parameter to the $resource factory function. The parameter must be an object of the following form:

```
action: {method:?, params:?, isArray:?, headers:?}
```

The action key is a new method name to be generated. A generated method will issue a HTTP request specified by method, params are holding default parameters specific to this particular action and the isArray specifies, if data returned from a back-end represent a collection (an array) or a single object. It is also possible to specify custom HTTP headers.

The $resource service can only work with JavaScript arrays and objects as data received from a back-end. Single values (primitive types) are not supported. Methods returning a collection (ones flagged with isArray) must return a JavaScript array. Arrays wrapped inside a JavaScript object won't be processed as expected.

Adding behavior to resource objects

The $resource factory is generating constructor functions that can be used as any other JavaScript constructor to create new resource instances using the new keyword. But we can also extend prototype of this constructor to add new behavior to resource objects. Let's say that we want to have a new method on the user level outputting a full name based on a first and last name. Here is the recommended way of achieving this:

```
.factory('Users', function ($resource) {
    var Users = $resource('https://api.mongolab.com/api/1/databases/
ascrum/collections/users/:id', {
      apiKey:'4fb51e55e4b02e56a67b0b66',
      id:'@_id.$oid'
```

```
    }, {
      update: {method:'PUT'}
    });

    Users.prototype.getFullName = function() {
      return this.firstName + ' ' + this.lastName;
    };

    return Users;
  })
```

Adding new methods on the class (constructor) level is also possible. Since, in JavaScript a function is a first-class object, we can define new methods on a constructor function. This way we can add custom methods "by hand" instead of relying on the AngularJS automatic method generation. This might prove useful, if we need some non-standard logic in one of the resources methods. For example, the MongoLab's REST API requires that the identifier of an object is removed from a payload while issuing PUT (update) requests.

$resource creates asynchronous methods

Let's have a second look at the `query` method example:

```
$scope.users = Users.query();
```

We might get the impression that generated resources behave in the synchronous way (we are not using any callbacks or promises here). In reality the `query` method call is asynchronous and AngularJS uses a smart trick to make it looks like synchronous.

What is going on here is that AngularJS will return immediately from a call to `Users.query()` with an empty array as a result. Then, when the asynchronous call is successful, and real data arrives from the server, the array will get updated with the data. AngularJS will simply keep a reference to an array returned at first, and will fill it in when data is available. This trick works in AngularJS since upon data arrival the content of the returned array will change and templates will get refreshed automatically.

But don't get mistaken, the `$resource` calls are asynchronous. This is often a source of confusion, as you might want to try to write the following code (or access the initial array in any other way):

```
$scope.users = Users.query();
console.log($scope.users.length);
```

And it doesn't work as expected!

Fortunately it is possible to use callbacks in the methods generated by the `$resource` factory and rewrite the preceding code to make it behave as intended:

```
Users.query(function(users){
    $scope.users = users;
    console.log($scope.users.length);
});
```

 Methods generated by the `$resource` factory are asynchronous, even if AngularJS is using a clever trick, and the syntax might suggest that we are dealing with the synchronous methods.

Limitations of the $resource service

The `$resource` factory is a handy service, and lets us to start talking to RESTful back-ends in virtually no time. But the problem with `$resource` is that it is a generic service; not tailored to any particular back-end needs. As such it takes some assumptions that might not be true for the back-end of our choice.

If the `$resource` factory works for your back-end and web-application, that's great. There are many use-cases where `$resource` might be enough, but for more sophisticated applications it is often better to use lower-level `$http` service.

Custom REST adapters with $http

The `$resource` factory is very handy, but if you hit its limitations it is relatively easy to create a custom, `$resource`-like factory based on the `$http` service. By taking time to write a custom resource factory we can gain full control over URLs and data pre/post processing. As a bonus we would no longer need to include the `angular-resource.js` file and thus save few KB of the total page weight.

What follows is a simplified example of a custom resource-like factory dedicated to the MongoLab RESTful API. Familiarity with the Promise API is the key to understanding this implementation:

```
angular.module('mongolabResource', [])

.factory('mongolabResource', function ($http, MONGOLAB_CONFIG) {

  return function (collectionName) {

    //basic configuration
    var collectionUrl =
      'https://api.mongolab.com/api/1/databases/' +
        MONGOLAB_CONFIG.DB_NAME +
```

```
                '/collections/' + collectionName;

      var defaultParams = {apiKey:MONGOLAB_CONFIG.API_KEY};

      //utility methods
      var getId = function (data) {
        return data._id.$oid;
      };

      //a constructor for new resources
      var Resource = function (data) {
        angular.extend(this, data);
      };

      Resource.query = function (params) {
        return $http.get(collectionUrl, {
          params:angular.extend({q:JSON.stringify({} || params)},
defaultParams)
        }).then(function (response) {
            var result = [];
            angular.forEach(response.data, function (value, key) {
              result[key] = new Resource(value);
            });
            return result;
          });
      };

      Resource.save = function (data) {
        return $http.post(collectionUrl, data, {params:defaultParams})
          .then(function (response) {
            return new Resource(data);
          });
      };

      Resource.prototype.$save = function (data) {
      return Resource.save(this);

      };

      Resource.remove = function (data) {
        return $http.delete(collectionUrl + '', defaultParams)
          .then(function (response) {
      return new Resource(data);
          });
      };

      Resource.prototype.$remove = function (data) {
```

```
return Resource.remove(this);
    };

    //other CRUD methods go here

    //convenience methods
    Resource.prototype.$id = function () {
      return getId(this);
    };

    return Resource;
  };
});
```

The example code starts by declaring a new module (mongolabResource) and a factory (mongolabResource) accepting a configuration object (MONGOLAB_CONFIG) those are the parts that should look familiar by now. Based on a provided configuration object we can prepare a URL to be used by a resource. Here we are in total control of how a URL is created and manipulated.

Then, the Resource constructor is declared, so we can create new resource objects from existing data. What follows is a definition of several methods; query, save and remove. Those methods are defined on the constructor (class) level, but instance-level methods are also declared (where appropriate) to follow the same convention as the original $resource implementation. Providing an instance-level method is as easy as delegating to the class-level one:

```
Resource.prototype.$save = function (data) {
      return Resource.save(this);
};
```

Usage of promise chaining is the crucial part of the custom resource implementation. The then method is always called on a promise returned from a $http call, and a resulting promise is returned to the client. A success callback on a promise returned from a $http call is used to register post-processing logic. For example, in the query method implementation we post-process raw JSON returned from a back-end, and create resource instances. Here, once again we've got full control over data extraction process from a response.

Let's examine how a new resource factory could be used:

```
angular.module('customResourceDemo', ['mongolabResource'])
  .constant('MONGOLAB_CONFIG', {
    DB_NAME: 'ascrum',
    API_KEY: '4fb51e55e4b02e56a67b0b66'
  })
```

```
    .factory('Users', function (mongolabResource) {
      return mongolabResource('users');
    })

    .controller('CustomResourceCtrl', function ($scope, Users,
      Projects) {

      Users.query().then(function(users){
        $scope.users = users;
      });
    });
```

The usage of our custom resource doesn't differ much from the original $resource equivalent. To start with we need to declare a dependency on the module where a custom resource factory is defined (mongolabResource). Next, we need to provide required configuration options in form of a constant. As soon as the initial setup is done we can define actual resources created by a custom factory. It is as easy as invoking the mongolabResource factory function and passing a MongoDB collection name as an argument.

During application's run-time a newly defined resource constructor (here: Users) can be injected as any other dependency. Then an injected constructor can be used to invoke either class-level or instance-level methods. An example of the later is shown here:

```
    $scope.addSuperhero = function () {
      new Users({name: 'Superhero'}).$save();
    };
```

The best part of switching to a custom, $http-based version of a resource factory is that we can enjoy the full power of the Promise API.

Using advanced features of $http

The $http service is extremely flexible and powerful. Its super-powers are result of clean, flexible API and usage of the Promise API. In this section, we are going to see how we can use some of the more advanced features of the $http service.

Intercepting responses

AngularJS built-in $http service allows us to register interceptors that will be executed around each and every request. Such interceptors are very useful in situations where we need to do special processing for many (potentially all) requests.

As the initial example, let's assume that we want to retry failed requests. To do so we can define an interceptor that inspects response status codes and retries a request, if the HTTP Service Unavailable (503) status code is detected. The sketch of the code could look like:

```
angular.module('httpInterceptors', [])

  .config(function($httpProvider){
    $httpProvider.responseInterceptors.push('retryInterceptor');
  })

  .factory('retryInterceptor', function ($injector, $q) {

    return function(responsePromise) {
      return responsePromise.then(null, function(errResponse) {
        if (errResponse.status === 503) {
          return $injector.get('$http')(errResponse.config);
        } else {
          return $q.reject(errResponse);
        }
      });
    };
  });
```

An interceptor is a function that accepts a promise of the original request as its argument, and should return another promise resolving to an intercepted result. Here we inspect the errResponse.status code to check if we are in the error condition where we can try to recover. If so, then we are returning a promise from a completely new $http call done with the same configuration object as the original request. If we happen to intercept an error that we can't handle we are simply propagating this error ($q.reject method).

AngularJS interceptors make have use of the promise API, and this is what makes them so powerful. In the example described here we can retry an HTTP request in a way that is completely transparent to clients using the $http service. *Chapter 7, Securing Your Application*, has a complete example of using response interceptors to provide sophisticated security mechanism.

Registering new interceptors is easy, and boils down to adding a reference to a new interceptor (here an AngularJS service created via factory) to an interceptor array maintained by the $httpProvider. Please note that we are using a provider to register new interceptors, and the providers are only available in configuration blocks.

Testing code that interacts with $http

Testing code calling external HTTP services is often problematic due to network latency and changing data. We want our test to run fast and be predictable. Fortunately, AngularJS provides excellent mocks to simulate HTTP responses.

In AngularJS the $http service depends on another, lower-level service $httpBackend. We can think of the $httpBackend as a thin wrapper over the XMLHttpRequest object. This wrapper masks browsers incompatibilities and enables JSONP requests.

> Application code should never call the $httpBackend directly as the $http service provides a much better abstraction. But having a separate $httpBackend service means that we can swap it for a mock one during testing.

To see the $httpBackend mock applied to a unit tests we are going to examine a test for a sample controller triggering a GET request via the $http service. Here is the code for the controller itself:

```
.controller('UsersCtrl', function ($scope, $http) {

  $scope.queryUsers = function () {
$http.get('http://localhost:3000/databases/ascrum/collections/
  users')

      .success(function (data, status, headers, config) {
        $scope.users = data;
      }).error(function (data, status, headers, config) {
        throw new Error('Something went wrong...');
      });
  };
});
```

To test this controller's code we can write:

```
describe('$http basic', function () {

  var $http, $httpBackend, $scope, ctrl;
  beforeEach(module('test-with-http-backend'));
  beforeEach(inject(function (_$http_, _$httpBackend_) {
    $http = _$http_;
    $httpBackend = _$httpBackend_;
  }));
  beforeEach(inject(function (_$rootScope_, _$controller_) {
    $scope = _$rootScope_.$new();
    ctrl = _$controller_('UsersCtrl', {
```

```
        $scope : $scope
    });
  }));

  it('should return all users', function () {

    //setup expected requests and responses
    $httpBackend
.whenGET('http://localhost:3000/databases/ascrum/collections/users').
respond([{name: 'Pawel'}, {name: 'Peter'}]);

    //invoke code under test
    $scope.queryUsers();

    //simulate response
    $httpBackend.flush();

    //verify results
    expect($scope.users.length).toEqual(2);
  });

  afterEach(function() {
    $httpBackend.verifyNoOutstandingExpectation();
    $httpBackend.verifyNoOutstandingRequest();
  });
});
```

First of all we can see that the $httpBackend mock allows us to specify expected requests (whenGET (...)) and prepare fake responses (respond (...)). There is a whole family of whenXXX methods for each HTTP verb. The signature of the whenXXX family of methods is quite flexible, and allows us to specify URLs as regular expressions.

To stub data normally returned from a back-end we can use the respond method. It is possible to mock response headers as well.

The best part about the $httpBackend mock is that it allows us to get precise control over responses and their timing. By using the flush() method we are no longer on the mercy of the asynchronous events, and we can simulate an HTTP response arriving from a back-end at a chosen moment. The unit tests using the $httpBackend mock can run synchronously, even if the $http service is asynchronous by design. This makes unit tests executing fast and in predictable manner.

The verifyNoOutstandingExpectation method verifies that all the expected calls were made ($http methods invoked and responses flushed), while the verifyNoOutstandingRequest call makes sure that code under test didn't trigger any unexpected XHR calls. Using those two methods we can make sure that the code under the test invokes all the expected methods and only the expected ones.

Summary

This chapter guided us through different methods of communicating with a back-end end to retrieve and manipulate data. We've started our journey by looking at the $http APIs which is the fundamental service for issuing XHR and JSONP request in AngularJS. Not only we got familiar with the basic APIs of the $http service, but also we had a close look at different ways of dealing with the cross-origin requests.

Many of the AngularJS asynchronous services rely on the Promise API to provide elegant interfaces. The $http service heavily depends on promises so we had to exhaustively cover promises implementation in AngularJS. We saw that the $q service provides a general purpose Promise API, and is tightly integrated with the rendering machinery. Having a good understanding of the Promise API with $q allowed us to fully understand values returned from the $http method calls.

AngularJS can easily communicate with RESTful endpoints. There is the dedicated $resource factory that makes it very easy write code interacting with RESTful back-ends. The $resource factory is very convenient but it is very generic, and as such might not cover all your needs. We shouldn't shy away from creating custom $resource-like factories based on the $http API.

Towards the end of the chapter, we've covered some of the advanced usages of the $http API with response interceptors.

Lastly, as any JavaScript code, methods using the $http APIs should be thoroughly tested, and we saw that AngularJS provides excellent mock object to facilitate unit testing of code talking to a back-end.

With all the data loaded on the client side, and available in JavaScript we are ready to dive into various ways of rendering those data with AngularJS. The next chapter is fully devoted to templates, directives and rendering.

4
Displaying and Formatting Data

Now that we know how to get data from a back-end into a browser we can focus on displaying and manipulating that data using AngularJS. This chapter starts with an overview of AngularJS built-in directives used in templates. As soon as the basics are covered we will see different directives in action and discuss their usage patterns. There is also extensive coverage of AngularJS filters.

In this chapter you will learn about:

- Naming conventions for AngularJS directives.
- Solutions for conditionally showing and hiding blocks of markup.
- Usage patterns and pitfalls of the repeater (ng-repeat) directive.
- Registering DOM event handlers so users can interact with an application.
- Limitations of the AngularJS DOM-based template language and possible workarounds.
- Filters: their purpose and usage samples. We will go over built-in filters as well as how to create and test a custom filter.

Referencing directives

Before we go over examples of different AngularJS built-in directives it is important to highlight that we can use a variety of naming conventions to reference directives in HTML markup.

In the AngularJS documentation all the directives are indexed under their camel-case name (For example, ngModel). In a template, however, we need to use either snake-case form (ng-model), colon-separated (ng:model) or the underscore-separated (ng_model) form. Additionally, each reference to a directive can be prefixed with either x or data.

> Each single directive can be referenced by a number of different (but equivalent) names. Taking the ngModel as an example we can write in our template one of: ng-model, ng:model, ng_model, x-ng-model, x-ng:model, x-ng_model, data-ng-model, data-ng:model, data-ng_model, x:ng-model, data_ng-model, and so on.

The data prefix is very convenient for keeping our HTML documents HTML5-compliant, and making them pass HTML5 validators tests. Otherwise you are free to choose whatever naming schema that pleases you; they are all equivalent.

> All the examples in this book are using the shortest snake-case form (for example, ng-model). We find this syntax concise and readable.

Displaying results of expression evaluation

AngularJS offers various ways of rendering data. The net effect is always the same model content is displayed to users, but there are also subtleties worth noting.

The interpolation directive

The **interpolation directive** is the most fundamental directive that deals with model data display. It accepts expressions delimited by a pair of curly braces:

```
<span>{{expression}}</span>
```

This directive will simply evaluate the expression and render its result on a screen.

The delimiter used by AngularJS is configurable; changing defaults might be needed if you plan to mix AngularJS with other language template on the server-side. Re-configuration is really simple and boils down to setting properties on the $interpolateProvider:

```
myModule.config(function($interpolateProvider) {
  $interpolateProvider.startSymbol('[[');
  $interpolateProvider.endSymbol(']]');
});
```

Here we are changing default {{}} to [[]] so later on we can write in the templates:

```
[[expression]]
```

Rendering model values with ngBind

The interpolation directive has an equivalent directive called `ng-bind`. It can be used as an HTML attribute:

```
<span ng-bind="expression"></span>
```

The curly braces form is easier to use but there are cases where the `ng-bind` directive might come handy. Usually the `ng-bind` directive is used to hide expressions before AngularJS has a chance of processing them on the initial page load. This prevents UI flickering and provides better user experience. The topic of optimizing the initial page load is covered in more details in *Chapter 12, Packaging and Deploying AngularJS Web Applications*.

HTML content in AngularJS expressions

By default AngularJS will escape any HTML markup that made it into an expression (model) evaluated by the interpolation directive. For example, given the model:

```
$scope.msg = 'Hello, <b>World</b>!';
```

And the markup fragment:

```
<p>{{msg}}</p>
```

The rendering process will escape the `<b>` tags, so they will appear as plain text and not as markup:

```
<p>Hello, &lt;b&gt;World&lt;/b&gt;!</p>
```

The interpolation directive will do the escaping of any HTML content found in the model in order to prevent HTML injection attacks.

If, for any reason, your model contains HTML markup that needs to be evaluated and rendered by a browser you can use the `ng-bind-html-unsafe` directive to switch off default HTML tags escaping:

```
<p ng-bind-html-unsafe="msg"></p>
```

Using the `ng-bind-html-unsafe` directive we will get the HTML fragment with the `<b>` tags interpreted by a browser.

Extreme care should be taken when using the `ng-bind-html-unsafe` directive. Its usage should be limited to cases where you fully trust or can control the expression being evaluated. Otherwise malicious users might inject any arbitrary HTML on your page.

AngularJS has one more directive that will selectively sanitize certain HTML tags while allowing others to be interpreted by a browser: `ng-bind-html`. Its usage is similar to the unsafe equivalent:

```
<p ng-bind-html="msg"></p>
```

In terms of escaping the `ng-bind-html` directive is a compromise between behavior of the `ng-bind-html-unsafe` (allow all HTML tags) and the `interpolation` directive (allow no HTML tags at all). It might be a good alternative for cases where we want to allow some HTML tags entered by users.

> The ng-bind-html directive resides in a separate module (ngSanitize) and requires inclusion of an additional source file: angular-sanitize.js.

Don't forget to declare dependency on the `ngSanitize` module if you plan to use the `ng-bind-html` directive:

```
angular.module('expressionsEscaping', ['ngSanitize'])
  .controller('ExpressionsEscapingCtrl', function ($scope) {
    $scope.msg = 'Hello, <b>World</b>!';
  });
```

> Unless you are working with existing legacy systems (CMS, back-ends sending HTML, and so on.), markup in the model should be avoided. Such markup can't contain AngularJS directives and requires the ng-bind-html-unsafe or ng-bind-html directive to obtain desired results.

Conditional display

Showing and hiding parts of the DOM based on some conditions is a common requirement. AngularJS comes equipped with four different sets of directives for this occasion (`ng-show`/`ng-hide`, `ng-switch-*`, `ng-if` and `ng-include`).

The ng-show/ng-hide family of directives can be used to hide (by applying CSS display rules) parts of the DOM tree based on a result of expression evaluation:

```
<div ng-show="showSecret">Secret</div>
```

The previous code rewritten using ng-hide would look as follows:

```
<div ng-hide="!showSecret">Secret</div>
```

> The ng-show/ng-hide directives do the trick by simply applying style="display: none;" to hide DOM elements. Those elements are not removed from the DOM tree.

If we want to physically remove or add DOM nodes conditionally the family of ng-switch directives (ng-switch, ng-switch-when, ng-switch-default) will come handy:

```
<div ng-switch on="showSecret">
  <div ng-switch-when="true">Secret</div>
  <div ng-switch-default>Won't show you my secrets!</div>
</div>
```

The ng-switch directive is really close to the JavaScript switch statement as we may have several ng-switch-when occurrences inside for one ng-switch.

> The main difference between the ng-show/ng-hide and the ng-switch directives is the way the DOM elements are treated. The ng-switch directive will add/remove DOM elements from the DOM tree while the ng-show/ng-hide will simply apply style="display: none;" to hide elements. The ng-switch directive is creating a new scope.

The ng-show/ng-hide directives are easy to use but might have unpleasant performance consequences if applied to large number of DOM nodes. If you spot performance issues related to the size of DOM tree you should lean towards using more verbose ng-switch family of directives.

The problem with the ng-switch family of directives is that the syntax can get quite verbose for simple use-case. Fortunately AngularJS has one more directive in its arsenal: ng-if. It behaves similarly to the ng-switch directive (in the sense that it adds / removes elements from the DOM tree) but has very simple syntax:

```
<div ng-if="showSecret">Secret</div>
```

The ng-if directive is available only in the most recent version of AngularJS: 1.1.x or 1.2.x.

Including blocks of content conditionally

The ng-include directive, while not directly acting as the if/else statement, can be used to conditionally display blocks of dynamic, AngularJS-powered markup. The discussed directive has a very nice property. It can load and conditionally display partials based on a result of expression evaluation. This allows us to easily create highly dynamic pages. For example, we could include different user edit forms depending on the user's role. In the following code snippet we load a different partial for users that have administrator role:

```
<div ng-include="user.admin && 'edit.admin.html' || 'edit.user.html'">
</div>
```

 The ng-include directive is creating a new scope for each partial it includes.

Additionally ng-include is the great tool that can be used to compose final pages from smaller markup fragments.

 The ng-include directive accepts an expression as its argument, so you need to pass a quoted string if you plan to use a fixed value pointing to a partial, for example, <div ng-include="'header. tpl.html'"></div>.

Rendering collections with the ngRepeat directive

The ng-repeat directive is probably one of the most used and the most powerful directives. It will iterate over a collection of items stamping out a new DOM element for each entry in a collection. But the ng-repeat directive will do much more than simply assuring the initial rendering of a collection. It will constantly monitor the source of data to re-render a template in response to changes.

> Repeater's implementation is highly optimized and will try to minimize number of DOM changes needed to reflect data structure in the DOM tree.

Internally the `ng-repeat` might choose to move DOM nodes around (if you move an element in array), delete a DOM node if an element is removed from the array and insert new nodes if additional elements end up in the array. Regardless of the strategy chosen by a repeater behind the scenes it is crucial to realize that it is not a simple `for` loop that will run once. The `ng-repeat` directive behaves more like an observer of a data that tries to map entries in a collection to DOM nodes. The process of data-observing is continuous.

Getting familiar with the ngRepeat directive

The basic usage and syntax is very simple:

```
<table class="table table-bordered">
  <tr ng-repeat="user in users">
    <td>{{user.name}}</td>
    <td>{{user.email}}</td>
  </tr>
</table>
```

Here the `users` array is defined on a scope and contains typical user objects with properties like: `name`, `email`, and so on. The `ng-repeat` directive will iterate over users' collection and create a `<tr>` DOM element for each entry in a collection.

> The `ng-repeat` directive creates a new scope for each element of a collection it iterates over.

Special variables

AngularJS repeater will declare a set of special variables in a scope created for each and every individual entry. Those variables can be used to determine a position of an element within a collection:

- `$index`: It will be set to a number indicating index of an element in a collection (indexes start at 0)
- `$first, $middle, $last`: These variables will get a Boolean value according to element's position

The mentioned variables come in very handy in many real-life situations. For example, in the sample SCRUM application we can rely on the $last variable to properly render links in a breadcrumb element. For the last (selected) part of the path there is no need to render links, while the <a> element is needed for other parts of the path.

We can model this UI using the following code:

```
<li ng-repeat="breadcrumb in breadcrumbs.getAll()">
  <span class="divider">/</span>
  <ng-switch on="$last">
    <span ng-switch-when="true">{{breadcrumb.name}}</span>
    <span ng-switch-default>
      <a href="{{breadcrumb.path}}">{{breadcrumb.name}}</a>
    </span>
  </ng-switch>
</li>
```

Iterating over an object's properties

Usually the ng-repeat directive is used to display entries from a JavaScript array. Alternatively it can be used to iterate over properties of an object. In this case the syntax is slightly different:

```
<li ng-repeat="(name, value) in user">
    Property {{$index}} with {{name}} has value {{value}}
</li>
```

In the preceding example, we can display all the properties of a user object as an unordered list. Please note that we must specify variable names for both a property name and its value using a bracket notation (name, value).

 The ng-repeat directive will, before outputting results, sort property names alphabetically. This behavior can't be changed so there is no way of controlling the iteration order while using ng-repeat with objects.

The $index variable can still be used to get a numerical position of a given property in a sorted list of all properties.

Iterating over objects' properties, while being supported, has limitations. The main issue is that we can't control iteration order.

 If you care about order in which properties are iterated over you should sort those properties in a controller and put sorted items in an array.

ngRepeat patterns

This section will walk us through some of the commonly used presentation patterns and ways of implementing them with AngularJS. In particular we are going to look into lists with details and altering classes on elements being part of a list.

Lists and details

It is a common use case to display a list whose items expand to show additional details, when they are clicked. There are two variants of this pattern: either only one element can be expanded or alternatively several expended elements are allowed. Here is the screenshot illustrating this particular UI design:

Name	e-mail
Pawel	pawel@domain.com
Pawel details go here...	
Peter	peter@domain.com

Displaying only one row with details

The requirement of having only one element expanded can be easily covered with the following code:

```
<table class="table table-bordered" ng-
controller="ListAndOneDetailCtrl">

  <tbody ng-repeat="user in users" ng-click="selectUser(user)" ng-
switch on="isSelected(user)">
    <tr>
      <td>{{user.name}}</td>
      <td>{{user.email}}</td>
</tr>
```

```
<tr ng-switch-when="true">
    <td colspan="2">{{user.desc}}</td>
  </tr>
 </tbody>
</table>
```

In the preceding example an additional row, containing user details, is only rendered if a given user was selected. A selection process is very simple and is covered by the selectUser and isSelected functions:

```
.controller('ListAndOneDetailCtrl', function ($scope, users) {
  $scope.users = users;

  $scope.selectUser = function (user) {
    $scope.selectedUser = user;
  };

  $scope.isSelected = function (user) {
    return $scope.selectedUser === user;
  };
})
```

Those two functions take advantage of the fact that there is one scope (defined on top of the table DOM element) where we can store a pointer (selectedUser) to an active item of a list.

Displaying many rows with details

Assuming that we would like to allow multiple rows with additional details we need to change a strategy. This time selection details need to be stored on each and every element level. As you remember the ng-repeat directive is creating a new scope for each and every element of a collection it iterates over. We can take advantage of this new scope to store "selected" state for each item:

```
<table class="table table-bordered">
  <tbody ng-repeat="user in users" ng-controller="UserCtrl"
    ng-click="toggleSelected()" ng-switch on="isSelected()">
    <tr>
      <td>{{user.name}}</td>
      <td>{{user.email}}</td>
    </tr>
    <tr ng-switch-when="true">
      <td colspan="2">{{user.desc}}</td>
    </tr>
  </tbody>
</table>
```

This example is interesting since we are using the `ng-controller` directive for each item. A provided controller can augment scope with functions and variables to control selection state:

```
.controller('UserCtrl', function ($scope) {

  $scope.toggleSelected = function () {
    $scope.selected = !$scope.selected;
  };

  $scope.isSelected = function () {
    return $scope.selected;
  };
});
```

It is important to understand that specifying a controller on the same DOM element as the `ng-repeat` directive means that the controller will be managing a new scope created by a repeater. In practice it means that we can have a controller dedicated to managing individual items of a collection. It is a powerful pattern that allows us to neatly encapsulate item-specific variables and behavior (functions).

Altering tables, rows, and classes

Zebra-striping is often added to lists in order to improve their readability. AngularJS has a pair of directives (`ngClassEven` and `ngClassOdd`) that make this task trivial:

```
<tr ng-repeat="user in users"
ng-class-even="'light-gray'" ng-class-odd="'dark-gray'">
  . . .
</tr>
```

The `ngClassEven` and `ngClassOdd` directives are just specialization of the more generic `ngClass` directive. The `ngClass` is very versatile and can be applied in many different situations. To demonstrate its power we could rewrite the preceding example like follows:

```
<tr ng-repeat="user in users"

ng-class="{'dark-gray' : !$index%2, 'light-gray' : $index%2}">
```

Here the `ngClass` directive is used with an object argument. Keys of this object are class names and values; conditional expressions. A class specified as a key will be added or removed from an element based on result of a corresponding expression evaluation.

The ng-class directive can also accept arguments of type string or array. Both arguments can contain a list of CSS classes (coma-separated in case of string) to be added to a given element.

DOM event handlers

Our UI wouldn't be very useful if users couldn't interact with it (either by using a mouse, a keyboard or touch events). The good news is that registering event handlers is a child's play with AngularJS! Here is an example of reacting to a click event:

```
<button ng-click="clicked()">Click me!<button>
```

The clicked() expression is evaluated against a current $scope which makes it very easy to call any method defined on that scope. We are not limited to simple function calls; it is possible to use expressions of an arbitrary complexity, including ones that accept arguments:

```
<input ng-model="name">
<button ng-click="hello(name)">Say hello!<button>
```

Developers new to AngularJS often try to register event handler as follows: ng-click="{{clicked()}}" or ng-click="sayHello({{name}})" that is using interpolation expression inside an attribute value. This is not needed and it won't work correctly. What would happen is that AngularJS would parse and evaluate an interpolation expression while processing the DOM. This first step of processing would evaluate an interpolation expression and use the result of this evaluation as an event handler!

AngularJS has the built-in support for the different events with the following directives:

- **Click events**: ngClick and ngDblClick

- **Mouse events**: ngMousedown, ngMouseup, ngMouseenter, ngMouseleave, ngMousemove and ngMouseover

- **Keyboard events**: ngKeydown, ngKeyup and ngKeypress

- **Input change event** (ngChange): The ngChange directive cooperates with the ngModel one, and let us to react on model changes initiated by user input.

Mentioned DOM event handlers can accept a special argument `$event` in their expression, which represents the raw DOM event. This allows us to get access to lower-level properties of an event, prevent it default action, stop its propagation, and so on. As an example we can see how to read the position of a clicked element:

```
<li ng-repeat="item in items" ng-click="logPosition(item, $event)">
    {{item}}
</li>
```

Where the `logPosition` function is defined on a scope like follows:

```
$scope.readPosition = function (item, $event) {
  console.log(item + ' was clicked at: ' + $event.clientX + ',' +
$event.clientY);
};
```

> While the `$event` special variable is exposed to event handlers it shouldn't be abused to do extensive DOM manipulations. As you remember from *Chapter 1, Angular Zen* AngularJS is all about declarative UI and DOM manipulation should be restricted to directives. This is why the `$event` argument is mostly used inside directive's code.

Working effectively with DOM-based templates

It is not very common to see a template system employing live DOM and HTML syntax but this approach turns out to work surprisingly well in practice. People used to other, string-based template engines might need some time to adjust, but after a few initial hops writing DOM-based templates becomes a second nature. There are just a couple of caveats.

Living with verbose syntax

Firstly, the syntax for some of the constructs might be a bit verbose. The best example of this slightly annoying syntax for the `ng-switch` family of directives some common use cases might simply require a lot of typing. Let's consider a simple example of displaying a different message based on a number of items in a list:

```
<div ng-switch on="items.length>0">
  <span ng-switch-when="true">
    There are {{items.length}} items in the list.
  </span>
```

```
    <span ng-switch-when="false">
      There are no items in the list.
    </span>
  </div>
```

Of course it would be possible to move the message-preparing logic to a controller to avoid switch statements in a template, but it feels like this type of simple conditional logic has its place in the view layer.

Fortunately, the latest version of AngularJS: the `ng-if` directive built-in is a very handy tool for cases where you don't need power of a full `if/else` expression.

ngRepeat and multiple DOM elements

A slightly more serious issue is connected with the fact that, in its simplest form, the `ng-repeat` repeater only knows how to repeat one element (with its children). This means that `ng-repeat` can't manage a group of sibling elements.

To illustrate this let's imagine that we've got a list of items with a name and description. Now, we would like to have a table where both the name and the description are rendered as separate rows (`<tr>`). The problem is that we need to add the `<tbody>` tag just to have a place for the `ng-repeat` directive:

```
<table>
  <tbody ng-repeat="item in items">
    <tr>
      <td>{{item.name}}</td>
    </tr>
    <tr>
      <td>{{item.description}}</td>
    </tr>
  </tbody>
</table>
```

It looks like the `ng-repeat` directive needs a container element and forces us to create a certain HTML structure. This might or might not be a problem depending on how strictly you need to follow markup structure outlined by your web designers.

In the previous example we were lucky since an appropriate HTML container exists (`<tbody>`), but there are cases where there is no valid HTML element where the `ng-repeat` directive could be placed. We could think of another example where we would like to have an HTML output like:

```
<ul>
  <!-- we would like to put a repeater here -->
  <li><strong>{{item.name}}</strong></li>
```

```
  <li>{{item.description}}</li>
  <!-- and end it here -->
</ul>
```

A new version of AngularJS (1.2.x) is going to extend the basic syntax of the ngRepeat directive to allow more flexibility in choosing DOM elements to be iterated over. In the future it will be possible to write:

```
<ul>
  <li ng-repeat-start="item in items">
    <strong>{{item.name}}</strong>
  </li>
  <li ng-repeat-end>{{item.description}}</li>
</ul>
```

By using the ng-repeat-start and the ng-repeat-end attributes it will be possible to indicate a group of sibling DOM elements to be iterated over.

Elements and attributes that can't be modified at runtime

Since AngularJS operates on the live DOM tree in a browser it can only do as much as browsers permit. It turns out that there are some corner cases where some browsers disallow any changes to elements and their attributes, after those elements were put in the DOM tree.

To see the consequences of those restrictions in practice let's consider a rather common use case of specifying an input element's type attribute dynamically. Many users have tried (and failed!) to write code along those lines:

```
<input type="{{myinput.type}}" ng-model="myobject[myinput.model]">
```

The trouble is that some browsers (yes! you've guessed it: Internet Explorer!) won't change type of a created input. Those browsers see {{myinput.type}} (un-evaluated) as an input type, and since it is unknown it is interpreted as type="text".

There are several approaches to tackling the problem described earlier, but we need to learn more about AngularJS custom directives before we can discuss those solutions. *Chapter 9, Building Advanced Directives*, offers one of the possible solutions. The other simple approach is to use the built-in ng-include directive to encapsulate static templates for different input types:

```
<ng-include src="'input'+myinput.type+'.html'"></ng-include>
```

Where the included fragment specifies input's type as static string.

 Pay attention to scoping issues when using this technique as ng-include creates a new scope.

Custom HTML elements and older versions of IE

Lastly, we need to mention that custom HTML elements and attributes are not well supported by Internet Explorer Version 8 and earlier. There are additional steps that must be undertaken to take full advantage of AngularJS directives in IE8 and IE7, and those are described in the details in *Chapter 12, Packaging and Deploying AngularJS Web Applications*, devoted to the real-life deployment scenarios.

Handling model transformations with filters

AngularJS expressions can get fairly complex and contain function invocations. Those functions might serve different purposes but model transformations and formatting are common needs. To cater for those common use-cases AngularJS expressions support special formatting (transforming) functions called filters:

```
{{user.signedUp| date:'yyyy-MM-dd'}}
```

In this example the date filter is used to format user's sign-up date.

A filter is nothing more than a global, named function that is invoked in view using the pipe (|) symbol with parameters separated by the colon (:) character. In fact we could re-write our sample code like so (provided that the formatDate function is defined on a scope):

```
{{formatDate(user.signedUp, 'yyyy-MM-dd')}}
```

Advantages of filters are two-fold: they don't require registration of functions on a scope (so are readily available for each and every template), and usually offer more convenient syntax as compared to regular function calls.

The simple example also shows that filters can be parameterized (or in other words, arguments can be passed to a filter function): here we specify a date format as an argument to the date filter.

Several filters can be combined (chained) to form a transformation pipeline. As an example we can format a string by limiting its length to 80 characters and convert all the characters to lowercase:

```
{{myLongString | limitTo:80 | lowercase}}
```

Working with built-in filters

AngularJS comes with several filters bundled as part of the core library. In general we can divide built-in filters into two groups: formatting filters and array-transforming filters.

Formatting filters

Here is a list of built-in formatting filters. Their purpose and usage scenarios are easy to decipher:

- `currency`: It formats numbers with two decimal places and a currency symbol.
- `date`: It formats date according to a specified data format. Model can contain dates expressed as Date objects or as Strings (in this case Strings will be parsed to a Date object before formatting).
- `number`: It will format input with a number of decimal places specified as an argument to this filter.
- `lowercase` and `uppercase`: As the same implies, those filters can be used to format strings into their lowercase or uppercase form.
- `json`: This filter is mostly useful for debugging purposes as it can assure "pretty-print" for JavaScript objects. Typical usage looks like follows: `<pre>{{someObject | json}}</pre>`. It is mostly used for debugging purposes.

Array-transforming filters

By default AngularJS provides three filters operating on arrays:

- `limitTo`: It returns an array shrunk to the specified size. We can retain elements either from the beginning of a collection or from its end (in this case the limit parameter must be provided as a negative number).
- `Filter`: This is a general-purpose filtering utility. It is very flexible and supports many options to precisely select elements from a collection.
- `orderBy`: Ordering filter can be used to sort individual elements in an array based on provided criteria.

The listed filters work on arrays only (`limitTo` being an exception, it can cope with strings as well).When applied to an object other that an array those filters have no effect and will simply return a source object.

The array-related filters are often used with the `ng-repeat` directive to render filtered results. In the following sections we are going to build a full example of a table that can be sorted, filtered and paginated. Examples are built around SCRUM backlog list from the sample application, and will illustrate how to combine filters and the repeater directive.

Filtering with the "filter" filter

First we need to clarify that AngularJS has a filter named `filter`. The name is a bit unfortunate since the word "filter" might refer to any filter in general (a transforming function) or this specific filter named "filter".

The **"filter" filter** is a general-purpose filtering function that can be used to select a subset of an array (or put differently exclude some elements). There are number of parameter formats that can be supplied to this filter in order to drive element selection process. In the simplest form we can provide a string in the case all fields of all elements in a collection will be checked for a presence of a given substring.

As an example let's consider a product backlog list that we would like to filter based on search criteria. Users would be presented with an input box where they could type-in search criteria. The resulting list should have only elements where any field of a given element contains a provided substring. The following screenshot illustrates finished UI:

Search for: rev

Name	Description	Priority	Estimation	Done?
Review draft	Re-read and review the 1st draft	4	5	false
Incorporate reviewers remarks	Go over and reviewers remarks	6	3	false

If we assume that our data model has the following properties: name, desc, priority, estimation and done, we could write a template for the discussed UI as follows:

```
<div class="well">
<label>
  Search for:<input type="text" ng-model="criteria">
</label>
</div>
<table class="table table-bordered">
  <thead>
    <th>Name</th>
    <th>Description</th>
    ...
  </thead>
  <tbody>
    <tr ng-repeat="backlogItem in backlog | filter:criteria">
      <td>{{backlogItem.name}}</td>
      <td>{{backlogItem.desc}}</td>
      ...
    </tr>
  </tbody>
</table>
```

As you can see it is extremely easy to add a filter based on user's input; we just need to wire up value of an input field as an argument to the filter. The rest will be taken care of by AngularJS automatic data binding and refresh mechanism.

> The matching criteria can be negated by prefixing with the ! operator.

In the previous example all the properties of source objects are searched for a substring match. If we want to have a more precise control over properties matching we can do so by providing an object argument to a filter. Such an object will act as a "query be example". Here we want to limit matching to the name property and include only items that are not done yet:

```
ng-repeat="item in backlog | filter:{name: criteria, done: false}"
```

In this code snippet all properties of an object specified as an argument must match. We could say that conditions expressed by the individual properties are combined using the AND logical operator.

Additionally AngularJS provides a catch-all property name: $. Using this wildcard as a property name we can combine AND and OR logical operators. Let's say that we want to search for a string match in all properties of a source object, but take into account only not completed items. In this case a filtering expression could be re-written as follows:

```
ng-repeat="item in backlog | filter:{$: criteria, done: false}"
```

It might happen that the combination of required search criteria is so complex that it is not possible to express it using object's syntax. In this case a function can be provided as an argument to the filter (so called `predicate` function). Such a function will be invoked for each and every individual element of a source collection. The resulting array will contain only elements for which the filtering function returns `true`. As a slightly contrived example we could imagine that we want to see only backlog items that are already completed and required over 20 units of effort. The filtering function for this example is both easy to write:

```
$scope.doneAndBigEffort = function (backlogItem) {
    return backlogItem.done && backlogItem.estimation > 20;
};
```

And use:

```
ng-repeat="item in backlog | filter:doneAndBigEffort"
```

Counting filtered results

Often at times, we would like to display a number of items in a collection. Normally it is as simple as using the `{{myArray.length}}` expression. Things get a bit more complicated while using filters as we would like to show the size of a filtered array. A naive approach could consist of duplicating filters in both a repeater and a counting-expression. Taking our last example of filtering in a repeater:

```
<tr ng-repeat="item in backlog | filter:{$: criteria, done: false}">
```

We could try to create a summary row like:

```
Total: {{(backlog | filter:{$: criteria, done: false}).length}}
```

This has obviously several drawbacks; not only code is duplicated but also the same filters need to be executed several times in two different places, not ideal from the performance standpoint.

To remedy this situation we can create an intermediate variable (`filteredBacklog`) that would hold a filtered array:

```
ng-repeat="item in filteredBacklog = (backlog | filter:{$: criteria,
done: false})"
```

Then, counting filtered results boils down to displaying the length of a saved array:

```
Total: {{filteredBacklog.length}}
```

The preceding pattern for counting filtering objects, while not very intuitive, allows us to have filtering logic in one place only.

The other possibility is to move the whole filtering logic to a controller and only expose filtered results on a scope. This method has one more advantage: it moves filtering code to a controller where it is very easy to unit test. To use this solution you will need to learn how to access filters from the JavaScript; something that is covered later on in this chapter.

Sorting with the orderBy filter

Quite often a tabular data can be sorted freely by users. Usually clicking on a header of an individual column selects a given field as sort criteria, while clicking again reverses the sort order. In this section, we are going to implement this common pattern with AngularJS.

The `orderBy` filter will be our primary tool for this job. When finished, our sample table holding list of backlog items will get fully functional sorting icons shown as follows:

Name ∧	Description	Priority	Estimation	Done?
Incorporate reviewers remarks	Go over and reviewers remarks	6	3	false
Prepare outline	Prepare book outline with estimated page count	2	2	true
Prepare samples	Think of code samples	3	5	true
Review draft	Re-read and review the 1st draft	4	5	false
Total: 4				

The `orderBy` filter is easy and intuitive to use so we can immediately dive into the code example, without spending too much time on theoretical introductions. Firstly we will make sorting work and then add sorting indicators. Here is relevant part of markup taking part in sorting:

```
<thead>
  <th ng-click="sort('name')">Name</th>
  <th ng-click="sort('desc')">Description</th>
   . . .
</thead>
<tbody>
  <tr ng-repeat="item in filteredBacklog = (backlog |
    filter:criteria | orderBy:sortField:reverse)">
    <td>{{item.name}}</td>
    <td>{{item.desc}}</td>
    ...
  </tr>
</tbody>
```

The actual sorting is taken care of by the `orderBy` filter, which in our example takes two arguments:

- `sortField`: a property name to be used as a sorting predicate
- sort order (`reverse`): this argument indicates if a sorted array should be reversed

The `sort` function, triggered by a click event on a cell header, is responsible for selecting the sort field as well as toggling sort direction. Here are relevant bits of the controller's code:

```
$scope.sortField = undefined;
$scope.reverse = false;

$scope.sort = function (fieldName) {
  if ($scope.sortField === fieldName) {
    $scope.reverse = !$scope.reverse;
  } else {
    $scope.sortField = fieldName;
    $scope.reverse = false;
  }
};
```

Our sorting example builds on top of the previous, filtering one, so now our backlog list can be both filtered and sorted. With AngularJS it is surprisingly easy to combine both filters to create interactive tables.

> The orderBy filter was deliberately placed after the filter filter. The reason for this is performance: sorting is more costly as compared to filtering so it is better to execute ordering algorithm on a minimal data set.

Now that the sorting works we just need to add icons indicating which field we are sorting and whether it is ascending or descending. Once again the ng-class directive will prove very useful. Here is the example of visual indicators for the "name" column:

```
<th ng-click="sort('name')">Name
<i ng-class="{'icon-chevron-up': isSortUp('name'), 'icon-chevron-down': isSortDown('name')}"></i>
</th>
```

The isSortUp and isSortDown functions are very simple and look like:

```
$scope.isSortUp = function (fieldName) {
  return $scope.sortField === fieldName && !$scope.reverse;
};

$scope.isSortDown = function (fieldName) {
  return $scope.sortField === fieldName && $scope.reverse;
};
```

Of course there are many ways of displaying sort indicators, and the one just presented strives to keep CSS classes out of JavaScript code. This way presentation can be easily changed just be tweaking a template.

Writing custom filters – a pagination example

So far we've managed to display backlog items in a dynamic table that support sorting and filtering. Pagination is another UI pattern that is often used with larger data sets.

AngularJS doesn't provide any filter that would help us to precisely select a subset of an array based on start and end indexes. To support pagination we need to create a new filter, and this is a good occasion to get familiar with the process of writing custom filters.

To get the idea of an interface for the new filter; let's call it pagination we will write a sketch of markup first:

```
<tr ng-repeat="item in filteredBacklog = (backlog |
  pagination:pageNo:pageSize">
  <td>{{item.name}}</td>
  . . .
</tr>
```

The new pagination filter needs to take two parameters: page to be displayed (its index) and its size (number of items per page).

What follows is the very first, naive implementation of the filter (error handling was deliberately omitted to focus on filter writing mechanics):

```
angular.module('arrayFilters', [])

  .filter('pagination', function(){

  return function(inputArray, selectedPage, pageSize) {
      var start = selectedPage*pageSize;
      return inputArray.slice(start, start + pageSize);
    };
  });
```

A filter, as any other provider, needs to be registered on an instance of a module. The filter method should be called with a filter name and a factory function that will create an instance of a new filter. The registered factory function must return the actual filter function.

The first argument of pagination filtering function represents input to be filtered while subsequent parameters can be declared to support filter options.

Filters are very easy to unit test; they work on a supplied input, and when done properly they shouldn't have any side effects. Here is an example test for our custom pagination filter:

```
describe('pagination filter', function () {

  var paginationFilter;
  beforeEach(module('arrayFilters'));
  beforeEach(inject(function (_paginationFilter_) {
    paginationFilter = _paginationFilter_;
  }));

  it('should return a slice of the input array', function () {
```

```
var input = [1, 2, 3, 4, 5, 6];

expect(paginationFilter(input, 0, 2)).toEqual([1, 2]);
    expect(paginationFilter(input, 2, 2)).toEqual([5, 6]);
  });

  it('should return empty array for out-of bounds', function () {

    var input = [1, 2];
expect(paginationFilter(input, 2, 2)).toEqual([]);
  });
});
```

Testing a filter is as simple as testing a single function, and most of the time is really straightforward. The structure of the sample test just presented should be easy to follow as there are almost no new constructs here. The only thing that requires explanation is the way of accessing instances of a filter from the JavaScript code.

Accessing filters from the JavaScript code

Filters are usually invoked from markup (using the pipe symbol in expressions), but it is also possible to get access to filters instances from JavaScript code (controllers, services, other filters, and so on). This way we can combine the existing filters to provide a new functionality.

Filters can be injected to any objects managed by AngularJS **Dependency Injection** system. We can express dependency on a filter using two distinct methods, requiring either:

* The `$filter` service
* A filter name with the `Filter` suffix

The `$filter` service is a lookup function that allows us to retrieve an instance of a filter based on its name. To see it in action we can write a filter that behaves similarly to the `limitTo` one and can trim lengthy strings. Additionally our custom version will add the "…" suffix if a string is trimmed. Here is the relevant code:

```
angular.module('trimFilter', [])
  .filter('trim', function($filter){

var limitToFilter =  $filter('limitTo');

    return function(input, limit) {
      if (input.length > limit) {
```

```
            return limitToFilter(input, limit-3) + '...';
        }
        return input;
    };
});
```

The `$filter('limitTo')` function call allows us to get a hand on a filter instance based on the filter's name.

While the previous method certainly works there is an alternative one that is often faster to code and easier to read:

```
.filter('trim', function(limitToFilter){

    return function(input, limit) {
        if (input.length > limit) {
            return limitToFilter(input, limit-3) + '...';
        }
        return input;
    };
});
```

In the second example, presented here it is enough to declare a dependency named as `[filter name]Filter` where the `[filter name]` is a name of a filter we want to retrieve.

> Accessing filter instances using the `$filter` service results in an odd syntax, and this is why we find it easier to work with the form using the `Filter` suffix. The only occasions where the `$filter` service might be more convenient is when we need to retrieve several filter instances in one place or retrieve a filter instance based on a variable, for example, `$filter(filterName)`.

Filters dos and don'ts

Filters do a marvelous job when used to format and transform data invoked from a template offering nice and concise syntax. But filters are just a tool for a specific job and can as any other tools cause damage if used incorrectly. This section describes situations where filters should be avoided and an alternative solution would be a better fit.

Filters and DOM manipulation

At times it might be tempting to return HTML markup as a result of filter's execution. In fact AngularJS contains one filter that does exactly that: `linky` (in the separate `ngSanitize` module).

It turns out, in practice, that filters outputting HTML are not the best idea. The main problem is that to render output of such a filter we need to use one of the binding directives described earlier on `ngBindUnsafeHtml` or `ngBindHtml`. Not only does it make the binding syntax more verbose (as compared to simply using `{{expression}}`) but potentially makes a web page vulnerable to HTML injection attacks.

To see some issues involving filters outputting HTML we can examine a simple `highlight` filter:

```
angular.module('highlight', [])

  .filter('highlight', function(){

    return function(input, search) {
      if (search) {
        return input.replace(new RegExp(search, 'gi'),
          '<strong>$&</strong>');
      } else {
        return input;
      }
    };
  });
```

You can immediately see that this filter contains hardcoded HTML markup. As a result we can't use it with the interpolation directive but need to write a template like:

```
<input ng-model="search">
<span ng-bind-html="phrase | highlight:search"></span>
```

On top of this the HTML markup outputted from a filter can't contain any AngularJS directives as those wouldn't be evaluated.

A custom directive will, most of the time, solve the same problem in a more elegant way, without introducing potential security hazards. Directives are covered in *Chapter 9, Building Advanced Directives* and *Chapter 10, Building AngularJS Web Applications for an International Audience*.

Costly data transformations in filters

Filters, when used in a template, become integral part of the AngularJS expression, and as such are frequently evaluated. In fact, such filter functions are called multiple times on each digest cycle. We can easily see this in practice by creating a logging wrapper around the uppercase filter:

```
angular.module('filtersPerf', [])
  .filter('logUppercase', function(uppercaseFilter){
    return function(input) {
      console.log('Calling uppercase on: '+input);
      return uppercaseFilter(input);
    };
  });
```

Upon using this newly defined filter in a markup like:

```
<input ng-model="name"> {{name | logUppercase}}
```

We will see that the log statement is written at least once (usually twice) for each keystroke! This experiment alone should convince you that filters are executed often so it is highly preferable that they execute fast.

 Don't be surprised to see that a filter is called multiple times in a row; this is AngularJS dirty checking at work. Strive to write your filters so they do light, fast processing.

Unstable filters

Since filters are called multiple times it is reasonable to expect that a filter responds with the same return value if the input doesn't change. Such functions are called stable with respect to their parameters.

Things can get easily out of hand if a filter doesn't have this property. To see the disastrous effects of unstable filters let's write a malicious random filter that selects a random element from an input array (it is unstable):

```
angular.module('filtersStability', [])

  .filter('random', function () {

    return function (inputArray) {
      var idx =  Math.floor(Math.random() * inputArray.length);
      return inputArray[idx];
    };
  })
```

Given an array of different items stored in the `items` variable on a scope, the `random` filter could be used in a template like:

```
{{items | random}}
```

The preceding code, upon execution, will print out a random value so it might seem that it behaves correctly. It is only upon expecting browser's console we can realize that in fact an error is logged:

```
Uncaught Error: 10 $digest() iterations reached. Aborting!
```

This error means that an expression is yielding different results each time it is being evaluated. AngularJS sees a constantly changing model and re-evaluates an expression, hoping that it will stabilize. After repeating this process ten times the digest is aborted, the last result printed and the error logged in a console. *Chapter 11, Writing Robust AngularJS Web Applications* goes into deeper discussion of these topics, and explains inner workings of AngularJS that should make reasons for this error easier to understand.

In situations like those the solution is to calculate a random value in a controller, before a template is rendered:

```
.controller('RandomCtrl', function ($scope) {

  $scope.items = new Array(1000);
  for (var i=0; i<$scope.items.length; i++) {
    $scope.items[i] = i;
  }

  $scope.randomValue = Math.floor(Math.random() * $scope.items.length);
});
```

Like this a random value will be calculated before template processing and we can safely use the `{{randomValue}}` expression to output the prepared value.

If your function can generate different results for the same input it is not a good candidate for a filter. Invoke this function from a controller instead and leave AngularJS to render pre-calculated value.

Summary

This chapter walked us through a set of patterns used to display data contained in the model.

We started by quickly covering directive's naming conventions and then moved to the overview of built-in AngularJS directives. The `ng-repeat` got special attention as it is the very powerful and one of the most frequently used directives.

While the DOM-based, declarative template, on which AngularJS is based, works perfectly most of the time, there are some corner cases where we hit the limits of this approach. It is important to recognize those situations and be prepared to slightly change target markup when necessary.

Filters offer a very convenient syntax for UI-specific model formatting. We saw that AngularJS provides several useful filters by default, but when a specific need arises it is very easy to create a custom filter. Filtering functions shouldn't be abused and we had a careful look into scenarios where an alternative constructs should be considered.

Directives, filters and display patterns covered in this chapter focused on data display. But before data can be displayed users need to be able to enter them using variety of input elements. The next chapter dives into AngularJS-way of dealing with form elements and data input problematic.

5
Creating Advanced Forms

AngularJS builds upon standard HTML forms and input elements. This means that you can continue to create your UI from the same HTML elements that you already understand using standard HTML design tools.

So far, in our SCRUM application, we've created some basic forms with input elements bound to model data and buttons for saving and deleting and so on. AngularJS takes care of wiring up both the element-model binding and the event-handler binding.

In this chapter, we will look at how AngularJS forms work in detail and then add validation and dynamic user interaction to our application's forms.

In this chapter we will cover:

- Model data binding and input directives
- Form Validation
- Nested and Repeated Forms
- Form Submission
- Resetting a Form

Comparing traditional forms with AngularJS forms

Before we begin to improve our application's forms we should understand how AngularJS forms work. In this section, we explain the differences between standard HTML input elements and AngularJS input directives. We will show how AngularJS modifies and expands the behavior of HTML input elements and how it manages updates to and from the model for you.

In a standard HTML form, the value of an input element is the value that will be sent to the server on submission of the form.

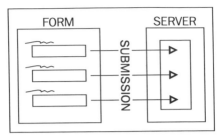

The trouble with the input elements holding the value of your submission is that you are stuck with having to work with the input values as they are shown to the user. This is often not what you want. For instance, a date input field may allow the user to enter a string in some predefined format, for example, "12 March 2013". But in your code you might want to work with the value as a JavaScript Date object. Constantly coding up these transformations is tedious and error-prone.

AngularJS decouples the model from the view. You let input directives worry about displaying the values and AngularJS worry about updating your model when the values change. This leaves you free to work with the model, via controllers for instance, without worrying about how the data is displayed or entered.

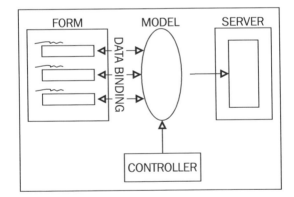

To achieve this separation, AngularJS enhances HTML forms with the form and input directives, validation directives, and controllers. These directives and controllers override the built-in behavior of HTML forms but, to the casual observer, forms in AngularJS look very similar to standard HTML forms.

First of all, the ngModel directive lets you define how inputs should bind to the model.

Introducing the ngModel directive

We have already seen how AngularJS creates data binding between fields on the scope object and HTML elements on the page. One can set up data binding by using curly braces, {{}}, or directives such as ngBind. But using such bindings is only one way. When binding to the value of an input directive, we use ngModel:

```
<div>Hello <span ng-bind="name"/></div>
<div>Hello <input ng-model="name"/></div>
```

Try it at http://bit.ly/Zm55zM.

In the first div, AngularJS binds scope.name of the current scope to the text of the span. This binding is one way: if the value of scope.name changes, the text of the span changes; but if we change the text of the span, the value of scope.name will not change.

In the second div, AngularJS binds scope.name of the current scope to the value of the input element. Here the data binding really is two way, since if we modify the value of the input box by typing in it, the value of the scope.name model is instantly updated. This update to scope.name is then seen in the one way binding to the span.

Why do we have a different directive to specify the binding on inputs? The ngBind directive only binds (one way) the value of its expression to the text of the element. With ngModel, data binding is two way, so changes to the value of the input are reflected back in the model.

In addition, AngularJS allows directives to transform and validate the ngModel directive values as the data binding synchronizes between the model and the input directive. You will see how this works in the ngModelController section.

Creating a User Information Form

In this section we will describe a simple User Information Form from our example SCRUM application. Throughout this chapter we will incrementally add functionality to this form to demonstrate the power of AngularJS forms. Here is our basic working form:

```html
<h1>User Info</h1>
<label>E-mail</label>
<input type="email" ng-model="user.email">

<label>Last name</label>
<input type="text" ng-model="user.lastName">

<label>First name</label>
<input type="text" ng-model="user.firstName">

<label>Website</label>
<input type="url" ng-model="user.website">

<label>Description</label>
<textarea ng-model="user.description"></textarea>

<label>Password</label>
<input type="password" ng-model="user.password">

<label>Password (repeat)</label>
<input type="password" ng-model="repeatPassword">

<label>Roles</label>
<label class="checkbox">
  <input type="checkbox" ng-model="user.admin"> Is Administrator
</label>

<pre ng-bind="user | json"></pre>
```

Try it at http://bit.ly/10ZomqS.

While it appears that we simply have a list of standard HTML inputs, these are actually AngularJS input directives. Each input has been given an ngModel directive that defines what current scope to bind the value of the input element. In this case, each input is bound to a field on the user object, which itself is attached to the current scope. In a controller we could log the value of a model field like so:

```
$log($scope.user.firstName);
```

Notice that we have not used a `form` element or put `name` or `id` attributes on any of the `input` elements. For simple forms with no validation this is all we need. AngularJS ensures that the values of the input elements are synchronized with the values in the model. We are then free to work with the user model in a controller, for example, without worrying about how they are represented in the view.

> We have also bound a `pre` element with a JSON representation of the user model. This is so that we can see what is being synchronized to the model by AngularJS.

Understanding the input directives

In this section we describe the AngularJS input directives that are provided out of the box. Using input directives is very natural to people used to HTML forms because AngularJS builds on top of HTML.

You can use all the standard HTML input types in your forms. The input directives work with the `ngModel` directive to support additional functionality, such as validation or binding to the model. The AngularJS `input` directive checks the `type` attribute to identify what kind of functionality to add to the input element.

Adding the required validation

All the basic input directives support the use of the `required` (or `ngRequired`) attribute. Adding this attribute to your input element will tell AngularJS that the `ngModel` value is invalid if it is `null`, `undefined`, or `""` (the empty string). See the following section on Field Validation for more about this.

Using text-based inputs (text, textarea, e-mail, URL, number)

The basic input directive, `type="text"` or `textarea`, accepts any string for its value. When you change the text in the input, the model is instantly updated with the value.

The other text-based input directives, such as e-mail, URL, or number, act similarly except that they only allow the model to update if the value in the input box matches an appropriate regular expression. If you type into the e-mail input, the e-mail field in the model is blank until the input box contains a valid e-mail string. This means that your model never contains an invalid e-mail address. This is one of the benefits of decoupling the model from the view.

In addition to these validations all the text-based directives allow you to specify minimum and maximum lengths for the text as well as an arbitrary regular expression that must match. This is done with the ngMinLength, ngMaxLength, and ngPattern directives:

```
<input type="password" ng-model="user.password"
  ng-minlength="3" ng-maxlength="10"
  ng-pattern="/^.*(?=.*\d)(?=.*[a-zA-Z]).*$/">
```

Try it at http://bit.ly/153L87Q.

Here, the user.password model field must have between 3 and 10 characters, inclusive, and it must match a regular expression that requires it to include at least one letter and one number.

 Note that these built-in validation features do not stop the user from entering an invalid string. The input directive just clears the model field if the string is invalid.

Using checkbox inputs

Checkboxes simply indicate a boolean input. In our form, the input directive assigns true or false to the model field that is specified by ngModel. You can see this happening in our User Info Form for the "Is Administrator" field.

```
<input type="checkbox" ng-model="user.admin">
```

The value of user.admin is set to true if the checkbox is checked and false otherwise. Conversely, the checkbox will be ticked if the value of user.admin is true.

You can also specify different strings for true and false values to be used in the model. For example, we could have used admin and basic in a role field.

```
<input type="checkbox" ng-model="user.role" ng-true-value="admin" ng-
false-value="basic">
```

Try it at http://bit.ly/Yidt37.

In this case, the user.role model, would contain either admin or basic depending on whether the checkbox was ticked or not.

Using radio inputs

Radio buttons provide a fixed group of choices for a field. AngularJS makes this really simple to implement: Just bind all the radio buttons in a group to the same model field. The standard HTML `value` attribute is then used to specify what value to put in the model when the radio is selected:

```
<label><input type="radio" ng-model="user.sex" value="male"> Male</
label>
<label><input type="radio" ng-model="user.sex" value="female">
Female</label>
```

Try it at `http://bit.ly/14hYNsN`.

Using select inputs

The `select` input directive allows you to create a drop-down list, from which the user can select one or more items. AngularJS lets you specify options for the drop down statically or from an array on the scope.

Providing simple string options

If you have a static list of options from which to select you can simply provide them as `option` elements below the `select` element:

```
<select ng-model="sex">
  <option value="m" ng-selected="sex=='m'">Male</option>
  <option value="f" ng-selected="sex=='f'">Female</option>
</select>
```

Be aware that since the `value` attribute can only take a string, the value to which you bind can only be a string.

 If you want to bind to values that are not strings or you want your list of options to be created dynamically from data, then use `ngOptions` as follows.

Providing dynamic options with the ngOptions directive

AngularJS provides an additional syntax for dynamically defining a complex list of options for a `select` directive. If you want to bind the value of a `select` directive to an object, rather than a simple string, then use `ngOptions`. This attribute accepts a **comprehension expression** that defines what options are to be displayed. The form of this expression is:

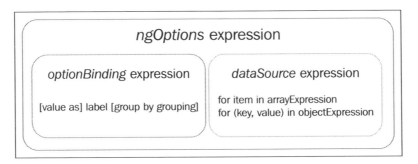

The `dataSource expression` describes the source of the information about the options to be displayed. It describes elements in an array or properties on an object. One select option will be generated for each item in the `dataSource expression`.

The `optionBinding` expression describes what should be extracted from each data source item and how that item should be bound to the `select` option.

Common examples of ngOptions

Before we explain the details of how to define these **comprehension expressions**, here are some typical examples.

Using array data sources

Select a user object with `user.email` as the label:

```
ng-options="user.email for user in users"
```

Select a user object with a computed label (the function would be defined on the scope):

```
ng-options="getFullName(user) for user in users"
```

Select a user's e-mail rather than the whole user object, with their full name as the label:

```
ng-options="user.email as getFullName(user) for user in users
```

Select a user object with the list grouped by sex:

```
ng-options="getFullName(user) group by user.sex for user in users"
```

Try it at http://bit.ly/1157jqa.

Using object data sources

Let's provide two objects that relate country names to codes:

```
$scope.countriesByCode = {
  'AF' : 'AFGHANISTAN',
  'AX' : 'ÅLAND ISLANDS',
  ...
};

$scope.countriesByName = {
  'AFGHANISTAN' : 'AF',
  'ÅLAND ISLANDS' : 'AX',
  ...
};
```

To select a country code by country name, ordered by country code:

```
ng-options="code as name for (code, name) in countriesByCode"
```

To select a country code by country name, ordered by country name:

```
ng-options="code as name for (name, code) in countriesByName"
```

Try it at http://bit.ly/153LKdE.

Now that we have seen some examples, we can show the full specification of these expressions.

Understanding the dataSource expression

If the data source will be an array then the arrayExpression should evaluate to an array. The directive will iterate over each of the items in the array, assigning the current item in the array to the value variable.

 The list of select options will be displayed in the same order as the items appear in the array.

If the data source will be an object then the objectExpression should evaluate to an object. The directive will iterate over each property of the object, assigning the value of the property to the value variable and the key of the member to the key variable.

The list of select options will be ordered alphabetically by the value of the key.

Understanding the optionBinding expression

The optionBinding expression defines how to get the label and value for each option and how to group the options from the items provided by the dataSource expression. This expression can take advantage of all the AngularJS expression syntax, including the use of filters. The general syntax is:

```
value as label group by grouping
```

If the value expression is not provided then the data item itself will be used as the value to assign to the model when this item is selected. If you provide a grouping expression, it should evaluate to the name of the group for the given option.

Using empty options with the select directive

What should the select directive do when the bound model value doesn't match with any of the values in the option list? In this case, the select directive will show an empty option at the top of the list of options.

 The empty option will be selected whenever the model does not match any of the options. If the user manually selects the empty option then the model will be set to null. It will not be set to undefined.

You can define an empty option by adding an option element as a child of the select element that has an empty string for its value:

```
<select ng-model="..." ng-options="...">
  <option value="">-- No Selection --</option>
</select>
```

Try it at http://bit.ly/ZeNpZX.

Here, we defined an empty option, which will display the -- No Selection -- label.

 If you define your own empty option then it will always be shown in the list of options and can be selected by the user.

If you do not define your own empty option in the declaration of the select directive it will generate its own.

If the directive generates the empty option, it will be shown only when the model does not match any items in the list. So the user will not be able to manually set the select value to null/undefined.

It is possible to hide the empty option by defining your own and setting its style to display: none.

```
<option style="display:none" value=""></option>
```

Try it at http://bit.ly/ZeNpZX.

In this case the select directive will use our empty option but the browser will not show it. Now, if the model does not match any options the select directive will be blank and invalid but there will not be a blank option shown in the list.

Understanding select and object equivalence

The select directive matches the model value to the option value using the object equivalence operator (===). This means that if your option values are objects and not simply values (like numbers and strings) you must use a reference to the actual option value for your model value. Otherwise the select directive will think that the objects are different and will not match it to the option.

In a controller we might set up the options and selected items as an array of objects:

```
app.controller('MainCtrl', function($scope) {
  $scope.sourceList = [
    {'id': '10005', 'name': "Anne"},
    {'id': '10006', 'name': "Brian"},
    {'id': '10007', 'name': "Charlie"}
  ];
  $scope.selectedItemExact = $scope.sourceList[0];
  $scope.selectedItemSimilar = {'id': '10005', 'name': "Anne"};
});
```

Here, selectedItemExact actually references the first item in the sourceList, while selectedItemSimilar is a different object, even though the fields are identical:

```
<select
  ng-model="selectedItemExact"
  ng-options=" item.name for item in sourceList">
</select>
<select
  ng-model="selectedItemSimilar"
  ng-options="item.name for item in sourceList">
</select>
```

Try it at `http://bit.ly/Zrachk`.

Here, we create two `select` directives that are bound to these values. The one bound to `selectedItemSimilar` will not have an option selected. Therefore, you should always bind the value of the select to an item in the `ng-options` array. You may have to search the array for the appropriate option.

Selecting multiple options

If you want to select multiple items, you simply apply the `multiple` attribute to the `select` directive. The `ngModel` bound to this directive is then an array containing a reference to the value of each selected option.

 AngularJS provides the `ngMultiple` directive, which takes an expression to decide whether to allow multiple selections. Currently, the `select` directive does not watch changes as to whether it accepts multiple selections, so the `ngMultiple` directive has limited use.

Working with traditional HTML hidden input fields

In AngularJS, we store all our model data in the scope so that there is rarely any need to use hidden input fields. Therefore, AngularJS has no hidden input directive. There are two cases where you might use hidden input fields: embedding values from the server and supporting traditional HTML form submission.

Embedding values from the server

You use a server-side templating engine to create the HTML and you pass data from the server to AngularJS via the template. In this case, it is enough to put an `ng-init` directive into the HTML that is generated by the server, which will add values to the scope:

```
<form ng-init="user.hash='13513516'">
```

Here the HTML sent from the server contains a form element that includes an `ng-init` directive that will initialize user, hash on the scope of the form.

Submitting a traditional HTML form

Traditionally, you might have wanted to submit values to the server that are not in the view, that is, not a visible input control. This would have been achieved by adding hidden fields to your form. In AngularJS, we work from a model that is decoupled from the form, so we do not need these hidden fields. We simply add such values to the scope and then simulate the form submission using the `$http` service. See *Chapter 3, Communicating with a Back-end Server* for how to do this.

Looking inside ngModel data binding

Until now we have seen that `ngModel` creates a binding between the model and the value in an input field. In this section we look deeper into what else this directive provides and how it works.

Understanding ngModelController

Each `ngModel` directive creates an instance of `ngModelController`. This controller is made available to all the directives on the `input` element.

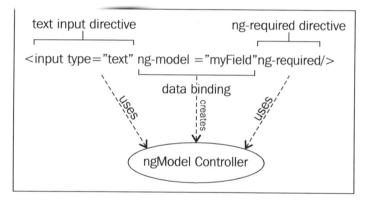

The `ngModelController` is responsible for managing the data binding between the value stored in the model (specified by `ngModel`) and the value displayed by the `input` element.

The `ngModelController` also tracks whether the view value is valid and whether it has been modified by the input element.

Transforming the value between the model and the view

The ngModelController has a transformation pipeline that it applies each time the data binding is updated. This consists of two arrays: $formatters that transforms from model into view and $parsers that transforms from view to model. Each directive on the input element can add in their own formatters and parsers to this pipeline in order to modify what happens to the data binding as shown in the following image:

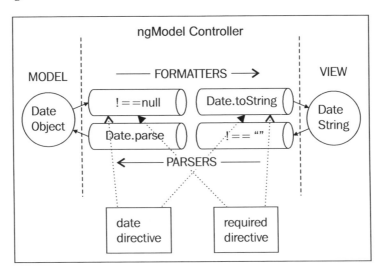

Here two directives are adding to the transformation pipeline. The date directive is parsing and formatting dates. The ng-required directive is checking that the value is not missing.

Tracking whether the value has changed

Along with transforming the value between the model and the view, the ngModelController tracks whether the value has changed since it was initialized and whether the value is valid.

When it is first initialized the ngModelController marks the value as pristine, that is, it has not been modified. It exposes this as an ng-pristine CSS class on the input element. When the view changes, say through typing in an input box, the value is marked as dirty. It replaces the ng-pristine CSS class with the ng-dirty CSS class.

By providing CSS styles for these classes, we can change the appearance of the input element based on whether the user has entered or modified the data:

```
.ng-pristine { border: solid black 1px; }
.ng-dirty { border: solid black 3px; }
```

Here we make the border of the element thicker if the user has made changes to the input.

Tracking input field validity

Directives on an input element can also tell the ngModelController whether they believe the value is valid or invalid. This is normally done by hooking into the transformation pipeline and checking the value rather than transforming it. The ngModelController tracks the validity and applies the ng-valid or ng-invalid CSS classes accordingly. We can provide further styles to change the appearance of the element based on these classes:

```
.ng-valid.ng-dirty { border: solid green 3px; }
.ng-invalid.ng-dirty { border: solid red 3px; }
```

Here, we are using a combination of pristine and invalid to ensure that only fields that have been changed by user input are styled: thick red border when invalid and thick green border when valid.

In the next section, Validating forms, we will see how we can work with the concepts of pristine, dirty, valid, and invalid programmatically.

Validating AngularJS forms

In this section we explain how to use validation directives and how they work with ngFormController to provide a full validation framework.

Understanding ngFormController

Each form (or ngForm) directive creates an instance of ngFormController. The ngFormController object manages whether the form is valid or invalid and whether it is pristine or dirty. Importantly, it works with ngModelController to track each ngModel field within the form.

When an ngModelController is created, it registers itself with the first ngFormController it comes across as it traverses up its list of parent elements. This way, the ngFormController knows what input directives it should track. It can check whether these fields are valid/invalid or pristine/dirty and set whether the form is valid/invalid or pristine/dirty accordingly.

Using the name attribute to attach forms to the scope

You can make the `ngFormController` appear on the local scope by giving the form a name. Any input elements within the form that also have names will have their `ngModelController` object attached as a property to this `ngFormController` object.

The following table shows how the scope contains the controllers associated with each of the elements in the form:

HTML	Scope	Controller
	`model1, model2, ...`	
`<form name="form1">`	`form1 : {`	`ngFormController`
	`$valid, $invalid,`	
	`$pristine, $dirty, ...`	

`<input`
`  name="field1"`
`  ng-model="model1"`
`/>`
	`field1: {`
	`    $valid, $invalid,`
	`    $pristine, $dirty, ...`
	`},`
		`ngModelController`

`<input`
`  name="field2"`
`  ng-model="model2"`
`/>`
	`field2: {`
	`    $valid, $invalid,`
	`    $pristine, $dirty, ...`
	`}`
		`ngModelController`

`</form>`	`},`	

Adding dynamic behavior to the User Information Form

Our form allows us to enter values into fields and we can change the appearance of the input elements based on the values entered. But for a more responsive user experience, we would like to show and hide validation messages and change the state of buttons on our form depending upon the state of the form fields.

Having the `ngFormController` and `ngModelControllers` objects on our scope allows us to work with the state of the form programmatically. We can use values like `$invalid` and `$dirty` to change what is enabled or visible to our user.

Showing validation errors

We can show error messages for inputs and for the form as a whole if something is not valid. In the template:

```
<form name="userInfoForm">
  <div class="control-group"
       ng-class="getCssClasses(userInfoForm.email)">

    <label>E-mail</label>
    <input type="email" ng-model="user.email"
           name="email" required>

    <span ng-show="showError(userInfoForm.email, 'email')" ...>
      You must enter a valid email
    </span>

    <span ng-show="showError(userInfoForm.email, 'required')" ...>
      This field is required
    </span>
  </div>

</form>
```

In the controller:

```
app.controller('MainCtrl', function($scope) {
  $scope.getCssClasses = function(ngModelContoller) {
    return {
      error: ngModelContoller.$invalid && ngModelContoller.$dirty,
      success: ngModelContoller.$valid && ngModelContoller.$dirty
    };
  };
  $scope.showError = function(ngModelController, error) {
    return ngModelController.$error[error];
  };
});
```

Try it at http://bit.ly/XwLUFZ.

This example shows the e-mail input from our User Form. We are using Twitter Bootstrap CSS to style the form, hence the `control-group` and `inline-help` CSS classes. We have also created two helper functions in the controller.

The ng-class directive will update the CSS classes on div that contains the label, the input, and the help text. It calls the getCssClasses() method, passing in an object and an error name.

 The object parameter is actually the ngModelController, which has been exposed on the ngFormController, which in turn is exposed on the scope.userInfoForm.email scope.

The getCssClasses() method returns an object that defines which CSS classes should be added. The key of each object refers to the name of a CSS class. The value of each member is true if the class is to be added. In this case getCssClasses() will return error if the model is dirty and invalid and success if the model is dirty and valid.

Disabling the save button

We can disable the save button when the form is not in a state to be saved.

```
<form name="userInfoForm">
  ...
  <button ng-disabled="!canSave()">Save</button>
</form>
```

In our view, we add a Save button with an ngDisabled directive. This directive will disable the button whenever its expression evaluates to true. In this case it is negating the result of calling the canSave() method. We provide the canSave() method on the current scope. We will do this in our main controller:

```
app.controller('MainCtrl', function($scope) {
  $scope.canSave = function() {
    return $scope.userInfoForm.$dirty &&
           $scope.userInfoForm.$valid;
  };
});
```

Try it at http://bit.ly/123zIhw.

The canSave() method checks whether the userInfoForm has the $dirty and $valid flags set. If so, the form is ready to save.

Disabling native browser validation

Modern browsers naturally try to validate the input values in a form. Normally this occurs when the form is submitted. For instance, if you have a required attribute on an input box, the browser will complain independently of AngularJS, if the field does not contain a value when you try to submit the form.

Since we are providing all the validation through AngularJS directives and controllers, we do not want the browser to attempt its own native validation. We can turn off this by applying the HTML5 `novalidate` attribute to the form element:

```
<form name="novalidateForm" novalidate>
```

Try it at `http://bit.ly/1110hS4`.

This form is called `novalidateForm` and the `novalidate` attribute will tell the browser not to attempt the validation on any of the inputs in the form.

Nesting forms in other forms

Unlike standard HTML forms, AngularJS forms can be nested inside each other. Since form tags inside other form tags are invalid HTML, AngularJS provides the `ngForm` directive for nesting forms.

> Each form that provides a name will be added to its parent form, or directly to the scope if it has no parent form.

Using subforms as reusable components

A nested form acts like a composite field that exposes its own validation information based on the fields that it contains. Such forms can be used to reuse as subforms by including them in container forms. Here we group two input boxes together to create a password and password confirmation widget:

```
<script type="text/ng-template" id="password-form">
  <ng-form name="passwordForm">
    <div ng-show="user.password != user.password2">
      Passwords do not match
    </div>
    <label>Password</label>
    <input ng-model="user.password" type="password" required>
```

```
        <label>Confirm Password</label>
        <input ng-model="user.password2" type="password" required>
    </ng-form>
</script>

<form name="form1" novalidate>
    <legend>User Form</legend>
    <label>Name</label>
    <input ng-model="user.name" required>
    <ng-include src="'password-form'"></ng-include>
</form>
```

Try it at http://bit.ly/10QWwyu.

We define our subform in a partial template. In this case it is inline in a script block but it could be in a separate file also. Next we have our container form, form1,which includes the subform by using the ngInclude directive.

The subform has its own validity state and related CSS classes. Also, notice that because the subform has a name attribute, it appears as a property on the container form.

Repeating subforms

Sometimes, we have fields in a form that needs to be repeated by an arbitrary number of times based on the data in the model. This is a common situation where you want to provide a single form that can display a one-to-many relationship in the data.

In our SCRUM app, we would like to allow users to have zero or more website URLs in their User Info profile. We can use an ngRepeat directive to set this up:

```
    <form ng-controller="MainCtrl">
    <h1>User Info</h1>
    <label>Websites</label>
    <div ng-repeat="website in user.websites">
        <input type="url" ng-model="website.url">
        <button ng-click="remove($index)">X</button>
    </div>
    <button ng-click="add()">Add Website</button>
    </form>
```

The controller initializes the model and provides the helper functions, `remove()` and `add()`:

```
app.controller('MainCtrl', function($scope) {
  $scope.user = {
    websites: [
      {url: 'http://www.bloggs.com'},
      {url: 'http://www.jo-b.com'}
    ]
  };
  $scope.remove = function(index) {
    $scope.user.websites.splice(index, 1);
  };
  $scope.add = function() {
    $scope.user.websites.push({ url: ''});
  };
});
```

Try it at `http://bit.ly/XHLEWQ`.

In the template, we have an `ngRepeat` directive that iterates over the websites in the user's profile. Each input directive in the repeat block is data bound to the appropriate `website.url` in the `user.websites` model. The helper functions take care of adding and removing items to and from the array and AngularJS data binding does the rest.

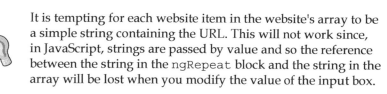 It is tempting for each website item in the website's array to be a simple string containing the URL. This will not work since, in JavaScript, strings are passed by value and so the reference between the string in the `ngRepeat` block and the string in the array will be lost when you modify the value of the input box.

Validating repeated inputs

The problem with this approach comes when you want to do work with validation on these repeated fields. We need each input to have a unique name within the form in order to access that field's validity, `$valid`, `$invalid`, `$pristine`, `$dirty`, and so on. Unfortunately, AngularJS does not allow you to dynamically generate the name attribute for `input` directives. The name must be a fixed string.

We solve this problem by using nested forms. Each exposes itself on the current scope, so if we place a nested form inside each repeated block that contains the repeated input directives, we will have access on that scope to the field's validity.

Template:

```
<form novalidate ng-controller="MainCtrl" name="userForm">
  <label>Websites</label>
  <div ng-show="userForm.$invalid">The User Form is invalid.</div>
  <div ng-repeat="website in user.websites" ng-form="websiteForm">
    <input type="url" name="website"
           ng-model="website.url" required>
    <button ng-click="remove($index)">X</button>
    <span ng-show="showError(websiteForm.website, 'url')">
      Pleae must enter a valid url</span>
    <span ng-show="showError(websiteForm.website, 'required')">
      This field is required</span>
  </div>
  <button ng-click="addWebsite()">Add Website</button>
</form>
```

Controller:

```
app.controller('MainCtrl', function($scope) {
  $scope.showError = function(ngModelController, error) {
    return ngModelController.$error[error];
  };
  $scope.user = {
    websites: [
      {url: 'http://www.bloggs.com'},
      {url: 'http://www.jo-b.com'}
    ]
  };
});
```

Try it at http://bit.ly/14i1sTp.

Here, we are applying the ngForm directive to div, to create a nested form, which is repeated for each website in the array of websites on the scope. Each of the nested forms is called websiteForm and each input in the form is called website. This means that we are able to access the validity of the ngModel for each website from within the ngRepeat scope.

We make use of this to show an error message when the input is invalid. The two ng-show directives will show their error messages when the showError function returns true. The showError function checks the passed in ngModelController to see if it has the relevant validation entry in the $error field. We can pass websiteForm.website to this function since this refers to the ngModelController object for our website input box.

Outside the `ngForm` we cannot reference the `websiteForm` (ngFormController) object on the scope or the `websiteForm.website` (ngModelController) object since they do not exist in this scope. We can, however, access the containing `userForm` (ngFormController) object. This form's validity is based upon the validity of all its child inputs and forms. If one of the `websiteForms` is invalid, so is the `userForm`. The div at the top of the form displays an overall error message only if `userForms.$valid` is true.

Handling traditional HTML form submission

In this section we take a look at how AngularJS handles submission of forms. Single Page AJAX Applications, for which AngularJS is perfect, don't tend to follow the same process of direct submission to the server as traditional web application do. But sometimes your application must support this. Here we show the various submission scenarios that you may wish to implement when submitting form data back to a server.

Submitting forms directly to the server

If you include an `action` attribute on a form in an AngularJS application, then the form will submit as normal to the URL defined in the action:

```
<form method="get" action="http://www.google.com/search">
  <input name="q">
</form>
```

Try it at `http://bit.ly/115cQgq`.

> Be aware that the Plnkr preview will block the redirection to Google.

Handling form submission events

If you don't include an `action` attribute, then AngularJS assumes that we are going to handle the submission on the client side by calling a function on the scope. In this case, AngularJS will prevent the form trying to directly submit to the server.

We can trigger this client-side function by using the `ngClick` directive on a `button` or the `ngSubmit` directive on the `form`.

You should not use both the ngSubmit and ngClick directives on the same form because the browser will trigger both directives and you will get double submission.

Using ngSubmit to handle form submission

To use ngSubmit on a form, you provide an expression that will be evaluated when the form is submitted. The form submission will happen when the user hits *Enter* in one of the inputs or clicks on one of the buttons:

```
<form ng-submit="showAlert(q)">
  <input ng-model="q">
</form>
```

Try it at http://bit.ly/ZQBLYj.

Here, hitting *Enter* while in the input will call the showAlert method.

 You should use ngSubmit only on a form that has only one input and not more than one button, such as our search form in the example.

Using ngClick to handle form submission

To use ngClick, on a button or input [type=submit], you provide an expression that will be evaluated when the button is clicked:

```
<form>
  <input ng-model="q">
  <button ng-click="showAlert(q)">Search</button>
</form>
```

Try it at http://bit.ly/153OvLS.

Here, clicking on the button or hitting *Enter* in the input field will call the showAlert method.

Resetting the User Info form

In our User Info form, we would like to cancel the changes and reset the form back to its original state. We do this by holding a copy of the original model with which we can overwrite any changes that the user has made.

Template:

```
<form name="userInfoForm">
  ...
  <button ng-click="revert()" ng-disabled="!canRevert()">Revert
Changes</button>
</form>
```

Controller:

```
app.controller('MainCtrl', function($scope) {
  ...
  $scope.user = {
    ...
  };
  $scope.passwordRepeat = $scope.user.password;

  var original = angular.copy($scope.user);

  $scope.revert = function() {
    $scope.user = angular.copy(original);
    $scope.passwordRepeat = $scope.user.password;
    $scope.userInfoForm.$setPristine();
  };

  $scope.canRevert = function() {
    return !angular.equals($scope.user, original);
  };

  $scope.canSave = function() {
    return $scope.userInfoForm.$valid &&
      !angular.equals($scope.user, original);
  };
});
```

Try it at http://bit.ly/17vHLWX.

Here, we have a button to revert the model back to its original state. Clicking on this button calls revert() on the scope. The button is disabled if canRevert() returns false.

In the controller, you can see that we use angular.copy() to make a copy of the model and place it in a local variable. The revert() method copies this original back over to the working user model and sets the form back to a pristine state so that all the CSS classes are no longer set to ng-dirty.

Summary

In this chapter we have seen how AngularJS extends standard HTML form controls to provide a more flexible and powerful system for getting input from the user. It enables a separation of the model from the view through `ngModel` and provides mechanisms to track changes and validity of input values through validation directives and the `ngFormController` object.

In the next chapter we will look at how to best manage navigation round our application. We will see how AngularJS supports deep linking to map URLs directly into aspects of our application and how to use `ngView` to automatically display relevant content to the user based on the current URL.

6
Organizing Navigation

In previous chapters, we've learnt how to fetch data from a back-end, edit those data using AngularJS-powered forms, and display the data on individual pages by employing various directives. In this chapter, we will see how to organize separate screens into a fully functional, easy-to-navigate-through application.

Well-designed and easy-to-remember **URLs (Uniform resource locators)** play a vital role in structuring an application for our users. It allows them to move effectively between different screens, using browser features with which they are comfortable. AngularJS includes various services and directives that bring URL support found in Web 1.0 applications to single-page web applications, most notably the following ones:

- Deep-linking URLs refer to a specific feature within a single-page web application. They can then be bookmarked or passed around (for example in an e-mail or in an instant message).

- The back and forward buttons in a browser behave as expected, allowing users to move between different screens of a single-page web application.

- URLs can have a nice, easy-to-remember format in browsers that support HTML5 history API.

- URL support in AngularJS is consistent across browsers, the same application code works correctly in browsers with full support for the HTML5 history API as well as in older browsers.

AngularJS has sophisticated machinery to handle URLs. In this chapter, we are going to learn about the following topics:

- The use of URLs in single-page web applications,

- The AngularJS approach to URLs and its abstractions over URLs: the `$location` and `$anchorScroll` services

- Organizing navigation in a client-side web application using the `$route` service (with its provider – `$routeProvider`) and the `ngView` directive
- Common patterns, tips, and tricks when using URLs in a single-page, AngularJS-powered web application

URLs in single-page web applications

Navigation between pages was straightforward in the early days of the web. One could type a URL in the browser's address bar to retrieve a precisely identified resource. After all, a URL is used to point to a single, physical resource (a file) on a server. When a page was loaded, we could follow hyperlinks to jump between resources as well as use the browser's back and forward buttons to move between visited items.

The rise of dynamically rendered pages broke this simple navigation paradigm. All of a sudden, the same URL could result in different pages being sent to a browser, depending on the application's internal state. The back and forward buttons were the first victims of the highly interactive web. Their usage became unpredictable, and many websites are still going as far as discouraging the use of the back and forward navigation buttons (encouraging users to rely on internal navigation links).

Single-page web applications didn't improve the situation, far from it! In modern, AJAX-heavy applications, it is not uncommon to see only a single URL in the browser's address bar (the one that was used to initially load the application). Subsequent HTTP interactions happen through the XHR object, without affecting the browser's address bar. In this setup, the back and forward buttons are completely useless, since pressing them would take us to completely different websites, instead of a place within the current application. Bookmarking or copying and pasting a link from the browser's address bar is not much use either. A bookmarked link will always point to the starting page of an application.

But the browser's back and forward buttons and ability to bookmark URLs are very useful. Users don't want to give them up while working with single-page web applications! Fortunately, AngularJS is well-equipped to help us handle URLs with the same efficiency as in the good, olden days of the static resources web!

Hashbang URLs in the pre-HTML5 era

It turns out that there is a trick that can bring back decent support for URLs in AJAX-heavy web applications.

The trick is based on the fact that we can modify parts of the URL in a browser's address bar, those after the # character without triggering a reload of the currently displayed page. This part of the URL is called the URL fragment. By changing the URL fragment, we can add new elements to the browser's history stack (the `window.history` object). The back and forward buttons rely on the browser's history. So if we manage to get the history right, the navigation buttons will work as expected.

Let's consider a set of typical URLs often used in CRUD-like applications. Ideally, we would like to have a URL pointing to a list of items, an edit form for an item, a form for new items, and so on. Taking the administration of users (from our sample SCRUM application), as an example, we would typically have the following distinct partial URLs:

- `/admin/users/list` – This URL shows a list of existing users
- `/admin/users/new` – This URL shows a form to add a new user
- `/admin/users/[userId]` – This URL shows a form to edit an existing user with ID equal to [userId]

We could translate these partial URLs to full URLs with fragments in a single-page web application using the # trick as follows:

- `http://myhost.com/#/admin/users/list`
- `http://myhost.com/#/admin/users/new`
- `http://myhost.com/#/admin/users/[userId]`

URLs pointing to inner parts of a single-page web applications, in this way are often referred to as "hashbang URLs".

Having set up the preceding URL scheme, we can change the URL in the browser's address bar without fully reloading the page. The browser will pick up different URLs (with the same prefix but different URL fragment after the # character) to drive its history and back/forward buttons. At the same time, it won't issue any calls to the server if the only changing part is the URL fragment.

Of course, changing the URL scheme is not enough. We need to have some JavaScript logic that will observe URL fragment changes, and modify the client-side state of the application accordingly.

HTML5 and the history API

As users, we love simple, memorable, and easy-to -bookmark URLs, but the hashbang tricks just described, make URLs excessively long and to be frank quite ugly. Fortunately there is an HTML5 specification that addresses this problem: The history API.

The history API is supported in most of the modern browsers. When it comes to Internet Explorer, it is only built in starting from Version 10. The earlier versions work only with hashbang URLs.

In short, using the history API, we can simulate visiting external resources without actually making round trips to the server. We can do so by pushing full, nicely formatted URLs on top of the browser's history stack using the new `history.pushState` method. The history API also has a built-in mechanism to observe changes in the history stack. We can listen to the `window.onpopstate` event and change the application's state in response to this event.

By using the HTML5 history API, we can once again work with nice URLs (without the # trick) in single-page web applications and enjoy good user experience by using bookmarkable URLs, back and forward buttons working as expected, and so on. The URLs from the previous example could be simply represented as follows:

- `http://myhost.com/admin/users/list`
- `http://myhost.com/admin/users/new`
- `http://myhost.com/admin/users/[userId]`

Those URLs look very much like "standard" URLs, pointing to real resources on a server. This is good, since we want to have nicely looking URLs. But if one of these URLs is entered into the browser's address bar, a user agent can't distinguish this URL from any other URL and it will issue a request to the server.

 For the HTML5 mode to work correctly in such situations, the server needs to be configured properly, and cooperate by always returning the application's landing page. We are going to cover server setup for the HTML5 URLs mode later in this chapter.

Using the $location service

AngularJS provides an abstraction layer over URLs (and their behavior) in the form of the $location service. This service masks the difference between the hashbang and the HTML5 URL modes allowing us, application developers, to work with a consistent API regardless of the browser and the mode being used. But the $location service does more heavy lifting, by providing the following functions:

- Provides convenient, clean API to easily access different parts of the current URL (protocol, host, port, path, query parameters, and so on)

- Lets us to programmatically manipulate different parts of the current URL and have those changes reflected in the browser's address bar

- Allows us to easily observe changes in different components of the current URL and take actions in response to those changes

- Intercepts the users' interactions with links on a page (such as clicking on the <a> tags) to reflect those interactions in the browser's history

Understanding the $location service API and URLs

Before we see practical examples of using the $location service, we need to get familiar with its API. Since the $location service works with URLs, the easiest way to get started is to see how the different components of a URL map to the API methods.

Let's consider a URL that points to a list of users. To make the example more complex, we will use a URL that has all the possible components: a path, a query string, and a fragment. The essential part of the URL could look as follows:

/admin/users/list?active=true#bottom

We could decipher this URL as: in the administration section, list all users that are active and scroll to the bottom of the retrieved list. This is the only part of a URL that is interesting from the point of view of our application, but in reality a URL is the "whole package", with a protocol, host, and so on. This URL in its full form, will be represented differently, depending on the mode (hashbang or HTML5) used. In the following URL, we can see examples of the same URL represented in both modes. In HTML5 it would look as follows:

http://myhost.com/myapp/admin/users/list?active=true#bottom

In hashbang mode it would take its longer, uglier form, which is as follows:

http://myhost.com/myapp#/admin/users/list?active=true#bottom

Regardless of the mode used, the $location service API will mask the differences and offer a consistent API. The following table shows a subset of the methods available on the API:

Method	Given the above example, would return
$location.url()	/admin/users/list?active=true#bottom
$location.path()	/admin/users/list
$location.search()	{active: true}
$location.hash()	Bottom

All of these methods are jQuery-style getters. In other words, they can be used to both get and set the value of a given URL's component. For example, to read the URL fragment value you would use: `$location.hash()`, while setting the value would require an argument to be supplied to the same function: `$location.hash('top')`.

The `$location` service offers other methods (not listed in the previous table) to access any part of a URL: the protocol (`protocol()`), the host (`host()`), the port (`port()`), and the absolute URL (`absUrl()`). The methods are getters only. They can't be used to mutate URLs.

Hashes, navigation within a page, and $anchorScroll

The side effect of using hashbang URLs is that the part of the URL after the # sign, normally used to navigate within a loaded document, is "taken" to represent the URL part interesting from a single-page web application point of view. Still, there are cases where we need to scroll to a specified place in a document loaded into the browser. The trouble is that, in hashbang mode, URLs would contain two # signs, for example:

```
http://myhost.com/myapp#/admin/users/list?active=true#bottom
```

Browsers have no way of knowing that the second hash (`#bottom`) should be used to navigate within a document, and we need a little bit of help from AngularJS here. This is where the `$anchorScroll` service comes into play.

By default the `$anchorScroll` service will monitor URL fragments. Upon detecting a hash that should be used to navigate within a document, it will scroll to the specified position. This process will work correctly in both the HTML5 mode (where only one hash is present in a URL) as well as in hashbang mode (where two hashes can make it into a URL). In short, the `$anchorScroll` service does the job which is normally performed by the browser, but taking the hashbang mode into account.

If we want to have more fine-grained control over the scrolling behavior of the `$anchorScroll` service you can opt out from its automatic URL fragment monitoring. To do so, you need to call the `disableAutoScrolling()` method on the `$anchorScrollProvider` service in a configuration block of a module as follows:

```
angular.module('myModule', [])
  .config(function ($anchorScrollProvider) {
    $anchorScrollProvider.disableAutoScrolling();
  });
```

By doing these configuration changes, we gain manual control over when scrolling takes place. We can trigger scrolling by invoking the service's function ($anchorScroll()) at any chosen point of time.

Configuring the HTML5 mode for URLs

By default AngularJS is configured to use hashbang mode for URLs. To enjoy nice-looking URLs in HTML5 mode, we need to change the default AngularJS configuration, as well as set up our server to support bookmarkable URLs.

Client side

Changing to HTML5 URL mode in AngularJS is trivial. It boils down to calling the html5Mode() method on $locationProvider with an appropriate argument as follows:

```
angular.module('location', [])
  .config(function ($locationProvider) {
    $locationProvider.html5Mode(true);
  })
```

Server side

For HTML5 mode to work correctly in all cases, we need a little help from the server that is responsible for serving the AngularJS application files to the browser. In a nutshell, we need to set up redirections on the web server, so that requests to any deep-linking application URL will be responded with the single-page web application's starting page (the one that contains the ng-app directive).

To understand why such redirections are needed, let's examine a situation where a user uses a bookmarked URL (in HTML5 mode) pointing to a product backlog of a specific project. Such a URL could look as follows:

http://host.com/projects/50547faee4b023b611d2dbe9/productbacklog

To the browser, such a URL looks like any other normal URL and the browser will issue a request to the server. Obviously such a URL only makes sense in the context of the single-page web application, at the client side. The /projects/50547faee4 b023b611d2dbe9/productbacklog resource doesn't exist physically on the server and can't be generated by the server dynamically. The only thing that a server can do with such URLs is to redirect them to the starting point of the application. This will result in the AngularJS application being loaded into the browser. When the application starts, the $location service will pick up the URL (still present in the browser's address bar), and this is where the client-side processing can take over.

Providing further details on how to configure different servers is beyond the scope of this book, but there are some general rules that apply to all servers. Firstly, there are roughly three types of URLs that a typical web server needs to handle:

- URLs pointing to static resources (images, CSS files, AngularJS partials, and so on)
- URLs for back-end data retrieval or modifications requests (for instance, a RESTful API)
- URLs that represent features of the application in HTML5 mode, where the server must respond with the application's landing page (typically a bookmarked URL used, or a URL typed in in a browser's address bar)

Since it is cumbersome to enumerate all the URLs that can hit a web server due to the HTML5 mode links, it is probably the best to use a well-known prefix for both static resources and URLs used to manipulate data. This is a strategy employed by the sample SCRUM application where all the static resources are served from the URLs with the /static prefix, while the ones prefixed with the /databases prefix are reserved for data manipulation on a back-end. Most of the remaining URLs are redirected to the starting point of the SCRUM application (index.html).

Handcrafting navigation using the $location service

Now that we are familiar with the $location service API and its configuration, we can put the freshly acquired knowledge into practice by building a very simple navigation scheme using the ng-include directive and the $location service.

Even the simplest navigation scheme in a single-page web application should offer some fundamental facilities to make developers life easier. As a bare minimum we should be able to perform the following activities:

- Define routes in a consistent, easy to maintain manner
- Update the application's state in response to URL changes
- Change the URL in response to the users navigating around the application (clicking on a link, using back and forward buttons in a browser, and so on)

 In the rest of this book, the term routing is used to denote a facility that helps synchronize the application's state (both screens and corresponding model) in response to URL changes. A single route is a collection of metadata used to transition an application to a state matching a given URL.

Structuring pages around routes

Before we dive into code samples, we should note that in a typical web application there are "fixed parts" of a page (header, footer, and so on) as well as "moving parts", which should change in response to the user's navigation actions. Taking this into account, we should organize markup and controllers on our page in such a way that fixed and moving parts are clearly separated. Building on the previously seen URL examples, we could structure the application's HTML as follows:

```html
<body ng-controller="NavigationCtrl">
<div class="navbar">
    <div class="navbar-inner">
      <ul class="nav">
        <li><a href="#/admin/users/list">List users</a></li>
        <li><a href="#/admin/users/new">New user</a></li>
      </ul>
    </div>
</div>
<div class="container-fluid" ng-include="selectedRoute.templateUrl">
    <!-- Route-dependent content goes here -->
</div>
</body>
```

The moving part in the preceding example is represented by a `<div>` tag with the `ng-include` directive referencing a dynamic URL: `selectedRoute.templateUrl`. But how does this expression gets changed based on URL changes?

Let's examine the JavaScript part, by having a closer look at `NavigationCtrl`. Firstly, we can define our `routes` variable as follows:

```javascript
.controller('NavigationCtrl', function ($scope, $location) {

    var routes = {
      '/admin/users/list': {templateUrl: 'tpls/users/list.html'},
      '/admin/users/new': {templateUrl: 'tpls/users/new.html'},
      '/admin/users/edit': {templateUrl: 'tpls/users/edit.html'}
    };
    var defaultRoute = routes['/admin/users/list'];
    ...
});
```

The `routes` object gives a basic structure to the application, it maps all possible partial templates to their corresponding URLs. By glancing over these routes definition, we can quickly see which screens make up our application and which partials are used in each route.

Mapping routes to URLs

Having a simple routing structure in place isn't enough. We need to synchronize the active route with the current URL. We can do this easily, by watching the path() component of the current URL as follows:

```
$scope.$watch(function () {
  return $location.path();
}, function (newPath) {
  $scope.selectedRoute = routes[newPath] || defaultRoute;
});
```

Here, each change in `$location.path()` component will trigger a lookup for one of the defined routes. If a URL is recognized, a corresponding route becomes the selected one. Otherwise, we fall back to a default route.

Defining controllers in route partials

When a route is matched, a corresponding template (partial) is loaded, and included into the page by the ng-include directive. As you remember the ng-include directive creates a new scope, and most of the time we need to set up this scope with some data that make sense for the newly loaded partial: a list of users, a user to be edited, and so on.

In AngularJS, setting up a scope with data and behavior is the job the controller. We need to find a way to define a controller for each and every partial. Obviously, the simplest approach is to use the ng-controller directive in the root element of each partial. For example, a partial responsible for editing users would look as follows:

```
<div ng-controller="EditUserCtrl">
    <h1>Edit user</h1>
    ...
</div>
```

The downside of this approach is that we can't reuse the same partial with different controllers. There are cases where it would be beneficial to have exactly the same HTML markup, and only change the behavior and the data set up behind this partial. One example of such a situation is an edit form, where we would like to reuse the same form both for adding new items editing an existing item. In this situation the form's markup could be exactly the same but data and behavior slightly different.

The missing bits in the handcrafted navigation

The ad-hoc solution presented here is not very robust, and should not be used as it is in real-life applications. Although incomplete, it illustrates several interesting features of the `$location` service.

To start with, the `$location` service API provides an excellent wrapper around various raw APIs exposed by browsers. Not only is this API consistent across browsers, but it also deals with different URL modes (hashbang and HTML5 history).

Secondly, we can really appreciate the facilities offered by AngularJS and its services. Anyone who had tried to write a similar navigation system in vanilla JavaScript would quickly see how much is offered by the framework. Still, there are numerous bits that could be improved! But instead of continuing with this custom development, based on the `$location` service, we will discuss the built-in AngularJS solution to these navigation-related issues: the `$route` service.

Using built-in AngularJS routing services

The AngularJS framework has a built-in `$route` service that can be configured to handle route transitions in single-page web applications. It covers all the features that we were trying to handcraft using the `$location` service and additionally offers other very useful facilities. We are going to get familiar with those step-by-step.

> Starting from Version 1.2, AngularJS will have its routing system delivered in a separate file (`angular-route.js`) with its own module (ngRoute). When working with the latest version of AngularJS, you will need to remember to include the `angular-route.js` file and declare a dependency on the ngRoute module.

Basic routes definition

Before diving into more advanced usage scenarios, let's abandon our naïve implementation by converting our route definitions to the syntax used by the `$route` service.

In AngularJS, routes can be defined during the application's configuration phase using the $routeProvider service. The syntax used by the $routeProvider service is similar to the one we were playing with in our custom $location based implementation:

```
angular.module('routing_basics', [])
  .config(function($routeProvider) {
    $routeProvider
      .when('/admin/users/list', {templateUrl: 'tpls/users/list.
html'})
        .when('/admin/users/new', {templateUrl: 'tpls/users/new.html'})
        .when('admin/users/:id', {templateUrl: 'tpls/users/edit.html'})

        .otherwise({redirectTo: '/admin/users/list'});
  })
```

The $routeProvider service exposes a fluent-style API, where we can chain method invocations for defining new routes (when) and setting up a default route (otherwise).

> Once initialized, an application can't be reconfigured to support additional routes (or remove existing ones). This is linked to the fact that AngularJS providers can be injected and manipulated only in configuration blocks executed during the application's bootstrap.

In the previous examples, you can see that templateUrl was the only property for each route but the syntax offered by the $routeProvider service is far richer.

> The content of a route can be also specified inline using the template property of a route definition object. While this is a supported syntax, hardcoding the route's markup in its definition is not very flexible (nor maintainable) so it is rarely used in practice.

Displaying the matched route's content

When one of the routes is matched against a URL, we can display the route's contents (defined as templateUrl or template) by using the ng-view directive. The $location-based version of the markup looked before as follows:

```
<div class="container-fluid" ng-include="selectedRoute.templateUrl">
    <!-- Route-dependent content goes here -->
</div>
```

With ng-view, this can be rewritten as follows:

```
<div class="container-fluid" ng-view>
    <!-- Route-dependent content goes here -->
</div>
```

As you can see, we simply substituted the ng-include directive for ng-view one. This time we don't need to provide an attribute value, since the ng-view directive "knows" that it should display the content of the currently matching route.

Matching flexible routes

In the naïve implementation, we were relying on a very simple route matching algorithm, which doesn't support variable parts in URLs. In fact it is a bit of a stretch to call it an algorithm, we are simply looking up a property on an object corresponding to URL's path! Due to the algorithm's simplicity, we were using a URL query parameter in the query string to pass around the user's identifier as follows:

/admin/users/edit?user={{user.id}}

It would be much nicer to have URLs where the user's identifier is embedded as part of a URL, for example:

/admin/users/edit/{{user.id}}

With the AngularJS router, this is very easy to achieve since we can use any string prefixed by a colon sign (:) as a wildcard. To support a URL scheme where the user's ID is part of a URL we could write as follows:

```
.when('/admin/users/:userid', {templateUrl: 'tpls/users/edit.html'})
```

This definition will match any URLs with an arbitrary string in place of the :userid wildcard, for example:

/users/edit/1234

/users/edit/dcc9ef31db5fc

On the other hand, routes with an empty :userid, or the :userid containing slashes (/) won't be matched.

> It is possible to match routes based on parameters that can contain slashes, but in this case we need to use slightly modified syntax: *id. For example, we could use the star-based syntax to match paths containing slashes: /wiki/pages/*page. The route-matching syntax will be further extended in AngularJS Version 1.2.

Defining default routes

The default route can be configured by calling the otherwise method, providing a definition of a default, catch-all route. Please notice that the otherwise method doesn't require any URL to be specified as there can be only one default route.

> A default route usually redirects to one of the already defined routes using the redirectTo property of the route definition object.

The default route will be used in both cases where no path was provided as well as for cases where an invalid URL (without any matching route) triggers a route change.

Accessing route parameter values

We saw that route URLs definition can contain variable parts that act as parameters. When a route is matched against a URL, you can easily access the values of those parameters using the $routeParams service. In fact, the $routeParams service is a simple JavaScript object (a hash), where keys represent route parameter names and values represent strings extracted from the matching URL.

Since $routeParams is a regular service, it can be injected into any object managed by the AngularJS Dependency Injection system. We can see this in action when examining an example of a controller (EditUserCtrl) used to update a user's data (/admin/users/:userid) as follows:

```
.controller('EditUserCtrl', function($scope, $routeParams, Users){
  $scope.user = Users.get({id: $routeParams.userid});
  ...
})
```

The $routeParams service combines parameter values from both the URL's path as well as from its search parameters. This code would work equally well for a route defined as /admin/users/edit with a matching URL: /admin/users/edit?userid=1234.

Reusing partials with different controllers

In the approach taken so far, we defined a controller responsible for initializing the partial's scope inside each partial using the ng-controller directive. But the AngularJS routing system makes it possible to define controllers at the route level. By pulling the controller out of the partial, we are effectively decoupling the partial's markup from the controller used to initialize the partial's scope.

Let's consider a partial providing a screen for editing a user's data:

```
<div ng-controller="EditUserCtrl">
    <h1>Edit user</h1>
    . . .
</div>
```

We could modify it by removing the ng-controller directive as follows:

```
<div>
    <h1>Edit user</h1>
    . . .
</div>
```

Instead of that we can define the controller service in the route level as follows:

```
.when('/admin/users/:userid', {
  templateUrl: 'tpls/users/edit.html'
  controller: 'EditUserCtrl'})
```

By moving the controller to the route definition level, we've gained the possibility of reusing the same controller for different partials and more importantly, reusing the same partials with different controllers. This additional flexibility comes in handy in several situations. A typical example would be a partial containing a form to edit an item. Usually we want to have exactly the same markup for both adding a new item and editing an existing item, but behavior for new items might be slightly different as compared to the existing ones (for example, creating rather than updating when persisting the item).

Avoiding UI flickering on route changes

While an application transitions between different screens, we usually need to get and display markup for a new screen as well as fetch the corresponding data (model). It turns out that there are two slightly different strategies that we can use to render a new screen, which are as follows:

- Display new markup as soon as possible (even if corresponding data are not yet ready) and then repaint the UI upon arrival of the data from the back-end.

- Make sure that all the requests to the back-end are completed and the data are ready before displaying markup for a new route

The first approach is the default one. For a route with both the templateUrl and the controller properties defined, AngularJS will match the route and render the contents of the partial, even if the data requested by a controller are not ready by this time. Of course, AngularJS will automatically repaint the partial when the data finally arrives (and is bound to the scope), but users might notice an unpleasant flickering effect. The UI flickering happens due to the same partial being rendered twice in a short timespan, firstly without data and then again when the data are ready.

The AngularJS routing system has excellent, built-in support for the second approach where the route change (and UI repaint) is postponed until both the partial and all the requested data are ready. By using the resolve property on a route definition object we can enumerate asynchronous dependencies for a route's controller. AngularJS will make sure that all these dependencies are resolved before the route change (and controller instantiation) takes place.

To illustrate the basic usage of the resolve property, let's rewrite our "edit user" route as follows:

```
.when('/admin/users/:userid', {
  templateUrl: 'tpls/users/edit.html'
  controller: 'EditUserCtrl',
    resolve: {
        user: function($route, Users) {
          return Users.getById($route.current.params.userid);
        }
    }
})
```

The resolve property is an object, where keys declare new variables that will be injected into the route's controller. The values of those variables are provided by a dedicated function. This function can also have dependencies injected by the AngularJS DI system. Here we are injecting the $route and Users services to retrieve and return user's data.

These resolve functions can either return simple JavaScript values, objects, or promises. When a promise is returned, AngularJS will delay the route change until the promise is resolved. Similarly if several resolve functions return promises, the AngularJS routing system will make sure that all the promises are resolved before proceeding with the route change.

 Functions in the resolve section of a route definition can return promises. The actual route change will take place, if and only if all the promises are successfully resolved.

Once all these route-specific variables (defined in the `resolve` section) are resolved, they are injected into the route's controller as follows:

```
.controller('EditUserCtrl', function($scope, user){
    $scope.user = user;
    ...
})
```

This is an extremely powerful pattern, as it allows us to define variables that are local to a given route and have those variables injected into a route's controller. There are multiple practical applications of this pattern and in the sample SCRUM application we are using it to reuse the same controller with different values for the `user` variable (either created in place or retrieved from a back-end). In the following code snippet, we can see an extract from the sample SCRUM application:

```
$routeProvider.when('/admin/users/new', {
    templateUrl:'admin/users/users-edit.tpl.html',
    controller:'UsersEditCtrl',
    resolve:{
      user: function (Users) {
        return new Users();
      }
    }
});


$routeProvider.when('/admin/users/:userId', {
    templateUrl:'admin/users/users-edit.tpl.html',
    controller:'UsersEditCtrl',
    resolve:{
      user: function ($route, Users) {
        return Users.getById($route.current.params.userId);
      }
    }
});
```

Defining local variables on a route level (in the `resolve` section) means that controllers defined as part of a route can be injected with those local variables. This greatly improves our ability to unit test the controllers' logic.

Preventing route changes

There are times where we might want to block a route change, based on certain conditions. For example, consider the following route to edit a user's data:

/users/edit/:userid

We need to decide what should happen if a user with the specified identifier doesn't exist. One reasonable expectation would be that users of an application can't navigate to a route pointing to a non-existing item.

As it turns out the `resolve` property of a route definition has a built-in support for blocking route navigation. If a value of one of the `resolve` keys is a promise that is rejected, AngularJS will cancel route navigation and won't change the view in the UI.

> If one of the promises returned in the `resolve` section of a route definition is rejected the route change will be canceled and the UI won't be updated.

It should be noted that the URL in a browser's address bar won't be reverted if route change is canceled. To see what it means in practice, let's assume that a list of users is displayed under the `/users/list` URL. All the users in a list might have links pointing to their edit forms (`/users/edit/:userid`). Clicking on one of those links will change the browser's address bar (so it will become something like `/users/edit/1234`) but it is not guaranteed that we will be able to edit user's details (user might have been deleted in the meantime, we don't have sufficient access rights, and so on). If the route's navigation is canceled the browser's address bar won't be reverted and will still read `/users/edit/1234`, even if UI will be still reflecting, content of the `/users/list` route.

> The Browser's address bar and the displayed UI might get out of sync if route navigation is canceled due to a rejected promise.

Limitations of the $route service

While the built-in `$route` service is very well-crafted and does an excellent job for many applications, there are cases where it falls short. This section lists those cases, so we can be aware and ready to change our application's design, or roll out a custom routing service!

> There is a community-driven effort in progress to provide a more powerful routing system for AngularJS applications: ui-router. The goal is to provide support for nested routes and routes that can influence multiple rectangles on a screen. At the time of writing this is still work in progress but you can follow its development at: `https://github.com/angular-ui/ui-router`.

One route corresponds to one rectangle on the screen

As you now know, the `ng-view` directive is used to indicate the DOM element whose content should be replaced with the content defined by the route (via the `template` or `templateUrl` property). This immediately tells us that in the `$route` service, a route can describe content for only one "hole" in the UI.

In reality, there are times where we would like to fill in multiple areas of a screen in response to a route change. A typical example would involve a menu that might be common to several routes and should change as we navigate from one area of an application to the other. The following figure illustrates this:

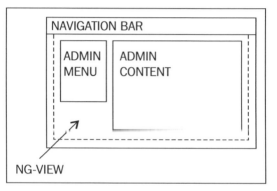

Taking the preceding figure as an example, we would like to keep the **ADMIN MENU** if a user navigates within the administration area. The only way to achieve this navigation scheme with the current version of AngularJS is to use a combination of the `ng-include` directive and the trick described in the next section.

Handling multiple UI rectangles with ng-include

Route definition objects are regular JavaScript objects and can contain custom properties, in addition to the ones interpreted by AngularJS. Defining a custom property won't interfere with the default `$route` behavior, but the AngularJS routing system will preserve those properties, so we can access them later on. Given this observation, we could define the custom `menuUrl` and `contentUrl` properties on a route level as follows:

```
$routeProvider.when('/admin/users/new', {
    templateUrl:'admin/admin.tpl.html',
```

```
        contentUrl:'admin/users/users-edit.tpl.html',
        menuUrl:'admin/menu.tpl.html',
        controller:'UsersEditCtrl',
        ...
    });
```

Then, we would have to point the `templateUrl` property to a new partial that will take care of including the menu and content subpartials as follows:

```
<div>
  <div ng-include='$route.current.contentUrl'>
    <!--menu goes here -->
  </div>
  <div ng-include='$route.current.menuUrl'>
    <!--content goes here -->
  </div>
</div>
```

While the preceding workaround gets us the desired visual effect, it will result in the `menu` DOM element being rerendered on each and every route change, even if we navigate within the `admin` section, where such a repaint is obviously unnecessary. This is not much of a problem if the partial is simple and doesn't need any data to be fetched from a back-end. But as soon as we need to do expensive processing for each partial, we need to think twice before triggering this processing with each route change.

No nested routes support

Another limitation of the existing routing system is the lack of support for nested routes. In practical terms, it means that we can have one and only one `ng-view` directive. Put differently, we can't use the `ng-view` directive inside any of the partials referenced in a route definition object. This can be problematic in larger applications where routes naturally form a hierarchy. In the sample SCRUM application, there is a set of such routes, which are as follows:

- `/projects`: It provides the list of all projects

- `/projects/[project id]/sprints`: It provides the list of sprints for a given project

- `/projects/[project id]/sprints/[sprint id]/tasks`: It provides the list of tasks for a given sprint within a given project

This navigation scheme forms a visual hierarchy that could be depicted as follows:

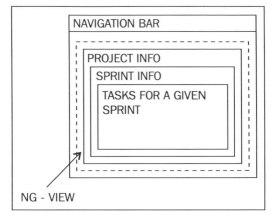

When switching between tasks views for different sprints within the same project, we would like to keep the data (and UI) for a given project since it doesn't change. Unfortunately, the "one route equals one rectangle" principle forces us to reload the whole dynamic part of the screen, including project-specific partial and its corresponding data. This in turn means that we need to retrieve the project's model on each route change, even if it doesn't change from one route to another!

While we can play with the `ng-include` directive to have proper nesting of visual UI elements, there is not much we can do about the increased number of data retrievals. We can only try to make sure that repetitive data retrievals from a back-end are as fast as possible, or cache subsequent calls to a back-end if suitable.

Routing-specific patterns, tips, and tricks

The earlier sections of this chapter gave us a good overview of the AngularJS APIs, related to handling navigation in single-page web applications. Here we are going to see practical examples of using those APIs, and discuss the best related practices.

Handling links

The HTML anchor tag (a) is a primary tool for creating navigation links. AngularJS has special treatment for those links and the following subsections will guide through AngularJS specifics.

Creating clickable links

AngularJS comes pre-bundled with the a directive, which prevents default actions on links when the `href` attribute is omitted. This allows us to create clickable elements using the a tag and the `ng-click` directive. For example, we can invoke a function defined on a scope by clicking a DOM element rendered as the a tag as follows:

```
<a ng-click='showFAQ()'>Frequently Asked Questions</a>
```

Having the a tags without a default navigation action is handy, as several CSS frameworks use the a tags to render different types of visual elements, where a navigation action doesn't make much sense. For example the Twitter's Bootstrap CSS framework uses the a tags to render headers in tabs and accordion components.

Given the special behavior of the a tag without the `href` attribute, you might wonder which method should be used to create actual navigation links. One might argue that we could use the following equivalent methods:

```
<a href="/admin/users/list">List users</a>
```

Another method is as follows:

```
<a ng-click="listUsers()">List users</a>
```

where the `listUsers` method could be defined on a scope as follows:

```
$scope.listUsers = function() {
  $location.path("/admin/users/list");
};
```

In practice, there are some subtle differences between the two approaches. To start with links created using the `href` attribute are more user-friendly, since visitors can right-click on such links and choose to open them in a separate tab (or window) of a browser. In general, we should prefer navigation links created with the `href` attribute, or even better with the AngularJS `ng-href` equivalent that makes it easy to create dynamic URLs:

```
<a ng-href="/admin/users/{{user.$id()}}">Edit user</a>
```

Working with HTML5 and hashbang mode links consistently

The `$location` service in an AngularJS application can be configured with either hashbang mode or HTML5 mode. This choice needs to be made upfront in a configuration block, and links need to be created according to the chosen strategy.

If we choose to use the hashbang mode we must create links as follows (notice the # character):

```
<a ng-href="#/admin/users/{{user.$id()}}">Edit user</a>
```

While in HTML5 mode the link would be slightly simpler as follows:

```
<a ng-href="/admin/users/{{user.$id()}}">Edit user</a>
```

As you can see from the preceding examples, all the links need to be created in accordance with the mode set on the `$locationProvider` service. The trouble here is that in a typical application there are many links so if we decide to change the configuration of `$location`, we will be forced to go over all the links in the whole application and add (or remove) hashes.

 Decide upon the URL mode very early in the application's development phase, otherwise you might need to review and change all the links in the entire application.

Linking to external pages

AngularJS assumes that links created with the a tag are internal to an application, and as such, should change the internal state of the application, instead of triggering a page reload in the browser. Most of the time this is the right assumption, but there are times where we might want to provide a link pointing to a resource that should be downloaded by the browser. In HTML5 mode it is impossible to distinguish, just by looking at the URL links pointing to the internal state from the ones meant to trigger a download of external resources. The solution is to use the `target` attribute on such a link as follows:

```
<a href="/static/form.pdf" target="_self">Download</a>
```

Organizing route definitions

In a large scale web application, it is not uncommon to have dozens and dozens of different routes. While the `$routeProvider` service offers a very nice, fluent style API, route definitions can get quite verbose (especially when the `resolve` property is used). If we combine a large number of routes with the relative verboseness of each definition, we quickly end up maintaining a huge JavaScript file with several hundreds of lines of code! Worse yet, having all routes defined in one huge file means that this file must be modified quite frequently by all developers working on a project – a recipe for creating a bottlenecks and disastrous merge issues.

Spreading route definitions among several modules

With AngularJS, we are not forced to define all the routes in one central file! If we take the approach described in *Chapter 2, Building and Testing* where each functional area has its own dedicated module, we can move routes linked to a certain part of an application to the corresponding module.

In the AngularJS module system, each and every module can have its associated `config` function, where we can inject `$routeProvider` service and define routes. For example, in the sample SCRUM application the administration module has two submodules: One for managing users and for managing projects. Each of these submodules defines its own routes as follows:

```
angular.module('admin-users', [])
.config(function ($routeProvider) {
  $routeProvider.when('/admin/users', {...});
  $routeProvider.when('/admin/users/new', {...});
  $routeProvider.when('/admin/users/:userId', {...});
});


angular.module('admin-projects', [])
.config(function ($routeProvider) {
  $routeProvider.when('/admin/users', {...});
  $routeProvider.when('/admin/users/new', {...});
  $routeProvider.when('/admin/users/:userId', {...});
});


angular.module('admin', ['admin-projects', 'admin-users']);
```

Taking this approach, we can spread routes definitions across different modules and avoid maintaining one giant file containing all the route definitions.

Fighting code duplication in route definitions

As mentioned in the previous section, route definitions can get quite verbose when the `resolve` property is used. But if we take a closer look at the code that needs to be written for routes in each functional area, we can quickly discover blocks of repeated code and configuration. This is particularly true for CRUD-like applications where routes for different functional blocks tend to follow the same pattern.

We can fight code duplication in route definitions by writing a custom provider, wrapping the `$routeProvider` service. By defining our own provider, we can come up with a higher-level API that captures URLs and functional patterns in our application.

A custom provider based on this idea will probably vary from one application to another, so we are not providing detailed, step-by-step instructions on how to build such a utility here. Nevertheless, the sample SCRUM application contains a custom provider that drastically reduces the amount of code needed to define routes for CRUD functionality. Its source code can be found on GitHub, where the whole application is hosted but the following is an example of a custom API in use:

```
angular.module('admin-users', ['services.crud'])
.config(function (crudRouteProvider) {
  crudRouteProvider.routesFor('Users')
    .whenList({
      users: function(Users) { return Users.all(); }
    })
    .whenNew({
      user: function(Users) { return new Users(); }
    })
    .whenEdit({
      user: function ($route, Users) {
        return Users.getById($route.current.params.itemId);
      }
    });
})
```

This is all that is needed to define a full set of CRUD routes for one functional area!

Summary

Effective design of navigation links within an application is paramount, as it forms the backbone around which the whole application is wrapped. Having a solid linking structure is important for our users, so that they can easily navigate within a web application. But it is also important for us, the developers, as it helps us to structure and organize code.

In this chapter we saw that applications built with AngularJS can offer an excellent user experience, when it comes to linking and navigation, one comparable to the Web 1.0 days. In practical terms, it means that we can once again allow our users to use the back and forward buttons in the browser to navigate through the application. On top of this, we can display nice, bookmarkable URLs in the browser's address bar.

The $route service (and its provider – $routeProvider) allows us to structure navigation in applications where only one part of the screen (one rectangle) should be updated in response to a route change. The built-in $route service is largely sufficient for many applications, but if the described "one route equals one rectangle change" characteristic is too limiting for your use case, you might consider keeping an eye on alternative, community-driven solutions. Or if you are brave enough, consider rolling out your own routing system. You should be well prepared for this now as this chapter covered the $location service, a lower-level service upon which the $route service is built.

Toward the end of the chapter we went over a number of patterns, tips, and solutions for problems that are commonly encountered in larger applications that use routing. Hopefully, the examples provided in this section of the chapter are readily applicable to your application as well! We would particularly encourage you to move route definitions to the corresponding functional modules in order to avoid maintaining a huge file containing all your route definitions.

Topics dealing with routing and navigation are linked to security considerations. Indeed, in applications where not all information is public we need to restrict certain users to a subset of available routes. The next chapter covers patterns for securing routes as well as many other security-related topics in detail.

7
Securing Your Application

In any web application, we must ensure that sensitive data and actions are not available to unauthorized users. The only really secure place in such an application is within the server. Outside of this, we have to assume that the code can be compromised, and so we must put checks in place at the point where data enters or leaves our server. The first part of this chapter looks at what we must do on both the client side and the server side to ensure this security, as given in the following points:

- Securing the server to prevent unauthorized access to data and HTML
- Encrypting the connection to prevent snooping
- Preventing **cross-site scripting (XSS)**, and **cross-site request forgery (XSRF)** attacks
- Blocking a JSON injection vulnerability

While security checks must always be done on the server, and this is most critical, we should also provide a good user experience with a client interface that only gives the user access to functionality that is appropriate to their permissions. We should also provide a clean authentication process that does not upset the flow of their interactions with the application. The second part of this chapter looks at how best to support this in AngularJS, as given in the following points:

- The difference in securing a stateful, rich client application compared to more traditional stateless, server-based applications
- Handling authorization errors from the server by intercepting HTTP responses
- Restricting access to parts of the application by securing routes

Providing server-side authentication and authorization

One thing that is common for all client/server applications is that the server is the only place where data is safe. We cannot rely on code on the client side to block access to sensitive information. Similarly, the server must never rely on the client to validate data that is sent to it.

> This is particularly pertinent in JavaScript applications, where it is quite straightforward to read the source code, and then even modify it to perform malicious actions.

In a real web application our server must provide the appropriate level of security. For our demo application, the server has fairly simple security measures in place. We implement authentication and authorization using Passport, which is an ExpressJS plugin. The authenticated user ID is stored as part of an encrypted session cookie. This is passed down to the browser, when the user is logged in. This cookie is sent back to the server on each request, to allow the server to authenticate that request.

Handling unauthorized access

When a request is made to a URL, the server determines whether this URL requires an authenticated user, and whether the authenticated user has sufficient privileges. In our application, we have arranged for the server to respond with an HTTP 401 unauthorized error, if the client tries to do any of the following:

- Any non-GET request (for example POST, PUT, or DELETE) on a database collection, when there is no current authenticated user

- Any non-GET request on the users or projects database collections, when the user is not an administrator

In this way, we are able to secure data (JSON requests) from unauthorized access. We could do the same with other assets such as HTML or images, if we wished to control access to those too.

Providing a server-side authentication API

To allow the client application to authenticate users, our server exposes the following HTTP API:

- POST /login: This message authenticates the user by the given username and password parameters, passed in the body of the POST request.

- `POST /logout`: This message logs out the current user by removing the authentication cookie.
- `GET /current-user`: This message retrieves the current user information.

This interface is enough for us to demonstrate how to handle authentication and authorization in our application.

> In a commercial application, the security requirements would be more complex, and you may also prefer to use a third-party authentication scheme such as OAuth2 (see `http://oauth.net/`).

Securing partial templates

There are some situations where you don't want users to be able to access the partial templates (HTML) for AngularJS routes to which they do not have authorization. Perhaps, the templates contain layout information that implicitly exposes sensitive information.

In this case, a simple solution is to ensure that requests for these partial templates are checked for authorization on the server. First, we should not preload such templates at application startup. And then, we should configure the server to check the current user whenever one of these partial templates is requested, once again returning an HTTP 401 unauthorized error, if unauthorized.

> If we are relying on the server to check authorization on each partial request, we need to ensure that the browser (or any proxy) is not caching the requests for partials. To do this, the server should provide the following HTTP headers, when serving up these partials:
>
> ```
> Cache-Control: no-cache, no-store, must-revalidate
> Pragma      : no-cache
> Expires     : 0
> ```

AngularJS caches all the templates that it downloads in the `$templateCache` service. If we want to secure our partials, we must also ensure that the partials are not cached in a way that allows unauthorized access. We must delete these templates from the `$templateCache` service before a new user logs in, to ensure that the new user doesn't inadvertently have access to the templates.

We could delete templates from the $templateCache service, either selectively or even completely at various points in the application. For instance, we could clear out restricted templates when navigating away from a restricted route, or when logging out. This can be complicated to manage, and the safest method is perhaps to completely reload the page, that is, to refresh the browser, when the user logs out.

 Reloading the application, by refreshing the browser page, has the added benefit of clearing out any data that may have been cached in AngularJS services.

Stopping malicious attacks

To be able to allow secure access to legitimate users, there has to be an element of trust between the server and the browser. Unfortunately, there are a number of attacks that can take advantage of this trust. With the correct support on the server, AngularJS can provide protection against these security holes.

Preventing cookie snooping (man-in-the-middle attacks)

Whenever you pass data over HTTP between a client and a server, there is an opportunity for third parties to snoop on secure information, or even worse, access your cookies to hijack your session and access the server, as though they were you. This is often referred to as a "man-in-the-middle" attack, see http://en.wikipedia.org/wiki/Man-in-the-middle_attack. The easiest way to prevent these attacks is to use HTTPS rather than HTTP.

 Any application, in which sensitive data passes between the application and the server should use HTTPS to ensure that this data is encrypted.

By encrypting the connection using HTTPS, we prevent sensitive data from being read as it passes between the client and the server, and also we prevent unauthorized users from reading authentication cookies from our requests and hijacking our session.

In our demo application, the requests to the MongoLab DB are already sent over HTTPS from our server. To provide complete security from this kind of snooping, we should also ensure that our client interacts with our server over HTTPS as well. Mostly, this is just a case of getting the server to listen over HTTPS, and the client to make requests over HTTPS.

Implementing this on the server is dependent on your choice of back-end technology, and is beyond the scope of this book. But in `Node.js` you could use the `https` module as shown in the following code:

```
var https = require('https');
var privateKey =
  fs.readFileSync('cert/privatekey.pem').toString();
var certificate =
  fs.readFileSync('cert/certificate.pem').toString();
var credentials = {key: privateKey, cert: certificate};
var secureServer = https.createServer(credentials, app);
secureServer.listen(config.server.securePort);
```

On the client side, we just have to ensure that the URL used to connect to the server is not hardcoded to the HTTP protocol. The easiest way to do this is not to provide a protocol at all in the URL.

```
angular.module('app').constant('MONGOLAB_CONFIG', {
  baseUrl: '/databases/',
  dbName: 'ascrum'
});
```

In addition, we should also ensure that the authentication cookie is restricted to HTTPS requests only. We can do this by setting the `httpOnly` and `secure` options to `true`, when creating the cookie on the server.

Preventing cross-site scripting attacks

A cross-site-scripting attack (XSS) is where an attacker manages to inject client-side script into a web page, when viewed by another user. This is particularly bad if the injected script makes a request to our server, because the server assumes that it is the authenticated user who is making the request and allows it.

There are a wide variety of forms in which XSS attacks can appear. The most common are where user-provided content is displayed without being properly escaped to prevent malicious HTML from being rendered. The next section explains how we can do this on the client, but you should also ensure that any user-provided content is sanitized on the server, before being stored or sent back to the client.

Securing HTML content in AngularJS expressions

AngularJS escapes all HTML in text that is displayed through the `ng-bind` directive, or template interpolation (that is text in {{curly braces}}). For example, using the following model:

```
$scope.msg = 'Hello, <b>World</b>!';
```

And the markup fragment looks as follows:

```
<p ng-bind="msg"></p>
```

The rendering process will escape the `<b>` tags, so they will appear as plain text, and not as markup:

```
<p>Hello, &lt;b&gt;World&lt;/b&gt;!</p>
```

This approach provides a pretty good defense against XSS attacks in general. If you actually want to display text that is marked up with HTML, then you must either trust it completely, in which case you can use the `ng-bind-html-unsafe` directive, or sanitize the text by loading the `ngSanitize` module, and then using the `ng-bind-html` directive.

Allowing unsafe HTML bindings

The following binding will render the `<b>` tags as HTML to be interpreted by the browser:

```
<p ng-bind-html-unsafe="msg"></p>
```

Sanitizing HTML

AngularJS has one more directive that will selectively sanitize certain HTML tags, while allowing others to be interpreted by a browser, which is `ng-bind-html`. Its usage is similar to the unsafe equivalent:

```
<p ng-bind-html="msg"></p>
```

In terms of escaping, the `ng-bind-html` directive is a compromise between behavior of `ng-bind-html-unsafe` (allow all HTML tags) and `ng-bind` (allow no HTML tags at all). It might be a good option for cases where we want to allow some HTML tags to be entered by users.

> The sanitization uses a whitelist of safe HTML tags, which is quite extensive. The main tags that will be sanitized include the `<script>` and `<style>` elements, as well as attributes that take URLs such as `href`, `src`, and `usemap`.

The `ng-bind-html` directive resides in a separate module (`ngSanitize`), and requires inclusion of an additional source file: `angular-sanitize.js`. You must declare a dependency on the `ngSanitize` module if you plan to use the `ng-bind-html` directive, as shown in the following code:

```
angular.module('expressionsEscaping', ['ngSanitize'])
  .controller('ExpressionsEscapingCtrl', function ($scope) {
    $scope.msg = 'Hello, <b>World</b>!';
  });
```

The ng-bind-html directive uses the $sanitize service, which is also found inside the ngSanitize module. This service is a function that takes a string, and then returns a sanitized version of the string, as described in the following code:

```
var safeDescription = $sanitize(description);
```

 Unless you are working with any existing legacy systems (For example CMS, back-ends sending HTML, and so on), markup in the model should be avoided. Such markup can't contain AngularJS directives and requires the ng-bind-html-unsafe or ng-bind-html directive to obtain the desired results.

Preventing the JSON injection vulnerability

There is a JSON injection vulnerability that allows evil third party websites to access your secure JSON resources, if they return JSON arrays. This is done by effectively loading the JSON as a script in a web page, and then executing it. See http://haacked.com/archive/2008/11/20/anatomy-of-a-subtle-json-vulnerability.aspx.

The $http service has a built-in solution to protect against this. To prevent the browser from being able to execute the JSON returned from the secure resource, you can arrange for your server to prefix all the JSON requests with the ")]}',\n" string, which is not legal JavaScript, and so cannot be executed. The $http service automatically strips this prefix string, if it appears from any JSON response. For example, if your JSON resource returns the following array:

```
['a','b','c']
```

This is vulnerable to the JSON injection attack. Instead, the server should return:

```
)]}',
['a','b','c']
```

This is not valid JavaScript. It cannot be executed by the browser, and so is no longer vulnerable to attack. The $http service will automatically strip off this invalid prefix, if found, before returning the valid JSON in its response object.

Preventing cross-site request forgery

In any application where the server must trust who the user is, that is, they are logged in, and allows them access to actions on the server based on that trust, there is the potential for other sites to pretend to be you, and then get access to those actions themselves. This is called cross-site request forgery (XSRF). If you visit an evil site when you are already logged into a secure site, the evil site's web page could post to your secure site, since it trusts that you are currently authenticated.

This attack is often in the form of a fraudulent `src` attribute on an `<img>` tag, which the user inadvertently loads by browsing to an evil page, while still logged into a secure site. When the browser tries to load the image, it actually makes a request to the secure site.

```
<img src="http://my.securesite.com/createAdminUser?username=badguy">
```

The solution is for the server to provide a secret to the browser, which can only be accessed by JavaScript running on the browser, and so would not be available in the `src` attribute. Any request to the server should include this secret in its headers to prove it is authentic.

The `$http` service has this solution built-in, in order to protect against such an attack. You must arrange for the server to set a token in the session cookie called `XSRF-TOKEN`, on the first `GET` request by the application. This token must be unique for this session.

In the client application, the `$http` service will extract this token from the cookie, and then attach it as a header (called `X-XSRF-TOKEN`) to every HTTP request it makes. The server must check the token on each request, and then block access if it is not valid. The AngularJS team recommends that the token is a digest of your site's authentication cookie with salt for added security.

Adding client-side security support

The rest of this chapter will look at what we should do in our AngularJS application running in the browser to provide security and give a consistent experience for the user, when dealing with authentication and authorization.

Out of the box, AngularJS does not provide functionality to deal with authentication and authorization. In our sample application, we developed services and directives that can be used in our templates and controllers to display security-related information, handle authorization failures, and manage logging in and logging out.

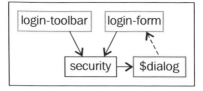

This diagram shows two user interface elements, the `login-toolbar` and `login-form`, both of which rely on the `security` service. The `security` service uses the `$dialog` service to create a modal dialog box from the `login-form` element.

Creating a security service

The `security` service is a component, which we have developed provides the primary API for our application to manage logging in and out, and to get information about the current user. We can inject this service into controllers and directives. These can then attach the following properties and methods of the service to the scope, to have access to them in templates:

- `currentUser`: This property contains information about the currently authenticated user, if any
- `getLoginReason()`: This method returns a localized message, explaining why we need to login, for example, **The current user does not have authorization**.
- `showLogin()`: This method causes the login form to be shown. This is called when the user clicks on the **login** button on the login toolbar, and when an HTTP 401 unauthorized error response is intercepted.
- `login(email, password)`: This method sends the specified credentials to the server to be authenticated. This is called when the user submits the login form. If the login is successful, the login form is closed, and any unauthorized requests are retried (that is, the request is made again).
- `logout(redirectTo)`: This method logs out the current user and redirects. This is called when the user clicks on the **logout** button on the login toolbar.
- `cancelLogin(redirectTo)`: This method gives up trying to login, any unauthorized requests are discarded, and then the application redirects to another `$route`. This is called if the user closes or cancels the login form.

Showing a login form

We need to allow the user to login to the application. The login form provides this. It is actually comprised of a template (`security/login/form.tpl.html`), and a controller (`LoginFormController`). The `security` service opens (`showLogin()`) or closes (`login()` or `cancelLogin()`) the login form, when authentication is required or requested.

```
Sign in

    You must be logged in to access this part of the application.

    Please enter your login details

E-mail

Password

                                      Sign in    Clear    Cancel
```

We are using the AngularUI bootstrap project's `$dialog` service for this. This service allows us to display a form as a modal dialog box, by specifying a template and a controller for the form.

You can find out more about the `$dialog` service at its website: `http://angular-ui.github.io/bootstrap/#/dialog`.

In our `security` service, we have the two helpers: `openLoginDialog()` and `closeLoginDialog()`.

```
var loginDialog = null;
function openLoginDialog() {
  if ( !loginDialog ) {
    loginDialog = $dialog.dialog();
    loginDialog.open(
      'security/login/form.tpl.html',
```

```
      'LoginFormController')
    .then(onLoginDialogClose);
  }
}
function closeLoginDialog(success) {
  if (loginDialog) {
    loginDialog.close(success);
    loginDialog = null;
  }
}
```

To open the dialog box, we call `openLoginDialog()`, passing in the URL of the login form template, `security/login/form.tpl.html`, and the name of the controller, `LoginFormController`. This returns a `promise` object that will be resolved, when the dialog box is closed, which we do by calling `closeLoginDialog()`. When the dialog box closes, we call the `onLoginDialogClose()` method, which will clean up and then run the code based on whether the user logged in successfully or not.

There is nothing very special about the template and controller, they just provide a simple form for entering an email and a password, and connect it up to the `security` and `service`. The **Sign in** button is handled by `security.login()`, and the **Cancel** button is handled by `security.cancelLogin()`.

Creating security-aware menus and toolbars

For a good user experience, we should not display things for which the user has no permission. Hiding elements from the user, however, will not prevent a determined user from accessing the functionality, it is purely to prevent the user being confused by trying to use features to which they have no permission. It is common to do this selective display in navigation menus and toolbars. To make it easier to write templates that react to the current authentication and authorization state of the user, we can create a `currentUser` service.

Hiding the menu items

We should only show menu items that are appropriate for the current user's permissions.

Our navigation menu has a set of `ng-show` directives on the elements that check whether the current user has relevant authorization, and then shows or hides the menu items accordingly.

```
<ul class="nav" ng-show="isAuthenticated()">
  <li ...><a href="/projects">My Projects</a></li>
  <li ... ng-show="isAdmin()">
    <a ... >Admin ...</a>
    <ul ...>
      <li><a ... >Projects</a></li>
      <li><a ... >Users</a></li>
    </ul>
  </li>
</ul>
```

Here, you can see that the whole navigation tree is hidden if the user is not authenticated. Further, the admin options are hidden, if the user is not an administrator.

Creating a login toolbar

We can create a reusable `login-toolbar` widget directive that simply displays a **Log in** button if no one is logged in, or the current user's name and a **Log out** button, if someone is logged in.

Here is the template for this directive. It injects the `currentUser` and `security` service onto the directive's scope, so we can display user information, as well as show or hide the **Log in** and **Log out** buttons.

```
<ul class="nav pull-right">

<li class="divider-vertical"></li>

<li ng-show="isAuthenticated()">
  <a href="#">{{currentUser.firstName}} {{currentUser.lastName}}</a>
</li>

<li ng-show="isAuthenticated()">
  <form class="navbar-form">
    <button class="btn" ng-click="logout()">Log out</button>
  </form>
```

```
  </li>

  <li ng-hide="isAuthenticated()">
    <form class="navbar-form">
      <button class="btn" ng-click="login()">Log in</button>
    </form>
  </li>

  </ul>
```

Supporting authentication and authorization on the client

Securing a rich client application, such as we are building here with AngularJS, is significantly different to securing a traditional, server-based web application. This has an impact on how and when we authenticate and authorize users.

Server-based web applications are generally stateless on the browser. We trigger a round-trip request for a complete new page from the server on every action. So, the server can compute the user's authorization levels on each request, and then redirect to some login page, if necessary.

 In a traditional, server-based web app, we would simply send the browser to some login page, and then once login is successful, we redirect back to the original page that was requesting the secure resource.

Rich clients do not send full-page requests on each action. They tend to maintain their own state and only pass data to and from the server. The server doesn't know the current state of the application, which makes it difficult to implement the traditional redirect back, after being sent to a login page. The client would have to serialize all its current state, and then send it to the server. Then, after a successful login, the server would have to pass this state back to the client, so that it could continue where it left off.

Handling authorization failures

When the server refuses to process an unauthorized request, returning an HTTP 401 unauthorized error, we need to give the user an opportunity to authenticate, and then retry the request. The request could have been part of some complex process on the client, which has no URL to identify it. If we redirected to a login page, then we would have to stop the current action, and the user would probably have to restart what they were doing again after authentication.

Instead, we will intercept the responses of unauthorized requests to the server, before they get back to the caller. We will suspend the current flow of the application business logic, do the authentication, and then retry the failed requests to resume the flow.

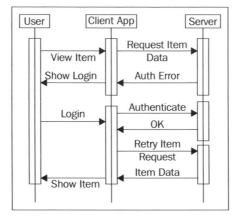

Intercepting responses

Remember that the $http requests return promises, which are resolved with the response from the server. The power of promises is that we can chain them, transform the response data that is returned, and even return a promise to a completely different deferred object. As described in *Chapter 3, Communicating with a Back-end Server*, AngularJS lets you create interceptors that can work with the server response, before it is received by the original caller.

HTTP response interceptors

A response interceptor is simply a function that receives a promise object for a response from the server, and then returns a promise object for the same. On each $http request, the response promise object will be passed to each interceptor, in turn giving them each an opportunity to modify the promise object, before it is returned to the original caller.

Generally, an interceptor function will use a call to then() to chain handlers onto the promise object it is passed, and then creates a new promise, which it then returns. Inside these handlers, we can read and modify the response object, such as the headers and data, as shown in the following example:

```
function myInterceptor(promise) {
    return promise.then(function(response) {
```

```
    if ( response.headers()['content type']  == "text/plain") {
      response.data = $sanitize(response.data);
    };
    return response;
  });
}
```

This interceptor checks the `response` object's `content-type`. If it is `text/plain`, we sanitize the `response` object's data, and then return the response `promise` object.

Creating a securityInterceptor service

We will create a `securityInterceptor` service that will work with the response `promise` object from the server. In our interceptor, we check to see if the response `promise` object is rejected with a 401 authorization error. In that case, we can create a new `promise` for a retry of the original request, and then return that to the caller, instead of the original.

> The original idea for this came from an excellent blog post by *Witold Szczerba*: http://www.espeo.pl/2012/02/26/authentication-in-angularjs application.

We create the `securityInterceptor` as a service, and then add it to the `$http` service `responseInterceptors` array.

```
.config(['$httpProvider', function($httpProvider) {
  $httpProvider.responseInterceptors.push(
    'securityInterceptor');
}]);
```

> We have to add the `securityInterceptor` service by name, rather than the object itself, because it depends upon services that are not available in the `config` block.

For our `securityInterceptor` service we implement the interceptor as a service, so that we can have other services injected into it.

> We can't inject `$http` directly into our interceptor, because it would create a circular dependency. Instead, we inject `$injector` service, and then use it to access the `$http` service at call time.

```
.factory('securityInterceptor',
  ['$injector', 'securityRetryQueue',
```

```
    function($injector, queue) {
    return function(promise) {
      var $http = $injector.get('$http');
      return promise.then(null, function(response) {
        if(response.status === 401) {
          promise = queue.pushRetryFn('unauthorized-server',
                        function() {return $http(response.config); }
                    );
        }
        return promise;
      });
    };
  }])
```

Our interceptor watches for error responses that have a 401 status. It does this by providing a handler for the second parameter of the call to then(). By providing null for the first parameter, we indicate that we are not interested in intercepting the promise object if it is resolved successfully.

When a request fails with a 401 error, the interceptor creates an entry in the securityRetryQueue service, which is described later. This service will repeat the failed request, when the queue is processed after a successful login.

The important thing to realize here is that promise handlers can either return a value or a promise object:

- If a handler returns a value, the value is passed straight on to the next handler in the chain

- If a handler returns a promise object, the next handler in the chain is not triggered until this new promise object has been resolved (or rejected).

In our case, when the original response returns a 401 unauthorized error, we actually return a new retry promise, for a retry item in the securityRetryQueue service instead of the original promise object for the response. This new retry promise object will be resolved, if the securityRetryQueue is retried and a new successful response is received from the server, or rejected if the securityRetryQueue is cancelled, or the response is another error.

While our original caller sits patiently waiting for some response to return from the server, we can pop up a login box, allow the user to authenticate, and then eventually retry the items in the queue. Once the original caller receives a successful response, they are able to carry on, as though they had been authenticated all along.

Creating the securityRetryQueue service

The securityRetryQueue service provides a place to store all those items that will be needed for retry, once the user authenticates successfully. It is basically a list, to which you add a function (to be called, when the item is retried) with pushRetryFn(). We process the items in the list by calling retryAll() or cancelAll(). Here is the retryAll() method.

```
retryAll: function() {
  while(retryQueue.length) {
    retryQueue.shift().retry();
  }
}
```

All items in the queue must have two methods, retry() and cancel(). The pushRetryFn() method makes it easier to set up these objects, as shown in the following code:

```
pushRetryFn: function(reason, retryFn) {
  var deferredRetry = $q.defer();
  var retryItem = {
    reason: reason,
    retry: function() {
      $q.when(retryFn()).then(function(value) {
        deferredRetry.resolve(value);
      },function(value) {
        deferredRetry.reject(value);
      });
    },
    cancel: function() {
      deferredRetry.reject();
    }
  };
  service.push(retryItem);
  return deferredRetry.promise;
}
```

This function returns a promise to retry the provided retryFn function. This retry promise object will be resolved or rejected, when the item in the queue is retried.

 We have to create our own new deferred object for this Retry promise object because its resolution or rejection is triggered, not by the response from the server, but by the call to retry() or cancel().

Notifying the security service

The last piece in the puzzle is how to notify the `security` service, when new items are added. In our implementation, we simply expose a method on the `securityRetryQueue` called `onItemAdded()`, which is called each time we push an item into the queue as follows:

```
push: function(retryItem) {
  retryQueue.push(retryItem);
  service.onItemAdded();
}
```

The `security` service overrides this method with its own, so that it can react whenever there are authorization failures, as given in the following code:

```
securityRetryQueue.onItemAdded = function() {
  if (securityRetryQueue.hasMore() ) {
    service.showLogin();
  }
};
```

This code is found in the `security` service, where the variable `service` is the `security` service itself.

Preventing navigation to secure routes

Preventing access to secure routes using client-side code is not secure. The only secure way to guarantee that users cannot navigate to unauthorized areas of the application is to require that the page be reloaded; this provides the server the opportunity to refuse access to the URL. Reloading the page is not ideal, because it defeats many of the benefits of a rich client application.

> While reloading the page to do security is not usually a good idea in a rich client application. It can be useful, if you have a clear distinction between areas of your application. For instance, if your application was really two subapplications, each having very different authentication requirements, you could host them at different URLs, and the server could ensure that the user had the necessary permissions, before allowing each subapplication to load.

In practice, since we can secure what data is displayed to the user, it is not so important to block access to routes using redirects to the server. Instead, we can simply block navigation to unauthorized routes on the client when the route changes.

This is not a security feature. It is really just a way to help users to authenticate correctly, if they navigate directly to a URL that requires some authorization.

Using route resolve functions

Each route defined with the `$routeProvider` service provider can contain a set of route `resolve` functions. Each of these is a function that returns a `promise` object, which must be resolved before navigation to the route can succeed. If any of the `promise` object is rejected, then navigation to that route is cancelled.

A very simple approach to authorization would be to provide a route `resolve` function that only resolves successfully if the current user has the necessary authorization.

```
$routeProvider.when('/admin/users', {
  resolve: [security, function requireAdminUser(security) {
    var promise = service.requestCurrentUser();
    return promise.then(function(currentUser) {
      if ( !currentUser.isAdmin() ) {
        return $q.reject();
      }
      return currentUser;
    });
  }]
});
```

Here, we request a promise for the current user from the `security` service, and then reject it if the user is not an administrator. The trouble with this method is that the user is not given an opportunity to log in and provide authorization. The route is just blocked.

In the same way that we dealt with HTTP `401` authorization errors from the server, we can also retry authorization failures, when navigating to a route. All we need is to add a retry item to the `securityRetryQueue` service, whenever such a route `resolve` fails, which will attempt the resolve again, once the user has logged in.

```
function requireAdminUser(security, securityRetryQueue) {
  var promise = security.requestCurrentUser();
  return promise.then(function(currentUser) {
    if ( !currentUser.isAdmin() ) {
      return securityRetryQueue.pushRetryFn(
      'unauthorized-client',
```

```
        requireAdminUser);
      }
    });
  }
```

Now, if a non-admin user attempts to access a route, which has this method as a `resolve`, a new item is added to the `securityRetryQueue` service. Adding this item to the queue will trigger the `security` service to display the login form, where the user can login with admin credentials. Once the login succeeds, the `requireAdminUser` method will be retried and, if successful, the route change will be allowed to succeed.

Creating the authorization service

To support these route `resolve` methods, we create a service, called `authorization`, which provides methods to check whether the current user has specified permissions.

 In a more complex application, we would create a service that could be configured with a range of roles and permissions to support the security requirements of the application.

For our application, this service is very simple, and only contains two methods: `requireAuthenticatedUser()` and `requireAdminUser()`, which can be described as follows:

- `requireAuthenticatedUser()`: This method returns a `promise` that will only be resolved when the user has logged in successfully.

- `requireAdminUser()`: This method returns a `promise` that will only be resolved when an administrator has logged in successfully.

Since these methods are in a service, which is not available directly while configuring the `$routeProvider`, we would normally have to call these methods in a `function`, wrapped in an array as follows:

```
['securityAuthorization', function(securityAuthorization) {
  return securityAuthorization.requireAdminUser();
}]
```

To prevent us from having to repeat ourselves, we can actually put this array into the provider for the authorization service, as given in the following code:

```
.provider('securityAuthorization', {
  requireAdminUser: [
  'securityAuthorization',
  function(securityAuthorization) {
    return securityAuthorization.requireAdminUser();
    }
  ],

  $get: [
    'security',
    'securityRetryQueue',
    function(security, queue) {
      var service = {
        requireAdminUser: function() {
        },
      };
    return service;
    }
  ]
});
```

The actual authorization service appears in the `$get` property. We place the route `resolve` helpers, such as `requireAdminUser()`, as methods on the provider. When configuring our routes, we simply inject the provider, and then use these methods as follows:

```
config([
  'securityAuthorizationProvider',
  function (securityAuthorizationProvider) {
    $routeProvider.when('/admin/users', {
      resolve: securityAuthorizationProvider.requireAdminUser
    });
  }
])
```

Now our routes are checked before we navigate to them, and the user is given an opportunity to authenticate with suitably authorized credentials, if necessary.

Summary

In this chapter, we have looked at some common security issues in rich client web applications, and how they compare to traditional, server-based web applications. In particular, while security checks must always be done at the server, the client and the server must also work together to prevent malicious attacks. We implemented a number of services and directives to support security in our application. We saw how the AngularJS promise-based $http service allows us to intercept responses to unauthorized server requests, and then give the user the opportunity to authenticate without having to interrupt or restart the flow of the application logic. Finally, we made use of route resolve functions in our application routes to check authorization, before the user is allowed to navigate to restricted parts of our application.

We are now going to look at how we can teach our browser some new tricks by developing our own directives, which will allow us to develop user interface components in a more declarative manner.

8

Building Your Own Directives

While you can get a long way using just controllers and the built-in directives that come with AngularJS, there will inevitably come a point in the development of your application where you will need to teach your browser some new tricks by building your own directives. The main reasons why you would want to develop custom directives are:

- You need to manipulate the DOM directly, such as with JQuery
- You want to refactor parts of your application to remove repeated codes
- You want to create new HTML mark-up for non-developers to use, such as designers

This chapter will introduce you to developing your own AngularJS directives. Directives appear in many different places and have different uses. In this chapter we will show:

- How to define a directive
- Examples of the most common types of directive and how to code them
- Directives that rely on each other
- How to unit test directives

What are AngularJS directives?

Directives are, arguably, the most powerful feature of AngularJS. They are the glue that joins your application logic to the HTML DOM. The following diagram illustrates how directives fit into the architecture of an AngularJS application:

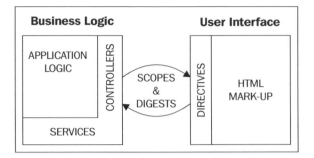

By extending and customizing how the browser behaves with regard to the HTML, directives let the application developer, or designer, focus their attention on what the application should do, or look like, in a declarative manner, rather than on programming low level interactions with the DOM. This makes the development process faster, more maintainable, and most importantly more fun!

AngularJS directives add new meaning and behavior to mark up in your HTML application. It is inside the directives, where you can get low level and dirty with DOM manipulation, usually working with jQuery or AngularJS's jqLite.

> If you load jQuery before AngularJS, then AngularJS will use jQuery for its DOM manipulation. Otherwise AngularJS assumes that you are not using jQuery and implements its own internal, minimal version of jQuery, which is often referred to as jqLite.

The job of a directive is to modify the DOM structure and to link the scope to the DOM. This means manipulating and binding DOM nodes based on data in the scope, but also binding DOM events to call methods on the scope.

Understanding the built-in directives

AngularJS comes with a number of built-in directives to the framework. There are the obvious custom HTML elements and attributes, such as `ng-include`, `ng-controller` and `ng-click`. There are also what appear to be standard HTML elements, such as `script`, `a`, `select`, and `input`. All of these directives are provided by the core AngularJS framework.

What is great is that the built-in directives are defined using the same directive API that we can use in our own applications. There is nothing special about them as compared to directives that application developers can build. Looking at the directives in the AngularJS source code can be a great way to learn how to develop your own directives.

 The built-in AngularJS directives can be found in the `src/ng/directive` folder of the AngularJS project (`https://github.com/angular/angular.js/tree/master/src/ng/directive/`).

Using directives in the HTML markup

Directives can appear as HTML **elements**, **attributes**, **comments**, or **CSS classes**. Also, any directive can be identified in the HTML in a number of different **formats**.

Here are some examples of using a directive in the HTML mark-up (not all of these would be appropriate depending on the use of the directive):

```
<my-directive></my-directive>
<input my-directive>
<!-- directive: my-directive-->
<input class="my-directive">
```

The canonical name, when used to define and refer to a directive in JavaScript, is the camelCased version, for example, `myDirective`.

Following the directive compilation life-cycle

When AngularJS compiles an HTML template it traverses the DOM supplied by the browser and tries to match each element, attribute, comment, and CSS class against its list of registered directives. When it matches a directive, AngularJS calls the directive's compile function, which returns a linking function. AngularJS collects all of these linking functions.

 The compilation stage is done before the scope has been prepared, and no scope data is available in the compile function.

Once all the directives have been compiled, AngularJS creates the scope and links each directive to the scope by calling each of the linking functions.

At the linking stage, the scope is being attached to the directive, and the linking function can then wire up bindings between the scope and the DOM.

The compile stage is mostly an optimization. It is possible to do almost all the work in the linking function (except for a few advanced things like access to the transclusion function). If you consider the case of a repeated directive (inside `ng-repeat`), the compile function of the directive is called only once, but the linking function is called on every iteration of the repeater, every time the data changes.

Transclusion functions are explained in detail in *Chapter 9, Building Advanced Directives*

The following table shows what compile functions are called when the AngularJS compiler matches the directives. You can see that each compile function is only called once when each directive is used in a template.

Template	Compile step
`<ul my-dir>`	`myDir` compile function
`  <li ng-repeat="obj in objs" my-dir>`	`ngRepeat` compile function
`  </li>`	`myDir` compile function
`</ul>`	

The following table shows what linking functions are called when the template is converted to the final HTML. You can see that the linking function for `myDir` is called on every iteration of the repeater:

HTML	Linking step
`<ul my-dir>`	`myDir` linking function
`<!-- ng-repeat="obj in objs" ->`	`ngRepeat` linking function
`  <li my-dir></li>`	`myDir` linking function
`  <li my-dir></li>`	`myDir` linking function
`  <li my-dir></li>`	`myDir` linking function
`</ul>`	

If you have some complex functionality that does not rely on the data in the scope, then it should appear in the compile function, so that it is only called once.

Writing unit tests for directives

Directives have low level access to the DOM and can be complex. This makes them prone to errors and hard to debug. Therefore, more than the other areas of your application, it is important that directives have a comprehensive range of tests.

Writing unit tests for directives can seem daunting at first but AngularJS provides some nice features to make it as painless as possible and you will reap the benefits when your directives are reliable and maintainable.

 AngularJS has a comprehensive set of tests for its built-in directives. They can be found in the `test/ng/directive` folder of the AngularJS project (`https://github.com/angular/angular.js/tree/master/test/ng/directive/`).

The general strategy when testing directives is as follows:

*   Load the module containing the directive
*   Compile a string of mark-up containing the directive to get linking function
*   Run the linking function to link it to the `$rootScope`
*   Check that the element has the properties that you expect

Here is a common skeleton unit test for a directive:

```
describe('myDir directive', function () {
  var element, scope;

  beforeEach(module('myDirModule'));

  beforeEach(inject(function ($compile, $rootScope) {
    var linkingFn = $compile('<my-dir></my-dir>');
    scope = $rootScope;
    element = linkingFn(scope);
  }));

  it('has some properties', function() {
    expect(element.someMethod()).toBe(XXX);
  });

  it('does something to the scope', function() {
    expect(scope.someField).toBe(XXX);
  });

  ...
});
```

Load the module that contains the directive into the test, then create an element containing this directive, using the $compile and $rootScope functions. Keep a reference of element and $scope so that it is available in all the tests later.

 Depending upon the kind of tests you are writing you may want to compile a different element in each it clause. In this case you should keep a reference to the $compile function too.

Finally, test whether the directive performs as expected by interacting with it through jQuery/jqLite functions and through modifying scope.

In cases where your directive is using $watch, $observe, or $q, you will need to trigger a $digest before checking your expectations. For example:

```
it("updates the scope via a $watch", function() {
  scope.someField = 'something';
  scope.$digest();
  expect(scope.someOtherField).toBe('something');
});
```

In the rest of this chapter we will introduce our custom directives through their unit tests, in keeping with the concept of **Test Driven Development (TDD)**.

Defining a directive

Each directive must be registered with a **module**. You call directive() on the **module** passing in the **canonical name** of the directive and a **factory function** that returns the **directive definition**.

```
angular.module('app', []).directive('myDir', function() {
  return myDirectiveDefinition;
});
```

The factory function can be injected with services to be used by the directive.

A directive definition is an object whose fields tell the compiler what the directive does. Some of the fields are declarative (for example, replace: true, which tells the compiler to replace the original element with what is in the template). Some fields are imperative (for example, link: function(...), which provides the linking function to the compiler.

This table describes all the fields that can be used in a directive definition:

Field	Description
name	The name of the directive.
restrict	In what kind of mark-up this directive can appear.
priority	Hint to the compiler of the order that directives should be executed.
terminal	Whether the compiler should continue compiling directives below this.
link	The link function that will link the directive to the scope.
template	A string that will be used to generate mark-up for this directive.
templateUrl	A URL where the template for this directive may be found.
replace	Whether to replace this directive's element with what is in the template.
transclude	Whether to provide the contents of this directive's element for use in the template and compile function.
scope	Whether to create a new child scope or isolated scope for this directive.
controller	A function that will act as a directive controller for this directive.
require	Requires a directive controller from another directive to be injected into this directive's link function.
compile	The compile function that can manipulate the source DOM and will create the link function and is only used if a link has not been provided above.

Most directives that you are likely to write will only need some of these fields. The rest of this chapter will show various custom directives from our SCRUM application. For each directive, we will look at the relevant parts of the directive definition.

Styling buttons with directives

We are using Bootstrap CSS styles for our application. This CSS library specifies mark-up and CSS classes to ensure that buttons are styled correctly. For instance a button might have mark-up of the form:

```
<button type="submit"

      class="btn btn-primary btn-large">Click Me!</button>
```

Having to remember to apply these classes is error prone and time consuming. We can build a directive to make this easier and more reliable.

Writing a button directive

All the buttons in our application should be styled as a Bootstrap CSS button. Instead of having to remember to add `class="btn"` to every button, we can add a button directive to do this for us. The unit tests for this look like:

```
describe('button directive', function () {
  var $compile, $rootScope;
  beforeEach(module('directives.button'));
  beforeEach(inject(function(_$compile_, _$rootScope_) {
    $compile = _$compile_;
    $rootScope = _$rootScope_;
  }));

  it('adds a "btn" class to the button element', function() {
    var element = $compile('<button></button>')($rootScope);
    expect(element.hasClass('btn')).toBe(true);
  });
});
});
```

We load the module, create a button, and check that it has the correct CSS class.

 Remember that the injector ignores a pair of underscores (for example, `_$compile_`) surrounding the parameter name. This allows us to copy the injected services into variables with the correct name for use later (for example, `$compile = _$compile_`).

Further any button with `type="submit"` should automatically be styled as a primary button and it would be nice to set the size of the button through an attribute size. We would like to simply write:

```
<button type="submit" size="large">Submit</button>
```

We would create unit tests like this:

```
it('adds size classes correctly', function() {
  var element = $compile('<button size="large"></button>')
($rootScope);
  expect(element.hasClass('btn-large')).toBe(true);
});

it('adds primary class to submit buttons', function() {
  var element = $compile('<button type="submit"></button>')
($rootScope);
  expect(element.hasClass('btn-primary')).toBe(true);
});
```

Let's look at how this directive could be implemented:

```
myModule.directive('button', function() {
  return {
    restrict: 'E',
    compile: function(element, attributes) {
      element.addClass('btn');
      if ( attributes.type === 'submit' ) {
        element.addClass('btn-primary');
      }
      if ( attributes.size ) {
        element.addClass('btn-' + attributes.size);
      }
    }
  };
});
```

 We are assuming that we have a myModule module already defined.

The name of our directive is 'button' and it is restricted to only appear as an element (restrict: 'E'). This means that this directive will be applied whenever the AngularJS compiler comes across the button element. In effect, we are adding behavior to the standard HTML button element.

The only other part of this directive is the compile function. This function will be called whenever the compiler matches this directive. The compile function is passed a parameter called element. This is a jQuery (or jqLite) object that references the DOM element where the directive appeared, in this case, the button element itself.

In our compile function we simply add CSS classes to the element. based on the values of the attributes on the element. We use the injected attributes parameter to access the value of the attributes on the element.

We can do all these modifications in the compile function rather than the linking function because our changes to the element do not rely on the scope data that will be bound to the element. We could have put this functionality into the linking function instead, but if the button appears in an ng-repeat loop, then addClass() would be called for each iteration of the button.

See *Following the directive compilation life-cycle* section for a detailed discussion of this.

By putting the functionality in the compile function, it is only called once, and the button is simply cloned by the ng-repeat directive. If you are doing complex work on the DOM then this optimization can make a significant difference, especially if you are iterating over a large collection.

Understanding AngularJS widget directives

One of the most powerful features of directives is to be able to create your own domain-specific tags. In other words, you can create custom elements and attributes that give new meaning and behavior to the mark-up in your HTML that is specific to the domain for which you are building the application.

For example, similar to standard HTML tags, you could create a <user> element displaying user information or a <g-map> element that lets you interact with a Google map. The possibilities are endless and the benefit is that your mark-up matches the domain in which you are developing.

Writing a pagination directive

In our SCRUM app, we often have large lists of tasks or backlog items that are unwieldy to display on the screen in one go. We use pagination to break up the lists into manageable pages of items. It is common to have a pagination control block on our screen that links to the pages in the list.

The Bootstrap CSS framework provides a clean design for styling such a widget.

We will implement this pagination block as a reusable widget directive that we use in our mark-up without having to think about the detail of how it works. The mark-up will look like this:

```
<pagination num-pages="tasks.pageCount"
            current-page="tasks.currentPage">
</pagination>
```

Writing tests for the pagination directive

The tests for this widget need to cover all the changes that can occur both on the $scope function and from the user clicking on the links. Here is a selection of the more significant tests:

```
describe('pagination directive', function () {
  var $scope, element, lis;
  beforeEach(module('directives'));
  beforeEach(inject(function($compile, $rootScope) {
    $scope = $rootScope;
    $scope.numPages = 5;
    $scope.currentPage = 3;
    element = $compile('<pagination num-pages="numPages" current-
page="currentPage"></pagination>')($scope);
    $scope.$digest();
    lis = function() { return element.find('li'); };
  }));

  it('has the number of the page as text in each page item',
function() {
    for(var i=1; i<=$scope.numPages;i++) {
      expect(lis().eq(i).text()).toEqual(''+i);
    }
  });

  it('sets the current-page to be active', function() {
    var currentPageItem = lis().eq($scope.currentPage);
    expect(currentPageItem.hasClass('active')).toBe(true);
  });

  ...

  it('disables "next" if current-page is num-pages', function() {
    $scope.currentPage = 5;
    $scope.$digest();
    var nextPageItem = lis().eq(-1);
    expect(nextPageItem.hasClass('disabled')).toBe(true);
  });

  it('changes currentPage if a page link is clicked', function() {
    var page2 = lis().eq(2).find('a').eq(0);
    page2.click();
    $scope.$digest();
```

```
        expect($scope.currentPage).toBe(2);
    });

...

    it('does not change the current page on "next" click if already at
last page', function() {
        var next = lis().eq(-1).find('a');
        $scope.currentPage = 5;
        $scope.$digest();
        next.click();
        $scope.$digest();
        expect($scope.currentPage).toBe(5);
    });

    it('changes the number of items when numPages changes', function() {
        $scope.numPages = 8;
        $scope.$digest();
        expect(lis().length).toBe(10);
        expect(lis().eq(0).text()).toBe('Previous');
        expect(lis().eq(-1).text()).toBe('Next');
    });

});
```

Using an HTML template in a directive

This widget requires that we generate some HTML tags to replace the directive. The simplest way to do this is to use a template for the directive. Here is the mark-up for this template:

```html
<div class="pagination"><ul>
  <li ng-class="{disabled: noPrevious()}">
    <a ng-click="selectPrevious()">Previous</a>
  </li>
  <li ng-repeat="page in pages"
      ng-class="{active: isActive(page)}">
    <a ng-click="selectPage(page)">{{page}}</a>
  </li>
  <li ng-class="{disabled: noNext()}">
    <a ng-click="selectNext()">Next</a>
  </li>
</ul></div>
```

The template uses an array called `pages` and a number of helper functions, such as `selectPage()` and `noNext()`. These are internal to the implementation of the widget. They need to be placed on a scope for the template to access them but they should not appear on the scope where the widget is used. To achieve this we can ask the compiler to create a new isolated scope for our template.

Isolating our directive from its parent scope

We do not know what the scope will contain at the point where our directive is used. It is a good practice, therefore, to provide our directive with a well-defined public facing interface. This ensures that the directive cannot rely on or be affected by arbitrary properties on the scope where it is used.

We have three options for the `scope` to be used in our directive and its template. This is defined in the directive definition:

- To reuse the scope, from the place where the widget is used. This is the default and corresponds to `scope: false`.

- To create a child scope, which prototypically inherits from the scope where the widget is used. You specify this with `scope: true`.

- To create an isolated scope, which does not prototypically inherit, so that it is completely isolated from its parent. You specify this by passing an object to the scope property: `scope: { ... }`.

We want to completely decouple our widget's template from the rest of the application, so that there is no danger of data leaking between the two. We will use isolated scope as shown in the following image:

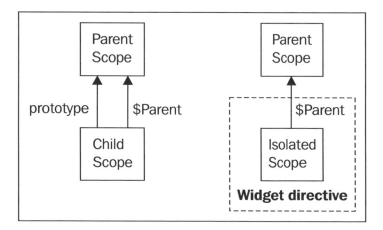

> While an isolated scope does not prototypically inherit from its parent, it can still access its parent's scope through the `$parent` property. But this is considered a bad practice because you are undermining the isolation of the directive from its surroundings.

Since our scope is now isolated from the parent scope, we need to explicitly map values between the parent scope and the isolated scope. This is done by referencing AngularJS expressions on the attributes of the element where the directive appears. In the case of our pagination directive, the `num-pages` and `current-page` attributes fulfill this role.

We can synchronize the expressions in these attributes with properties on the template scope through watches. We can set this up manually or we can ask AngularJS to wire them up for us. There are three types of interface we can specify between the element's attributes and the isolated scope: `interpolate` (`@`), `data bind` (`=`), and `expression` (`&`). You specify these interfaces as key-value pairs on the scope property of the directive definition.

The key is the name of the field on the isolated scope. The value is one of `@`, `=`, or `&` followed by the name of the attribute on the element:

```
scope: {
  isolated1: '@attribute1',
  isolated2: '=attribute2',
  isolated3: '&attribute3'
}
```

Here we have defined three fields on the isolated scope and AngularJS will map their values from the specified attributes on the element where the directive appears.

> If the attribute name is omitted from the value, then it is assumed that the attribute has the same name as the isolated scope field:
> ```
> scope: { isolated1: '@' }
> ```
> It will expect the attribute to be called `isolated1`.

Interpolating the attribute with @

The `@` symbol indicates that AngularJS should interpolate the value of the specified attribute and update the isolated scope property when it changes. Interpolation is used with `{{}}` curly braces to generate a string using values from the parent scope.

A common mistake is to expect an interpolated object to be the object itself. Interpolation always returns a string. So if you have an object, say user has a field called userName, then the interpolation of {{user}} will convert the user object to a string and you will not be able to access the userName property on the string.

This attribute interpolation is equivalent to manually $observe the attribute:

```
attrs.$observe('attribute1', function(value) {
  isolatedScope.isolated1 = value;
});
attrs.$$observers['attribute1'].$$scope = parentScope;
```

Binding data to the attribute with =

The = symbol indicates that AngularJS should keep the expression in the specified attribute and the value on the isolated scope in sync with each other. This is a two-way data binding that allows objects and values to be mapped directly between the inside and outside of the widget.

Since this interface supports two way data binding, the expression given in the attribute should be assignable (that is, refers to a field on the scope or an object) and not an arbitrary computed expression.

This binding is a bit like setting up two $watch functions:

```
var parentGet = $parse(attrs['attribute2']);
var parentSet = parentGet.assign;
parentScope.$watch(parentGet, function(value) {
  isolatedScope.isolated2 = value;
});
isolatedScope.$watch('isolated2', function(value) {
  parentSet(parentScope, value);
});
```

The actual implementation is more complex to ensure stability between the two scopes.

Providing a callback expression in the attribute with &

The & symbol indicates that the expression provided in the attribute on the element will be made available on the scope as a function that, when called, will execute the expression. This is useful for creating callbacks from the widget.

This binding is equivalent to $parse the expression in the attribute and exposing the parsed expression function on the isolated scope:

```
parentGet = $parse(attrs['attribute3']);
scope.isolated3 = function(locals) {
  return parentGet(parentScope, locals);
};
```

Implementing the widget

The following is the pagination directive definition object:

```
myModule.directive('pagination', function() {
return {
  restrict: 'E',
  scope: {
    numPages: '=',
    currentPage: '='
  },
  template: ...,
  replace: true,
```

The directive is restricted to appear as an element. It creates an isolated scope with numPages and currentPage data, which is bound to attributes num-pages and current-page, respectively. The directive element will be replaced with the template shown earlier:

```
link: function(scope) {
  scope.$watch('numPages', function(value) {
    scope.pages = [];
    for(var i=1;i<=value;i++) { scope.pages.push(i); }
    if ( scope.currentPage > value ) {
      scope.selectPage(value);
    }
  });

  ...

  scope.isActive = function(page) {
    return scope.currentPage === page;
  };

  scope.selectPage = function(page) {
    if ( ! scope.isActive(page) ) {
      scope.currentPage = page;
    }
```

```
    };

    ...

    scope.selectNext = function() {
      if ( !scope.noNext() ) {
        scope.selectPage(scope.currentPage+1);
      }
    };
}
```

The link function sets up a $watch property to create the pages array based on the value of numPages. It adds the various helper functions to the isolated scope that will be used in the directive's template.

Adding a selectPage callback to the directive

It would be useful to provide a function or an expression that is evaluated when the page changes. We can do this by specifying a new attribute on the directive and mapping it to the isolated scope using &.

```
<pagination
  num-pages="tasks.pageCount"
  current-page="tasks.currentPage"
  on-select-page="selectPage(page)">
</pagination>
```

What we are saying here is that whenever the selected page changes, the directive should call the selectPage(page) function passing it to the new page number as a parameter. Here is a test of this feature:

```
    it('executes the onSelectPage expression when the current page
changes', inject(function($compile, $rootScope) {
      $rootScope.selectPageHandler =
        jasmine.createSpy('selectPageHandler');
      element = $compile(
        '<pagination num-pages="numPages" ' +
                ' current-page="currentPage" ' +
                ' on-select-page="selectPageHandler(page)">' +
        '</pagination>')($rootScope);
      $rootScope.$digest();
      var page2 = element.find('li').eq(2).find('a').eq(0);
      page2.click();
      $rootScope.$digest();
      expect($rootScope.selectPageHandler).toHaveBeenCalledWith(2);
    }));
```

We create a spy to handle the call-back and then the `it` function gets called when we click on a new page.

To implement this we add an extra field to our isolate scope definition:

```
scope: {
    ...,
    onSelectPage: '&'
},
```

Now an `onSelectPage()` function will be available on the isolated scope. When called, it will execute the expression passed to the `on-select-page` attribute. We now change the `selectPage()` function on the isolated scope to call `onSelectPage()`:

```
scope.selectPage = function(page) {
    if ( ! scope.isActive(page) ) {
        scope.currentPage = page;
        scope.onSelectPage({ page: page });
    }
};
```

> Note that we pass the page variable to the expression in a map of variables. These variables are provided to the bound expression when it is executed, as though they were on the scope.

Creating a custom validation directive

In our SCRUM application we have a User Edit Form. On that form we require users to provide a password. Since the password field is obscured and the user cannot see what they are typing, it is helpful to have a `confirm password` field.

We need to check that the password and confirm password field are identical. We will create a custom validation directive that we can apply to an input element that checks whether the model of the input element matches another model value. In use, it will look like this:

```
<form name="passwordForm">
    <input type="password" name="password" ng-model="user.password">
    <input type="password" name="confirmPassword" ng-
model="confirmPassword" validate-equals="user.password">
</form>
```

This custom model validator directive must integrate with ngModelController to provide a consistent validation experience for the user.

We can expose the ngModelController on the scope by providing a name for the form and a name for the input element. This allows us to access model validity in the controller. Our validation directive will set the confirmPassword input to valid if its model value is the same as the user.password model.

Requiring a directive controller

Validation directives require access to the ngModelController, which is the directive controller for the ng-model directive. We specify this in our directive definition using the require field. This field takes a string or an array of strings. Each string must be the canonical name of the directive whose controller we require.

When the required directive is found, its directive controller is injected into the linking function as the fourth parameter. For example:

```
require: 'ngModel',
link: function(scope, element, attrs, ngModelController) { … }
```

If more than one controller is required, then the fourth parameter will be an array containing these controllers in the same order as they were required.

 If the current element does not contain the specified directive, then the compiler will throw an error. This can be a good way to ensure that the other directive has been provided.

Making the controller optional

You can make the require field of the controller optional by putting a '?' in front of the directive name, for example, require: '?ngModel'. If the directive has not been provided, then the fourth parameter will be null. If you require more than one controller then the relevant element in the array of controllers will be null.

Searching for parents for the controller

If the directive, whose controller you require, can appear on this or any ancestor of the current element, then you can put a '^' in front of the directive name, for example, `require: '^ngModel'`. The compiler will then search the ancestor elements starting from the element containing the current directive and return the first matching controller.

> You can combine optional and ancestor prefixes to have an optional directive that may appear in an ancestor. For example, `require: '^?form'` would let you find the controller for the form directive, which is what the `ng-model` directive does to register itself with the form if it is available.

Working with ngModelController

Once we have required the `ngModelController` we use its API to specify the validity of the input element. This is a common case for this kind of directive and the pattern is fairly straightforward. The `ngModelController` exposes the following functions and properties that we will use:

Name	Description
`$parsers`	A pipeline of functions that will be called in turn when the value of the input element changes.
`$formatters`	A pipeline of functions that will be called in turn when the value of the model changes.
`$setValidity(validationError Key, isValid)`	A function called to set whether the model is valid for a given kind of validation error.
`$valid`	True if there is no error.
`$error`	An object that contains information about any validation errors on the model.

The functions that go into `$parsers` and `$formatters` take a value and return a value, for example, `function(value) { return value; }`. The value they receive is the value returned from the previous function in the pipeline. It is inside these functions where we put our validation logic and call `$setValidity()`.

Writing custom validation directive tests

The pattern for testing validation directives is to compile a form containing an input that uses `ng-model` and our validation directive. For example:

```
<form name="testForm">
  <input name="testInput"
         ng-model="model.value"
         validate-equals="model.compareTo">
</form>
```

This directive is an attribute on the input element. The value of the attribute is an expression that must evaluate to the value on the model. The directive will compare this value with the input's value.

We specify the model bound to this input using the `ng-model` directive. This will create `ngModelController`, which will be exposed on the scope as `$scope.testForm.testInput` and the model value itself will be exposed on the scope as `$scope.value`.

We then make changes to the input value and the model value and check the `ngModelController` for changes to `$valid` and `$error`.

In the test setup we keep a reference to the model and the `ngModelController`.

```
describe('validateEquals directive', function() {
  var $scope, modelCtrl, modelValue;

  beforeEach(inject(function($compile, $rootScope) {
    ...
    modelValue = $scope.model = {};
    modelCtrl = $scope.testForm.testInput;
    ...
  }));

  ...
  describe('model value changes', function() {
    it('should be invalid if the model changes', function() {
      modelValue.testValue = 'different';
      $scope.$digest();
      expect(modelCtrl.$valid).toBeFalsy();
      expect(modelCtrl.$viewValue).toBe(undefined);
    });
    it('should be invalid if the reference model changes', function()
{
      modelValue.compareTo = 'different';
```

```
        $scope.$digest();
        expect(modelCtrl.$valid).toBeFalsy();
        expect(modelCtrl.$viewValue).toBe(undefined);
    });
    it('should be valid if the modelValue changes to be the same as
the reference', function() {
        modelValue.compareTo = 'different';
        $scope.$digest();
        expect(modelCtrl.$valid).toBeFalsy();

        modelValue.testValue = 'different';
        $scope.$digest();
        expect(modelCtrl.$valid).toBeTruthy();
        expect(modelCtrl.$viewValue).toBe('different');
    });
});
```

Here, we modify the scope, both the model of the input element itself (`modelValue.testValue`) and the model of the value with which to compare the input (`modelValue.compareTo`). Then we test the validity of the input (`modelCt1`). We have to call `$digest()` to ensure that the input has been updated from the model changes.

```
describe('input value changes', function() {
    it('should be invalid if the input value changes', function() {
        modelCtrl.$setViewValue('different');
        expect(modelCtrl.$valid).toBeFalsy();
        expect(modelValue.testValue).toBe(undefined);
    });

    it('should be valid if the input value changes to be the same as
the reference', function() {
        modelValue.compareTo = 'different';
        $scope.$digest();
        expect(modelCtrl.$valid).toBeFalsy();

        modelCtrl.$setViewValue('different');
        expect(modelCtrl.$viewValue).toBe('different');
        expect(modelCtrl.$valid).toBeTruthy();
    });
});
});
```

Here we modify the input value, by calling `$setViewValue()`, which is what happens if the user types or pastes into the input box.

Implementing a custom validation directive

Now we have our tests in place, so we can implement the functionality of the directive:

```
myModule.directive('validateEquals', function() {
  return {
    require: 'ngModel',
    link: function(scope, elm, attrs, ngModelCtrl) {
      function validateEqual(myValue) {
        var valid = (myValue === scope.$eval(attrs.validateEquals));
        ngModelCtrl.$setValidity('equal', valid);
        return valid ? myValue : undefined;
      }

      ngModelCtrl.$parsers.push(validateEqual);
      ngModelCtrl.$formatters.push(validateEqual);

      scope.$watch(attrs.validateEquals, function() {
        ngModelCtrl.$setViewValue(ngModelCtrl.$viewValue);
      });
    }
  };
});
```

We create a function called `validateEqual(value)`, which compares the passed in value with the value of the expression. We push this into the `$parsers` and `$formatters` pipelines, so that the validation function gets called each time either the model or the view changes.

In this directive we also have to take into account the model we are comparing against changing. We do this by setting up a watch on the expression, which we retrieve from the `attrs` parameter of the linking function. When it does change, we artificially trigger the `$parsers` pipeline to run by calling `$setViewValue()`. This ensures that all potential `$parsers` are run in case any of them modify the model value before it gets to our validator.

Creating an asynchronous model validator

Some validation can only be done by interacting with a remote service, say a database. In these cases, the response from the service will be asynchronous. This brings in complication not only in working with model validation asynchronously but also in testing this functionality.

In our Admin User Form, we would like to check whether the e-mail address that a user is entering has already been taken. We will create a uniqueEmail directive, which will check with our back-end server to find if the e-mail address is already in use:

```
<input ng-model="user.email" unique-email>
```

Mocking up the Users service

We use the Users resource service to query the database for the e-mail addresses that are already in use. We need to mock up the query() method in this service for our test.

 In this case, it is easiest to create a test module and mock out a Users service object instead of injecting the service and spying on the query() method since the Users service itself relies on a number of other services and constants.

```
angular.module('mock.Users', []).factory('Users', function() {
  var Users = { };
  Users.query = function(query, response) {
    Users.respondWith = function(emails) {
      response(emails);
      Users.respondWith = undefined;
    };
  };
  return Users;
});
```

The query() function creates Users.respondWith() that will call the response callback that was passed to query(). This allows us to simulate a response to the query in our tests.

 Before Users.query() has been called and after it has been handled with a call to Users.respondWith(), we set the Users.respondWith function to undefined.

We then load this module in addition to the module under test:

```
beforeEach(module('mock.users'));
```

This causes the original Users service to be overridden by our mock service.

Writing tests for asynchronous validation

We set up the test similar to the previous validation directive:

```
beforeEach(inject(function($compile, $rootScope, _Users_){
  Users = _Users_;
  spyOn(Users, 'query').andCallThrough();
  ...
}));
```

We are spying on the `Users.query()` function but we also want it to call through to our mocked out function so that we can simulate responses with `Users.respondWith()`.

The significant unit tests are as follows:

```
it('should call Users.query when the view changes', function() {
  testInput.$setViewValue('different');
  expect(Users.query).toHaveBeenCalled();
});

it('should set model to invalid if the Users.query response contains
users', function() {
  testInput.$setViewValue('different');
  Users.respondWith(['someUser']);
  expect(testInput.$valid).toBe(false);
});

it('should set model to valid if the Users.query response contains no
users', function() {
  testInput.$setViewValue('different');
  Users.respondWith([]);
  expect(testInput.$valid).toBe(true);
});
```

We are checking to see if `Users.query()` was called. Also, since `Users.query()` tracks the response callback, we can simulate a response from the server with `Users.respondWith()`.

One issue, which we need to test for, is that we don't want to query the server if the user re-enters the same value as was provided by the model. For instance, if we are editing a user rather than creating a user, then the user's original e-mail is in the database on the server but it is a valid e-mail address.

```
it('should not call Users.query if the view changes to be the same as
the original model', function() {
  $scope.model.testValue = 'admin@abc.com';
```

```
        $scope.$digest();
        testInput.$setViewValue('admin@abc.com');
        expect(Users.query).not.toHaveBeenCalled();
        testInput.$setViewValue('other@abc.com');
        expect(Users.query).toHaveBeenCalled();

        querySpy.reset();
        testInput.$setViewValue('admin@abc.com');
        expect(Users.query).not.toHaveBeenCalled();
        $scope.model.testValue = 'other@abc.com';
        $scope.$digest();
        testInput.$setViewValue('admin@abc.com');
        expect(Users.query).toHaveBeenCalled();
    });
```

We set the `model` and then check that `User.query()` is called only if the input value is set to an e-mail that does not match the original model value. We use `Users.query.reset()` when we want to check that the spy has not been called since the last time we checked.

Implementing the asynchronous validation directive

The implementation of this directive is similar in structure to the previous validation directive. We require the `ngModel` controller and add to the `$parsers` and `$formatters` in the linking function:

```
myModule.directive('uniqueEmail', ["Users", function (Users) {
    return {
        require:'ngModel',
        link:function (scope, element, attrs, ngModelCtrl) {
            var original;
            ngModelCtrl.$formatters.unshift(function(modelValue) {
                original = modelValue;
                return modelValue;
            });

            ngModelCtrl.$parsers.push(function (viewValue) {
                if (viewValue && viewValue !== original ) {
                    Users.query({email:viewValue}, function (users) {
                        if (users.length === 0) {
                            ngModelCtrl.$setValidity('uniqueEmail', true);
                        } else {
```

```
                    ngModelCtrl.$setValidity('uniqueEmail', false);
                }
            });
            return viewValue;
        }
    });
    }
  };
}]);
```

We are only checking with the server in the `$parser`, that is, when the user changes the input. If the value is updated programmatically, via the model, we assume that the application business logic ensures that this is a valid e-mail address. For example, if we are loading an existing user to edit, the e-mail address is valid even though it is already taken.

Normally, in a validation function you return `undefined` if the value is not valid. This prevents the model from being updated with an invalid value. In this case, at the point of returning, the validation function does not know whether the value is valid or not. So we return the value any-way and then let the response callback set the validity later.

We are using the `$formatters` pipeline to add a function that tracks the original value that was set in the model. This prevents the validation function from contacting the server if the user re-enters the original e-mail address, as it would incorrectly set the e-mail to invalid.

Wrapping the jQueryUI datepicker directive

Sometimes there is a third party widget that is complex enough and it is not worth writing a pure AngularJS version of it in the short term. You can accelerate your development by wrapping such as widget in an AngularJS directive but you have to be careful about how the two libraries would interact.

Here we will look at making a `datepicker` input directive that wraps the jQueryUI `datepicker` widget. The widget exposes the following API that we will use to integrate into AngularJS, where element is the jQuery wrapper around the element on which the widget is to be attached.

Function	Description
`element.datepicker(options)`	Create a new widget using the given options and attach it to the element.
`element.datepicker("setDate", date)`	Set the date on the widget.
`element.datepicker("getDate")`	Get the date on the widget.
`element.datepicker("destroy")`	Destroy and remove the widget from the element.

We want to be informed when the user selects a new date with the picker. The `options` that we pass to create a new widget can provide an `onSelect` callback that will be called when the user selects a date:

```
element.datepicker({onSelect: function(value, picker) { ... });
```

 To keep things simple, we will specify that the `datepicker` directive can only be linked to a JavaScript Date object in the model.

The general pattern for wrapping JQuery input widgets is similar, again, to building a validation directive. You require `ngModel` and place functions on the `$parsers` and `$formatters` pipeline to transform the values between the model and the view.

Also, we need to put data into the widget when the model changes and get data into the model when the widget changes. We override `ngModel.$render()` to update the widget. This function is called after all the `$formatters` have been executed successfully. To get the data out, we use the `onSelect` callback to call `ngModel.$setViewValue()`, which updates the view value and triggers the `$parsers` pipeline.

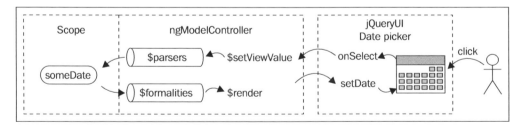

Writing tests for directives that wrap libraries

In a pure unit test we would create a mock jQueryUI `datepicker` widget that exposes the same interface. In this case we are going to take a more pragmatic approach and use a real `datepicker` widget in the tests.

The advantage of this is that we do not have to rely on the widget's interface being documented accurately. By calling the actual methods and checking that the user interface is updated correctly, we can be very sure that our directive is working. The disadvantages are that the DOM manipulation in the widget can slow down the test runs and there must be a way to interact with the widget to ensure that it is behaving correctly.

In this case, the jQueryUI `datepicker` widget exposes another function that allows us to simulate a user selecting a date:

```
$.datepicker._selectDate(element);
```

We create a helper function `selectDate()`, which we will use to simulate date selection on the widget:

```
var selectDate = function(element, date) {
  element.datepicker('setDate', date);
  $.datepicker._selectDate(element);
};
```

 This kind of simulation is sometimes hard to achieve, and if so, you should consider mocking out the widget altogether.

The tests themselves make use of the widget's API and this helper function. For example:

```
describe('simple use on input element', function() {
  var aDate, element;
  beforeEach(function() {
    aDate = new Date(2010, 12, 1);
    element = $compile(
      "<input date-picker ng-model='x'/>")($rootScope);
  });
  it('should get the date from the model', function() {
    $rootScope.x = aDate;
    $rootScope.$digest();
    expect(element.datepicker('getDate')).toEqual(aDate);
  });

  it('should put the date in the model', function() {
    $rootScope.$digest();
    selectDate(element, aDate);
    expect($rootScope.x).toEqual(aDate);
  });
});
```

Here, we check that model changes get forwarded to the widget and widget changes get passed back to the model. Notice that we do not call $digest() after selectDate(), since it is the directive's job to ensure that the digest occurs after a user interaction.

 There are more tests for all different scenarios for this directive. They can be found in the sample code.

Implementing the jQuery datepicker directive

The directive implementation is again making use of the functionality provided by the ngModelController. In particular, we add a function to the $formatters pipeline that ensures that the model is a Date object, we add our onSelect callback to the options, and we override the $render function to update the widget when the model changes.

```
myModule.directive('datePicker', function () {
  return {
    require:'ngModel',
    link:function (scope, element, attrs, ngModelCtrl) {
      ngModelCtrl.$formatters.push(function(date) {
        if ( angular.isDefined(date) &&
             date !== null &&
             !angular.isDate(date) ) {
          throw new Error('ng-Model value must be a Date object');
        }
        return date;
      });

      var updateModel = function () {
        scope.$apply(function () {
          var date = element.datepicker("getDate");
          element.datepicker("setDate", element.val());
          ngModelCtrl.$setViewValue(date);
        });
      };
      var onSelectHandler = function(userHandler) {
        if ( userHandler ) {
          return function(value, picker) {
            updateModel();
            return userHandler(value, picker);
          };
```

```
    } else {
      return updateModel;
    }
  };
```

The `onSelect()` handler calls our `updateModel()` function, which passes the new date value into the `$parsers` pipeline via `$setViewValue()`:

```
    var setUpDatePicker = function () {
      var options = scope.$eval(attrs.datePicker) || {};
      options.onSelect = onSelectHandler(options.onSelect);
      element.bind('change', updateModel);
      element.datepicker('destroy');
      element.datepicker(options);
      ngModelCtrl.$render();
    };

    ngModelCtrl.$render = function () {
      element.datepicker("setDate", ngModelCtrl.$viewValue);
    };

    scope.$watch(attrs.datePicker, setUpDatePicker, true);
    }
  };
});
```

Summary

In this chapter we looked at a variety of common patterns for defining, testing, and implementing directives. We saw how to integrate with the `ngModel` to implement validation, how to write a reusable encapsulated widget, and how to wrap a third party widget in an AngularJS directive. Throughout the chapter testing has been promoted and we looked at common strategies for testing directives in AngularJS.

In the next chapter we will take a deeper look into building directives, looking at some of the more advanced features such as transclusion, and compiling our own templates.

9
Building Advanced Directives

The previous chapter introduced how to develop and test your own custom directives. In this chapter we look at some of the more advanced things that you can do when developing AngularJS directives. This will include:

- Understanding transclusion: in particular use of **transclusion** functions and transclusion scopes

- Define your own directive controllers to create directives that can cooperate, and how these controllers differ from link functions

- Terminating the compilation process and taking control: loading your own templates dynamically and using the $compile and $interpolate services

Using transclusion

When you move elements from one part of the DOM to another, you have to decide what happens to their associated scope.

The naïve approach is to associate the elements with the scope that is defined at the new position. This is likely to break the application, since the elements may no longer have access to items from their original scope.

What we really need is to "bring the original scope with us". Moving elements and their scope in this way is called transclusion. We will look into how to move the scope in transclusion later in this chapter in the *Understanding transclusion scope* section. But first let's look at some examples.

Using transclusion in directives

Transclusion is necessary whenever a directive is replacing its original contents with new elements but wants to use the original contents somewhere in the new elements.

For example, `ng-repeat` will transclude and clone its original element, stamping out multiple copies of the transcluded element as it iterates over a list of items. Each of these elements will be associated with a new scope, which is a child of the original element's scope.

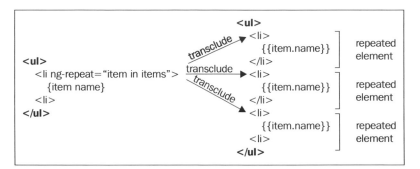

Transcluding into an isolated scope directive

The `ng-repeat` directive is quite unusual in that it makes clones of itself, which are then transcluded. It is more common to use transclusion when you are creating a templated widget directive, where you want to insert the original element's contents at some point in the template.

Creating an alert directive that uses transclusion

A simple example of such a templated widget is an `alert` element directive.

 Alerts are messages, which are displayed to the user to indicate the current status of the application.

Oh snap! Something went wrong.   ✕

Well done! It worked out in the end.   ✕

Add Alert

The contents of the `alert` element contains the message to display in the alert. This needs to be transcluded into the directive's template. A list of alerts can be displayed using `ng-repeat`:

```
<alert type="alert.type" close="closeAlert($index)"
        ng-repeat="alert in alerts">
  {{alert.msg}}
</alert>
```

The `close` attribute should contain an expression that will be executed when the user closes the alert. The implementation of the directive is quite straightforward as follows:

```
myModule.directive('alert', function () {
  return {
    restrict:'E',
    replace: true,
    transclude: true,
    template:
      '<div class="alert alert-{{type}}">' +
        '<button type="button" class="close"' +
                'ng-click="close()">&times;' +
        '</button>' +
        '<div ng-transclude></div>' +
      '</div>',
    scope: { type:'=', close:'&' }
  };
});
```

Understanding the replace property in the directive definition

The `replace` property tells the compiler to replace the original directive's element with the template given by the `template` field. If we had provided `template` but not `replace`, then the compiler would append the template to the directive's element.

 When you ask the compiler to replace the element with a template, it will copy over all the attributes from the original element to the template element as well.

Understanding the transclude property in the directive definition

The `transclude` property takes either `true` or `'element'`. This tells the compiler to extract the contents of the original `<alert>` element and make them available to be transcluded into the template.

- Using `transclude: true` means that the children of the directive's element will be transcluded. This is what happens in the `alert` directive, although we then replaced the directive's element with our template.

- Using `transclude: 'element'` means the entire element will be transcluded including any attribute directives that have not already been compiled. This is what happens in the `ng-repeat` directive.

Inserting the transcluded elements with ng-transclude

The `ng-transclude` directive gets the transcluded elements and appends them to the element in the template on which it appears. This is the simplest and most common way to use transclusion.

Understanding the scope of transclusion

All DOM elements that have been compiled by AngularJS have a scope associated with them. In most cases DOM elements do not have scopes defined directly on them but get their scope from some ancestor element. New scopes are created by directives that specify a `scope` property on their directive definition object.

> Only a few core directives define new scopes, these are `ng-controller`, `ng-repeat`, `ng-include`, `ng-view`, and `ng-switch`. They all create child scopes that prototypically inherit from their parent scopes.

We saw in *Chapter 8, Building Your Own Directives*, how to build widget directives that use isolated scope to ensure that the scopes inside and outside the widget do not contaminate each other. This means that expressions within the template have no access to the values on the parent scope, containing the widget. This is useful because we don't want properties on the parent scope affecting or being affected by what we do inside the template.

The original contents of the directive's element, which is going to be inserted into the template, needs to be associated with the original scope and not the isolated scope. By transcluding the original elements we are able to maintain the correct scope for these elements.

Our `alert` directive is a widget, using isolated scope. Consider what scopes are created with the `alert` directive. Before the alert directive has been compiled the DOM and its scopes look like this:

```
<!-- defines $rootScope -->
<div ng-app ng-init="type='success'">
  <!-- bound to $rootScope -->
  <div>{{type}}</div>
  <!-- bound to $rootScope -->
  <alert type="'info'" ...>Look at {{type}}</alert>
</div>
```

The `<div>{{type}}</div>` does not have a scope directly defined on it. Instead, it is implicitly bound to the `$rootScope` because it is a child of the `ng-app` element where `$rootScope` is defined and so `{{type}}` will evaluate to `'success'`.

On the alert element we have an attribute: `type="'info'"`. This attribute is mapped to a `type` property on the template's scope. Once the `alert` directive has been compiled, it is replaced with its template, the DOM and its scopes look like this:

```
<!-- defines $rootScope -->
<div ng-app ng-init="type='success'">
  <!-- bound to $rootScope -->
  <div>{{type}}</div>
  <!-- defines an isolated scope -->
  <div class="alert-{{type}}" ...>
    <!-- bound to isolated scope -->
    <button>...</button>
    <div ng-transclude>
      <!-- defines new translude scope -->
      <span>Look at {{type}}</span>
    </div>
  </div>
</div>
```

Inside the template, the `class="alert-{{type}}"` attribute is implicitly bound to the isolated scope and so will evaluate to `class="alert-info"`.

In contrast, the transcluded contents of the original `<alert>` element, `<span>Look at {{type}}</span>`, are now bound to a new transclude scope. If we had naïvely moved these contents into the template, their implicit scope binding would change from `$rootScope` to the isolated scope and then `{{type}}` would evaluate to `'info'`. This is not what we want.

Instead, the new transclude scope is a child of `$rootScope` and prototypically inherits from it. This means that the span will evaluate correctly to `<span>Look at **success**</span>`. The following image shows these scopes in Batarang:

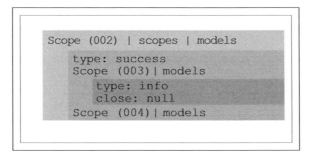

In the previous image, `Scope (002)` is the `$rootScope`, which contains the `type="success"`. `Scope (003)` is the isolated scope for the `alert` template and does not inherit from `$rootScope`. `Scope (004)` is the transcluded scope and does inherit from `$rootScope` and so in this scope, `type` will be `success`.

> When elements are moved by transclusion they get to take their original scope binding with them. More accurately, the transcluded elements will be bound to a new scope that is a prototypical child of the scope from where they were taken.

Creating and working with transclusion functions

Transclusion in AngularJS is made possible by the use of **transclusion** functions. These functions are simply link functions, which are created by calling the `$compile` service.

When a directive requests transclusion, AngularJS will extract the transcluded elements from the DOM and compile them. Here is an approximation of what happens with transclude: true:

```
var elementsToTransclude = directiveElement.contents();
directiveElement.html('');
var transcludeFunction = $compile(elementsToTransclude);
```

The first line gets the contents of the element containing the directive that requested the transclusion. The second line clears this element. The third line compiles the transcluded contents to produce the **transclusion** function, which will be passed back to the directive, for it to use.

Creating a transclusion function with the $compile service

The AngularJS compiler is exposed as the $compile service. This is the same function that is used when compiling any other part of an AngularJS application. To use this service we simply call it with a list of DOM nodes (or a string that will be parsed into a list of DOM nodes).

```
var linkingFn = $compile(
  '<div some-directive>Some {{"interpola-ted"}} values</div>');
```

The call to $compile service returns a linking function. You call this function with a scope to retrieve a DOM element containing the compiled DOM elements, bound to the given scope:

```
var compiledElement = linkingFn(someScope);
```

> Transclusion functions are just special instances of link functions.

Cloning the original elements when transcluding

If we pass in a call-back function as a parameter to a linking function then a clone of the elements will be returned instead of the original elements. The call-back function will be called synchronously with the cloned elements as a parameter.

```
var clone = linkingFn(scope, function callback(clone) {
  element.append(clone);
});
```

> This is very useful if you want to make copies of the original element's children, as it would happen in `ng-repeat`.

Accessing transclusion functions in directives

The compiler passes this **transclusion** function back to the directive. There are two places where you can get hold a **transclusion** function: the compile function and the directive controller. There is a section describing directive controllers in detail later in this chapter.

```
myModule.directive('myDirective', function() {
  return {
    transclude: true,
    compile: function(element, attrs, transcludeFn) { ... };
    controller: function($scope, $transclude) { ... },
  };
});
```

Here we have indicated that the directive should `transclude` its contents. We can access the **transclusion** functions in the compile function, via the `transcludeFn` parameter and in the directive controller, via the `$transclude` parameter.

Getting the transclusion function in the compile function with transcludeFn

The transclusion function is made available as the third parameter of the compile function of a directive. At this stage of the compilation, the scope is not known so the **transclusion** function is not bound to any scope. Instead, you will pass in the scope to this function, as its first parameter, when you call it.

The scope is available in the linking function and so this is where you will generally find the transclusion function being invoked.

```
compile: function(element, attrs, transcludeFn) {
  return function postLink(scope, element, attrs, controller) {
    var newScope = scope.$parent.$new();
    element.find('p').first().append(transcludeFn(newScope));
  };
}
```

We append the transcluded elements to the first `<p>` element below the directive's element. When calling the **transclusion** function, we bind the transcluded elements to a scope. In this case we create a new scope, which is a sibling of the directive's scope, that is, child of the `$parent` of the directive's scope.

This is necessary when the directive has an isolated scope; since the scope passed to the link function is the isolated scope and does not inherit the properties from the parent scope, which the transcluded elements need.

Getting the transclusion function in the directive controller with $transclude

We can access the **transclusion** function in a directive controller by injecting `$transclude`. In this case, `$transclude` is a function that is pre-bound to new a child of the parent scope, so you do not need to provide a scope.

```
controller: function($scope, $element, $transclude) {
  $element.find('p').first().append($transclude());
}
```

Once again, we append the transcluded elements to the first `<p>` element.

 With `$transclude`, the pre-bound scope will be a prototypical child of the original scope from where the transcluded elements came.

Creating an if directive that uses transclusion

Let's look at a simple directive that makes explicit use of transclusion functions rather than relying on the `ng-transclude` directive. While AngularJS 1.0 provides both `ng-show` and `ng-switch` directives for changing the visibility of content in an application, `ng-show` doesn't remove the element from the DOM when it is hidden and `ng-switch` is quite verbose for simple situations.

If we just want to remove the element from the DOM when it is not needed, we can create an `if` directive. It would be used similar to `ng-show`:

```
<body ng-init="model= {show: true, count: 0}">
  <button ng-click="model.show = !model.show">
    Toggle Div
  </button>
```

```
      <div if="model.show" ng-init="model.count=model.count+1">
        Shown {{model.count}} times
      </div>
    </body>
```

Here, each time the button is clicked the value of `model.show` is toggled between `true` and `false`. To show that the DOM element is being removed and reinserted on each toggle, we are incrementing `model.count`.

In the unit tests we will need to test that the DOM element is actually added and removed correctly:

```
it('creates or removes the element as the if condition changes',
function () {
    element = $compile(
      '<div><div if="someVar"></div></div>')(scope);
  scope.$apply('someVar = true');
  expect(element.children().length).toBe(1);
  scope.$apply('someVar = false');
  expect(element.children().length).toBe(0);
  scope.$apply('someVar = true');
  expect(element.children().length).toBe(1);
});
```

Here we check that the number of children on our container element increases or decreases as the expression toggles between `true` and `false`.

> Note that we need to wrap the element that contains the `if` directive in a `div` because our directive will use `jqLite.after()` to insert it into the DOM, which requires that the element has a parent.

Let's take a look at how to implement this directive:

```
myModule.directive('if', function () {
  return {
    transclude: 'element',
    priority: 500,
    compile: function (element, attr, transclude) {
      return function postLink(scope, element, attr) {
        var childElement, childScope;

        scope.$watch(attr['if'], function (newValue) {
          if (childElement) {
```

```
      childElement.remove();
      childScope.$destroy();
      childElement = undefined;
      childScope = undefined;
    }
    if (newValue) {
      childScope = scope.$new();
      childElement = transclude(childScope, function(clone){
        element.after(clone);
      });
    }
  });
...
```

The directive transcludes the entire element (transclude: 'element'). We provide a compile function, which gives us access to the **transclusion** function, which returns the link function, where we $watch the if attribute expression.

> We use $watch rather than $observe here because the if attribute should contain an expression to be evaluated rather than a string to be interpolated.

When the expression changes, we tidy up the scope and child element, if they exist. This is important to ensure that we don't have any memory leaks. If the expression evaluates to true, we create a new child scope and then use it with the **transclusion** function to clone a new copy of the transcluded elements. We insert these elements after the element that contained the directive.

Using the priority property in a directive

All directives have a priority, defaulting to zero, as in the case of the alert directive. On each element, AngularJS compiles the higher priority directives before lower priority ones. We can specify this using the priority property on the directive definition object.

If a directive has transclude: 'element', the compiler will only transclude attributes whose directives have a lower priority than the current directive, in other words, the element's directives that have not yet been processed.

The ng-repeat directive has `transclude: 'element'` and `priority: 1000`, so generally all attributes that appear on the ng-repeat element are transcluded to appear on the cloned repeated elements.

 We gave out `if` directive a priority of `500`, which is less than `ng-repeat`. This means that if you put it on the same element as an `ng-repeat`, the expression that `if` watches will refer to the scope created by each iteration of `ng-repeat`.

In this directive, transclusion allowed us to get hold of the contents of the directive's element, bound to the correct scope, and conditionally insert it into the DOM.

Next we are going to change tack and look at providing controllers specifically for directives.

Understanding directive controllers

A controller in AngularJS is an object attached to a DOM element that initializes and adds behaviour to the scope at that element.

 We have already seen many application controllers, instantiated by the `ng-controller` directive. These controllers should not interact directly with the DOM but should deal only with the current scope.

A directive controller is a special form of controller that is defined by a directive and instantiated each time that directive appears on a DOM element. Its role is to initialize and provide behavior for the directive rather than a scope.

You define a directive controller using the `controller` property on the directive definition object. The `controller` property can be a string containing the name of a controller already defined on a module:

```
myModule.directive('myDirective', function() {
  return {
    controller: 'MyDirectiveController'
  };
});
myModule.controller('MyDirectiveController', function($scope) {
  ...
});
```

Or it can be a constructor function that will be used to instantiate the controller:

```
myModule.directive('myDirective', function() {
  return {
    controller: function($scope, ...) { ... }
  };
});
```

> If the controller is defined on a module then it is easy to test it independently of the directive. But this also means that the controller is exposed to the whole application, via the injector, so you must be careful that its name does not conflict with controllers in other modules of the application.
>
> Defining the module inline, as an anonymous function, makes it more difficult to test it separately from the directive but allows us to keep it private to the directive.

Injecting special dependencies into directive controllers

Just like any controller, directive controllers are injected with dependencies by AngularJS. All controllers are injected with $scope and you can specify other services to be injected, such as $timeout or $rootScope. On top of these, directive controllers can also be injected with the following three special services:

- $element: This is a reference to the directive's DOM element. This will be wrapped in jQLite/jQuery.

- $attrs: This is a normalized list of the attributes that appear on the directive's DOM element.

- $transclude: This is a **transclusion** function that is already bound to the correct scope. This function is described in the **transclusion** functions.

Creating a controller-based pagination directive

There is a lot of overlap in functionality between directive controllers and link functions. It is often possible to use a controller instead of a link function. Here is the pagination directive from *Chapter 9, Building Advanced Directives*, but this time using a directive controller instead of a link function:

```
myModule.directive('pagination', function() {
  return {
    restrict: 'E',
    scope: { numPages: '=', currentPage: '=', onSelectPage: '&' },
    templateUrl: 'template/pagination.html',
    replace: true,
    controller: ['$scope, '$element', '$attrs',
                  function($scope, $element, $attrs) {
      $scope.$watch('numPages', function(value) {
        $scope.pages = [];
        for(var i=1;i<=value;i++) {
          $scope.pages.push(i);
        }
        if ( $scope.currentPage > value ) {
          $scope.selectPage(value);
        }
      });
      $scope.noPrevious = function() {
        return $scope.currentPage === 1;
      };
      ...
    }]
    ...
  });
```

In this simple case, the only difference between this version and the one that used a link function is that, while the link function is passed `scope`, `element`, `attrs`, and `controller` parameters, the directive controller must use the dependency injection annotations to be provided with the `$scope`, `$element`, and `$attrs` services.

Understanding the difference between directive controllers and link functions

When choosing between using link functions or directive controllers it is helpful to be aware of a few differences.

Injecting dependencies

First, as we saw previously, directive controllers must use dependency injection annotations to specify what services it needs, for example, $scope, $element, and $attrs. A link function is always passed the same four parameters: scope, element, attrs, and controller, regardless of the names of these parameters in the function definition.

The compilation process

Directive controllers and link functions are called at different times during the compilation process. Given a set of directives on DOM elements with this structure:

The directive controllers and link functions are invoked in this order:

- parent (controller)
- parent (pre-link)
    - child 1 (controller)
    - child 1 (pre-link)

    - child 1 a (controller)
    - child 1 a (pre-link)
    - child 1 a (post-link)
    - child 1 b (controller)
    - child 1 b (pre-link)
    - child 1 b (post-link)
    - child 1 (post-link)

- parent (post-link)

If an element contains multiple directives then for that element:

- A scope is created, if necessary
- Each directive's directive controller is instantiated
- Each directive's pre-link function is called
- Any child elements are linked
- Each directive's post-link function is called

This means that when a directive controller is instantiated the directive's element and its children have not yet been fully linked. But when the link functions (pre or post) are called, all the directive controllers for that element have already been instantiated. This is why directive controllers can be passed to link functions.

> The post-link function is called after the compiler has completely finished compiling and linking the current element and all its child elements. This means that any changes to the DOM at this stage will not be noticed by the AngularJS compiler.
>
> This is useful when you want to wire up third party libraries to elements, such as a JQuery plug-in, which may modify the DOM in a way that would confuse the AngularJS compiler.

Accessing other controllers

Link functions receive a fourth parameter that contains any directive controllers that have been `required` by the directive. We saw how this enabled us to access `ngModelController` in *Chapter 9, Building Advanced Directives*.

```
myModule.directive('validateEquals', function() {
  return {
    require: 'ngModel',
    link: function(scope, elm, attrs, ngModelCtrl) {
      ...
    };
});
```

Here the `validateEquals` directive is requiring the `ngModel` directive controller, which is then passed to the link function as `ngModelCtrl`.

In contrast, a directive controller cannot have other directive controllers injected into it.

Accessing the transclusion function

As described in the section on **transclusion** functions, directive controllers can be injected with a $transclusion function, which is already bound to the correct scope.

Link functions can only access a **transclusion** function via the closure of a compile function, and this function is not pre-bound to a scope.

Creating an accordion directive suite

Directive controllers attach behavior to a directive's element, which can then be required by other directives. This lets us build suites of cooperating directives that can communicate and work together.

In this section we will look at how to implement an accordion widget. An accordion widget is a list of collapsible groups of content, with clickable headers. Clicking on the header of a group expands it and causes the other groups to collapse.

The HTML when using the accordion looks like this:

```
<accordion>
  <accordion-group heading="Heading 1">
    Group 1 <strong>Body</strong>
  </accordion-group>
  <accordion-group heading="Heading 2">
    Group 2 <strong>Body</strong>
  </accordion-group>
</accordion>
```

Here we have two new element directives: accordion, which is a container for the groups, and accordion-group, which specifies the content of each group.

Using a directive controller in accordion

To enable the groups to communicate with each other the `accordion` directive defines a directive controller, `AccordionController`. Each `accordion-group` directive will `require` this controller.

The `AccordionController` directive controller will expose two methods, `addGroup` and `closeOthers`, which the `accordion-group` directives will use to register themselves as part of the accordion and to tell the other `accordion-groups` to close when they are opened.

Unit testing a directive controller is very similar to testing an application controller. See *Chapter 2, Building and Testing, An Example App.* Here is a test for the `closeOthers` method:

```
describe('closeOthers', function() {
  var group1, group2, group3;
  beforeEach(function() {
    ctrl.addGroup(group1 = $scope.$new());
    ctrl.addGroup(group2 = $scope.$new());
    ctrl.addGroup(group3 = $scope.$new());
    group1.isOpen = group2.isOpen = group3.isOpen = true;
  });
  it('closes all groups other than the one passed', function() {
    ctrl.closeOthers(group2);
    expect(group1.isOpen).toBe(false);
    expect(group2.isOpen).toBe(true);
    expect(group3.isOpen).toBe(false);
  });
});
```

We add three groups, which are all set to `isOpen=true`. After calling `closeOthers` with `group2` we test that `group1` and `group2` have `isOpen` set to `false`.

Here is the implementation of the `AccordionController`:

```
myModule.controller('AccordionController', ['$scope', '$attrs',
function ($scope, $attrs) {
  this.groups = [];
  this.closeOthers = function(openGroup) {
    angular.forEach(this.groups, function (group) {
      if ( group !== openGroup ) {
        group.isOpen = false;
      }
    });
  }
```

```
  };
  this.addGroup = function(groupScope) {
    var that = this;
    this.groups.push(groupScope);
    groupScope.$on('$destroy', function (event) {
      that.removeGroup(groupScope);
    });
  };
  this.removeGroup = function(group) {
    var index = this.groups.indexOf(group);
    if ( index !== -1 ) {
      this.groups.splice(this.groups.indexOf(group), 1);
    }
  };
}]);
```

Notice that we automatically remove the group from the list when its scope
is destroyed. This is important because our list of groups may be generated
dynamically at run-time using an ng-repeat directive, which could remove
elements and so group scopes from the application. If we still held references
to the these group scopes then they could not be garbage collected.

Implementing the accordion directive

The main accordion directive just specifies AccordionController as its directive
controller and adds an accordion CSS class to its element in its link function:

```
myModule.directive('accordion', function () {
  return {
    restrict:'E',
    controller:'AccordionController',
    link: function(scope, element, attrs) {
      element.addClass('accordion');
    }
  };
})
```

Implementing the accordion-group directive

Each collapsible group will be defined by an accordionGroup directive. Each group
consists of a link and a body. Here is the template for this directive:

```
<div class="accordion-group">
  <div class="accordion-heading" >
    <a class="accordion-toggle"
```

```
            ng-click="isOpen=!isOpen">{{heading}}</a>
    </div>
    <div class="accordion-body" ng-show="isOpen">
      <div class="accordion-inner" ng-transclude></div>
    </div>
</div>
```

We transclude the original child elements of the directive into the body of the template. The template references `isOpen` and `heading`, on the current scope. We want to have complete control over these values so that the `accordion-group` directive will have an isolated scope.

In the tests, we set up an `accordion` and some `accordion-group` directives and then check that they open and close correctly. Here is an example of the unit tests:

```
describe('accordion-group', function () {
  var scope, element, groups;
  beforeEach(inject(function($rootScope, $compile) {
    scope = $rootScope;
    var tpl =
"<accordion>" +
"<accordion-group heading='title 1'>Content 1</accordion-group>" +
"<accordion-group heading='title 2'>Content 2</accordion-group>" +
"</accordion>";
    $compile(tpl)(scope);
    scope.$digest();
    groups = element.find('.accordion-group');
  });
  ...
  it('should change selected element on click', function () {
    groups.eq(0).find('a').click();
    expect(findGroupBody(0).scope().isOpen).toBe(true);
    groups.eq(1).find('a').click();
    expect(groups.eq(0).scope().isOpen).toBe(false);
    expect(groups.eq(1).scope().isOpen).toBe(true);
  });
  ...
});
```

We trigger a click event on groups and check that `isOpen` is `false` on the scope of the other groups.

The implementation of the directive is fairly straightforward:

```
myModule.directive('accordionGroup', function() {
  return {
    require:'^accordion',
```

```
        restrict:'E',
        transclude:true,
        replace: true,
        templateUrl:'template/accordion/accordion-group.html',
        scope:{ heading:'@' },
        link: function(scope, element, attrs, accordionCtrl) {
          accordionCtrl.addGroup(scope);
          scope.isOpen = false;
          scope.$watch('isOpen', function(value) {
            if ( value ) {
              accordionCtrl.closeOthers(scope);
            }
          });
        }
      };
    });
```

You can see that this directive requires the directive controller from the `accordion` directive to appear on an ancestor of this directive's DOM element. The required directive controller appears as the fourth parameter, `accordionCtrl`, on the link function. The `accordion-group` directive registers itself using the `addGroup()` function and calls `closeOthers()` whenever this group is opened.

Taking control of the compilation process

There are some situations where we need to have more control over how AngularJS compiles and links an element and its children. Perhaps we wish to load the directive's template dynamically or we want more control over the transclusion of elements into a directive's template. In these cases we can terminate the compilation process then modify and compile the directive's element and children manually.

Creating a field directive

When writing applications that use forms, it quickly becomes apparent that there is a lot of duplication and redundancy in the amount of boilerplate HTML requires for each field on the form.

For instance, and for every field there will be an `input` element and a `label` element surrounded by various `div` and `span` elements. On these elements, we need to provide a number of attributes, `ng-model`, `name`, `id`, and `for`, which are usually very similar or even identical, and various CSS classes. We also need to display validation messages for when the input values are invalid.

We end up with this kind of HTML repeated all over our forms:

```
<div class="control-group" ng-class="{'error' : form.email.$invalid
&& form.email.$dirty, 'success' : form.email.$valid && form.
email.$dirty}">
  <label for="email">E-mail</label>
  <div class="controls">
    <input type="email" id="email" name="email" ng-model="user.email"
required>
    <span ng-show="form.email.$error['required'] && form.email.dirty"
class="help-inline">Email is required</span>
    <span ng-show=" form.email.$error['email'] && form.email.dirty"
class="help-inline">Please enter a valid email</span>
  </div>
</div>
```

We can eliminate much of this duplication by creating a `field` directive. The directive will insert a suitable template containing a labeled input control. Here is an example of using the `field` directive:

```
<field type="email" ng-model="user.email" required >
  <label>Email</label>
  <validator key="required">$fieldLabel is required</validator>
  <validator key="email">Please enter a valid email</validator>
</field>
```

Now we simply provide `ng-model`, `type`, and validation directives for the input, as attributes on the `field`. Then we provide the `label` and validation messages as child elements of the `field` element. Note, also that we can use a `$fieldLabel` property inside the validation messages. This property will be added to the scope of the validation messages by the `field` directive.

The `field` directive has a number of requirements that are hard to achieve with the built-in directive API.

- Rather than specifying a single template for the whole directive, we need to insert a different template depending upon the type of field that is being displayed. We cannot use the `template` (or `templateUrl`) property on the directive definition object.

- We need to generate and apply unique `name` and `id` attributes for the `input` and wire up the `label` elements `for` attribute, before the `ng-model` directive is compiled.

- We want to extract the validation messages for the field from the child `validator` elements to be used in the template when there is an error with the field's value.

The directive definition object for this `field` directive looks like this:

```
restrict:'E',
priority: 100,
terminal: true,
compile: function(element, attrs) {
  ...
  var validationMgs = getValidationValidationMessages(element);
  var labelContent = getLabelContent(element);

  element.html('');

  return function postLink(scope, element, attrs) {
    var template = attrs.template || 'input.html';
    loadTemplate(template).then(function(templateElement) {
      ...
    });
  };
}
```

We terminate compilation at this directive, giving it a `priority` of `100`, to ensure that it runs before the `ng-model` directive that will be on the same element. In the compile function we extract the validation messages, `getValidationMessageMap`, and label information, `getLabelContent`, from the terminated element. Once this has been retrieved, we empty out the contents of the element so that we have a clean element in which to load the template. The `compile` function returns a `postLink` function, which will load a suitable template.

Using the terminal property in directives

If a directive has `terminal: true`, the compiler will stop and not process the child elements of this directive's element or any other directives on this directive's element that have a lower priority than this directive.

> Even if you terminate a directive, the directive controller, compile function, and link function for that directive are still executed.

Once we have terminated the compilation we can modify the directive's element and its children, but then we are responsible for setting up any new scopes, correctly transcluding content and also for further compiling of child elements that may contain directives.

Most of the time AngularJS takes care of interpolating strings into expressions, that is, when using {{}} brackets in templates. But in this directive we need to programmatically interpolate a string. This is done with the $interpolate service.

Using the $interpolate service

The getLabelContent simply copies across the HTML content from the label in the directive to the label in the template, where it will be compiled along with the template:

```
function getLabelContent(element) {
  var label = element.find('label');
  return label[0] && label.html();
}
```

But for validation messages, we are going to use ng-repeat to display strings only for validations that are currently failing. So we will need to store the validation messages on the template's scope, as $validationMessages. These validation messages may contain interpolated strings so we will interpolate them during compilation:

```
function getValidationMessageMap(element) {
  var messageFns = {};
  var validators = element.find('validator');
  angular.forEach(validators, function(validator) {
    validator = angular.element(validator);
    messageFns[validator.attr('key')] =
      $interpolate(validator.text());
  });
  return messageFns;
}
```

For each of the <validator> elements we use the $interpolate service create an interpolation function from the text of the element and add that function into a map based on the value of the validator element's key attribute. This map will be added to the template's scope as $validationMessages.

The $interpolate service is used throughout AngularJS to evaluate strings that contain {{}} curly braces. If we pass such a string to the service, it returns an interpolation function that takes a scope and returns the interpolated string:

```
var getFullName = $interpolate('{{first}}{{last}}');
var scope = { first:'Pete',last:'Bacon Darwin' };
var fullName = getFullName(scope);
```

Here, we create a getFullName interpolation function, from the '{{first}} {{last}}' string and then call it with a scope object, resulting in fullName being assigned as 'Pete Bacon Darwin'.

Binding to validation messages

To display the validation error messages in our field templates, we will have something like this:

```
<span class="help-inline" ng-repeat="error in $fieldErrors">
  {{$validationMessages[error](this)}}
</span>
```

We are repeating over all the validation error keys in $fieldErrors and binding to the result of calling the validation interpolation function for the given error key.

 We have to provide a scope to the interpolation function. We can do this, in a template, by passing this, which refers to the current scope. Failing to do this can lead to an unexpected and a difficult time in debugging errors.

The $fieldErrors property contains a list of the current invalid validation error keys. It is updated by a watch created in the success handler for loadTemplate().

Loading templates dynamically

The loadTemplate function loads in the specified template and converts it to a jqLite/jQuery wrapped DOM element:

```
function loadTemplate(template) {
  return $http.get(template, {cache:$templateCache})
    .then(function(response) {
      return angular.element(response.data);
    }, function(response) {
      throw new Error('Template not found: ' + template);
    });
}
```

The function is asynchronous and so it returns a promise to the wrapped element. Just as directives using templateUrl and ng-include do, we are using the $templateCache to cache the templates when we load them.

Setting up the field template

In the `field` directive's link function, we call `loadTemplate` with the value of the template attribute on the directive's element (or `'input.html'` if none is specified).

```
loadTemplate(template).then(function(templateElement) {
```

All the work of the directive happens once the promise is resolved.

```
var childScope = scope.$new();
childScope.$validationMessages = angular.copy(validationMsgs);
childScope.$fieldId = attrs.ngModel.replace('.', '_').toLowerCase()
+ '_' + childScope.$id;
childScope.$fieldLabel = labelContent;

childScope.$watch('$field.$dirty && $field.$error',
function(errorList) {
  childScope.$fieldErrors = [];
  angular.forEach(errorList, function(invalid, key) {
    if ( invalid ) {
      childScope.$fieldErrors.push(key);
    }
  });
}, true);
```

First we create a new child scope and attach useful properties, such as `$validationMessages`, `$fieldId`, `$fieldLabel`, and `$fieldErrors`:

```
var inputElement = findInputElement(templateElement);
angular.forEach(attrs.$attr, function (original, normalized) {
  var value = element.attr(original);
  inputElement.attr(original, value);
});
inputElement.attr('name', childScope.$fieldId);
inputElement.attr('id', childScope.$fieldId);
```

We copy over all the attributes from the field directive's element to the template's input element and add on computed values for the `name` and `id` attributes:

```
var labelElement = templateElement.find('label');
labelElement.attr('for', childScope.$fieldId);
labelElement.html(labelContent);
```

We copy in the labelContent and apply the for attribute to the label element:

```
    element.append(templateElement);
    $compile(templateElement)(childScope);
    childScope.$field = inputElement.controller('ngModel');
});
```

We append the templateElement to the original field element, then use the $compile service to compile and link it to our new childScope. Once the element is linked, the ngModelController is available for us to put into the $field property for the template to use.

Summary

In this chapter we have looked at some of the more advanced aspects of developing directives. We saw in our alert directive, how transclusion can be used with ng-transclude when creating widgets. The accordion directive suite neatly demonstrated how directive controllers can be used to coordinate communication between directives. We even took complete control of the compile process by terminating the current compilation in the field directive and the using the $compile service to manually compile the element's contents

In the next chapter we will be looking at what we can do to ensure that our application performance is fast and responsive.

10
Building AngularJS Web Applications for an International Audience

We live in a global village where anyone equipped with an internet connection can access your web application. You might start your project by providing only a single language version, but as your website becomes popular on the international scene you might want to offer content in languages, to which your users are comfortable with. Or you might be obliged to provide several localized versions due to customers' demand or law-enforced constraints. Whatever the reasons internalization problems are a fact of life for many web developers.

There are several aspects of **internationalization (i18n)** and **localization (i10n)**, but this chapter focuses on problems and solutions specific to AngularJS web applications. In particular, you will see how to:

- Configure date, number and currency formats as well as choose other locale-specific settings based on user's preferences

- Handle content translated into multiple languages (both embedded in AngularJS templates as well as one manipulated in JavaScript code)

The last part of this chapter presents some patterns, tips and tricks that you will find useful while building AngularJS applications for an international audience.

Using locale-specific symbols and settings

AngularJS deliverables contain a set of modules with the locale-specific settings. This section illustrates steps required to configure the locale-specific modules as well as it describes settings and constants available for each locale.

Configuring locale-specific modules

If you explore AngularJS deliverables carefully you will notice that each distribution contains a folder named i18n. Inside this folder there are files named according to the following pattern: `angular-locale_[locale name].js` where [locale name] corresponds to a locale name (expressed as a combination of a language code and a country code). For example, a file with local settings for the French language with Canadian specificities is named as `angular-locale_fr-ca.js`.

 AngularJS is distributed with over 280 files containing locale specific settings and constants for different languages and countries. Those files, while distributed with AngularJS, are not maintained as part of the project. Instead locale-specific settings are extracted from the closure library (`http://closure-library.googlecode.com/`) on a regular basis.

By default AngularJS will use i18n settings specific to the English locale in the United States (en-us). If you are writing an application for another locale (or want to choose different locale for different users) you need to include appropriate file and declare a dependency on the locale module. For example, to configure a web application to use the French-Canadian (fr-ca) locale you would organize scripts on your page as follows:

```
<!doctype html>
<html ng-app="locale">
<head>
<meta charset="utf-8">
<script src="lib/angular/angular.js"></script>
<script src="lib/angular/angular-locale_fr-ca.js"></script>
<script src="locale.js"></script>
</head>
<body ng-controller="LocaleCtrl">
...
</body>
```

Where the `locale.js` file should contain a module definition with a dependency on the `ngLocale` module:

```
angular.module('locale', ['ngLocale'])
```

Making use of available locale settings

Each and every localization file distributed with AngularJS contains definition of a module named `ngLocale`. The `ngLocale` module exposes only one service: `$locale`. The only documented, public API of the `$locale` service consists of the `$locale.id` variable, which can be used to retrieve a currently used locale.

In reality the `$locale` service exposes much more constants for a given locale. Among the exposed constants we can find ones holding date and time formats (`$locale. DATETIME_FORMATS`), as well as the number formats (`$locale.NUMBER_FORMATS`). The mentioned constants are JavaScript objects containing settings one might need to format dates, time, number and currencies. For example, we can find all the month names by inspecting `$locale.DATETIME_FORMATS.MONTH`.

Locale-specific settings and AngularJS filters

Having access to all the localization settings might come handy when writing custom directives and filters, but AngularJS already makes good use of those settings in the build in filters.

Date filter

The `date` filter converts dates according to a specified format. A target format can be specified either in a precise, locale-independent manner (For example, `mm/dd/yy hh:mm a`) or in a locale-dependent one. In the second case, instead of precisely enumerating each character of a desired format, we can use predefined, named ones. AngularJS understands the following names for predefined formats: `medium`, `short`, `fullDate`, `longDate`, `mediumDate`, `shortDate`, `mediumTime`, `shortTime`.

As an example, let's consider the `{{now | date:'fullDate'}}` expression (where now is initialized to `new Date()`), that will produce different results depending on a locale:

- Tuesday, April 9, 2013 in `en-us`(English locale in United States)
- mardi 9 avril 2013 in `fr-fr` (French locale in France)

Currency filter

The `currency` filter can format a number as currencies. By default it will use a currency symbol from the current locale. For example, the `{{100 | currency}}` expression will yield different results depending on the configured locale:

- $100.00 in `en-us` (English locale in United States)
- 100.00 € in `fr-fr` (French locale in France)

The default behavior of the currency filter might be confusing for the users of your web application, as usually we want to display numbers as a price in a specific currency. It would be rather bizarre, if we could reduce a price of an item from 100.00 € (euros) to 100.00 $ just be changing locale settings.

Unless you are using just one, fixed locale we recommend to always specify a currency symbol when using the currency filter:

```
{{100 | currency:'€'}}
```

There is a further complication though, while the currency filter allows us to specify a currency symbol, it won't let us specify a position of this symbol or a decimal separator (and will use defaults from the current locale). This means that the previous example would render as € 100.00, something that is unusual for the Euro currency symbol.

If the currency filter does the job for your use cases that's great; by all means use it. But there are times where it falls short, and we should be prepared to roll out a custom filter.

Number filter

The number filter behaves as expected, and will format numbers by applying both thousand and decimal separators according to local settings. For example:

```
{{1000.5 | number}}
```

It will render as:

- 1,000.5 in `en-us` (English locale in United States)
- 1000,5 € in `fr-fr` (French locale in France)

Handling translations

Being able to format dates and numbers according to local settings is only small part of the whole localization story. Usually when people think about localization it is the translation effort that comes to the mind first.

In an AngularJS application there are at least two places where we can find words to be translated to a target language: templates (partials) and strings used in JavaScript code.

For the rest of this chapter let's assume that we do have translated strings already available in a convenient format, for example JSON. Such JSON could be an object where keys correspond to logical names of fragments to be translated (For example, `crud.user.remove.success`), and the values are actual translated strings for a given locale. For example, JSON containing translations for the `en-us` locale could look like follows:

```
{
'crud.user.remove.success': 'A user was removed successfully.',
'crud.user.remove.error': 'There was a problem removing a user.'
  . . .
}
```

While the same JSON structure for the `pl-pl` locale would have the following content:

```
{
   'crud.user.remove.success': 'Użytkownik został usunięty.',
   'crud.user.remove.error': 'Wystąpił błąd podczas usuwania
     użytkownika.'
 . . .
}
```

Handling translated strings used in AngularJS templates

Typically, a vast majority of strings to be translated are located in the AngularJS partials. Let's considering the simple "Hello, World!" example:

```
<span>Hello, {{name}}!</span>
```

To make this partial work in different languages we need to find a way of substituting the `Hello` string with its translated value for a currently selected language. There are number of techniques that we can use here, each of them having their pros and cons as discussed in the following section.

Using filters

Assuming that we've got JSON structure with translated strings like:

```
{
  'greetings.hello': 'Hello'
  . . .
}
```

We could imagine writing a filter (let's call it i18n) to be used as follows:

```
<span>{{'greetings.hello' | i18n}}, {{name}}!</span>
```

Writing a basic version of the i18n filter wouldn't be difficult, and we could start off by sketching the code as shown in the following code:

```
angular.module('i18nfilter', ['i18nmessages'])
  .filter('i18n', function (i18nmessages) {
    return function (input) {
      if (!angular.isString(input)) {
        return input;
      }
      return i18nmessages[input] || '?'+input+'?';
    };
  });
```

The i18 filter would rely on a set of translated messages (i18nmessages). The messages themselves could be declared as a value is a separate module, for example:

```
angular.module('i18nmessages', [])
  .value('i18nmessages', {
    'greetings.hello': 'Hello'
  });
```

The i18n filter shown here is very simple, and there is plenty of room for extensions and improvements: loading translated strings via $http service with caching, switching locale on the fly and so on. While the presented i18n filter seems to be working well, and we could spend time elaborating it further, if there is performance-related problem with the filter-based approach to translations.

By turning static text "Hello" embedded in HTML into a filtered expression ({{'greetings.hello' | i18n}}) we've introduced one more expression to be evaluated by AngularJS. As we are going to see in *Chapter 11, Writing Robust AngularJS Web Applications* is strongly correlated with a number of expressions that need to be watched and evaluated by the framework. Adding a new watch expression for each individual string is wasteful, and might slow down your application to unacceptable levels.

While the filter-based approach to translation seems to be easy and flexible it has adverse performance implications. The performance penalty incurred might be acceptable for small pages with few strings to be translated. For bigger pages with many translations it might quickly become a bottleneck.

Using directives

To remedy the performance problems related to the filter-based approach we could turn our attention to directives. One could imagine using syntax as follows:

```
<span><i18n key='greetings.hello'></i18n>, {{name}}!</span>
```

By using a directive we could eliminate the need for an additional AngularJS watch expression and as a result address performance issues present in the filter-based approach. But usage of directives brings its own problems.

For a start the syntax is verbose and not very pretty. One could experiments with alternatives (For example, by using attribute directives) but in any case templates are becoming harder to read and modify. There is a more serious problem though: directives can't be used in certain places. Let's consider an input field with a `placeholder` attribute:

```
<input ng-model='name' placeholder='Provide name here'>
```

We can't use directive-based approach to translate the "`Provide name here`" string. There is simply no way of evaluating directives inside an HTML attribute.

As you can see the directive-based approach can't cover all the use cases so we need to continue our quest in search for a solution.

Translating partials during the build-time

The last approach explored in this chapter consists of moving translation efforts to the build system. The idea is to process all the partials and generate a set of language-specific templates to be downloaded by a browser. In this way the templates would appear to AngularJS as static ones and wouldn't require any language-specific processing on the client side.

The exact technology to be used to translate partials during the build time will depend on the build system used. For the Grunt.js based builds we could use Grunt's capability of creating templates. Considering the following partial, named hello.tpl.html:

```
<div>
<h3>Hello, {{name}}!</h3>
<input ng-model='name' placeholder='Provide name here'>
</div>
```

We could turn it into Grunt.js template to be processed during the build-time:

```
<div>
<h3><%= greeting.hello %>, {{name}}!</h3>
<input ng-model='name' placeholder='<%= input.name %>'>
</div>
```

Then, based on a list of supported locales and translation files, the Grunt.js build would produce translated partials, saving them in folders corresponding to a locale name. For example:

```
/en-us/hello.tpl.html
/fr-ca/hello.tpl.html
/pl-pl/hello.tpl.html
```

Setting up a build-time translation system might be a bit cumbersome, but usually it is a one-time effort done at the very beginning of a project. The benefit is that we avoid any kind of performance problems linked to localization, and can translate strings at any place of a partial.

Handling translated strings used in the JavaScript code

While most of the strings to be translated are located in AngularJS templates, there are times when we need to handle text in a JavaScript code. We might need to display a localized error message, an alert and so on. Whatever the reason may be, we need to be prepared for handling translated strings in the JavaScript code.

AngularJS doesn't provide any facility that would help us here, so we need to roll up our sleeves, and write a simple service that will serve us as a handy translation tool. Before writing any code let's consider an example usage scenario. Let's say we would like to prepare an alert message to be displayed when an item is successfully deleted from a persistent store, doesn't exist in a persistent store, and so on.

If we need to support multiple languages we can't simply hard-code a message's text in the JavaScript code. Instead we need to be able to retrieve a localized and parameterized message based on its key. For example, calling:

```
localizedMessages.get('crud.user.remove.success', {id: 1234})
```

It should return a message that could look like "A user with id '1234' was removed successfully." in en-us and "Użytkownik z identyfikatorem '1234' został usunięty." in pl-pl (Polish in Poland).

Writing a service that would look up a message based on its key and the current locale is of no use. The only difficulty that we are facing here is delays in handling parameters inside localized strings. Fortunately, we can lean on AngularJS here, and re-use the $$interpolate service; the same one that AngularJS uses to handle interpolation directives in its templates. This would allow us to specify localized messages as:

```
"A user with id '{{id}}' was removed successfully."
```

The sample SCRUM application has a complete implementation of the localization service based on the idea just described. A sketch of this implementation is presented here as well as it is very simple:

```javascript
angular.module('localizedMessages', [])
.factory('localizedMessages', function ($interpolate, i18nmessages) {

  var handleNotFound = function (msg, msgKey) {
    return msg || '?' + msgKey + '?';
  };

  return {
    get : function (msgKey, interpolateParams) {
      var msg =  i18nmessages[msgKey];
      if (msg) {
        return $interpolate(msg)(interpolateParams);
      } else {
        return handleNotFound(msg, msgKey);
      }
    }
  };
});
```

Patterns, tips, and tricks

The last part of this chapter is devoted to internationalization and localization related patterns. We will start by looking into ways of initializing an application and switching locale. Then we will move to patterns applicable inside a running application: overriding default locale-specific formats and handling users input in accordance with a selected locale.

Initializing applications for a given locale

As we've learned in the beginning of this chapter, AngularJS distribution contains files with locale specific settings. There is one file for each locale and each file contains definition of the ngLocale module. If we want to take advantage of locale-specific settings we need to declare a dependency on the ngLocale module in our application. As a remainder here is how one would initialize AngularJS application for a fixed locale:

```
<head>
<meta charset="utf-8">
<script src="lib/angular/angular.js"></script>
<script src="lib/angular/angular-locale_fr-ca.js"></script>
<script src="locale.js"></script>
</head>
```

This works fine if our application is supposed to work with only one fixed locale. In reality, though, we often want to initialize locale based on user's preferences. There is variety of sources we could consider for user preferences:

- Browser's settings
- HTTP request headers (For example, Accept-Language)
- URL or request parameters
- Server-side settings (user profile, geo-localization, and so on.)

Looking at the list provided earlier we can clearly see that we've got more means of determining a desired locale on the server side. This is why we would advocate server side processing for the initial page of an application.

To demonstrate locale selection process in practice, let's have a look into a strategy implemented in the sample SCRUM application. The approach taken consists of determining the target locale based on:

- Locale specified as part of a URL that trigger's application's bootstrap
- The Accept-Language request header
- A set of supported locales

Considering this strategy a user might target our sample application with following types of URLs:

- `http://host.com/fr-ca/admin/users/list`: Here a user is specifying a desired locale (`fr-ca`). We should cross check the requested locale with a list of supported ones and redirect a user to a different URL, if we don't happen to support the wished one. For example, we could redirect users to a URL with a default locale (say en-us), if the `fr-ca` is not supported: `http://host.com/en-us/admin/users/list`

- `http://host.com/admin/users/list`: Here a desired locale was not specified. We can try to guess a locale for a user based on the `Accept-Language` HTTP request header, and redirect a user to a URL with an identified locale. Obviously, we should cross check a locale extracted from request headers with a set of supported locales.

 In practice you are likely to have a more sophisticated algorithm combining settings from different sources with a robust fallback strategy and defaults. The exact strategy to determine user's locale based on his request will largely depend on your application requirements.

As soon a locale for a given user is identified we can send to a browser a page that bootstraps the whole application. The initial page (`index.html` or similar) needs to be generated dynamically on the server side. In the sample SCRUM application the `index.html` file is a template shown as follows:

```
<head>
<meta charset="utf-8">
<script src="lib/angular/angular.js"></script>
<script src="lib/angular/angular-locale_<%= locale %>.js"></script>
. . .
</head>
```

Here the target `locale` is identified according to the described algorithm and a template is processed on the server-side before being served to a browser.

Consequences of including locales as part of URLs

As soon as we add a new path element to the application's URLs we need to take care of two new issues: reconfiguring routes and downloading partials.

Normally a new path element should be handled as a part of routes definition. Of course we could go back to our application and re-define all the routes, for example: `/admin/users/list` would become `/:locale/admin/users/list`.

While this approach would work it is tedious and error-prone to prefix all the routes with `/:locale`. What we can do instead is to define a base tag in a landing's page HTML and point it to a locale folder:

```
<head>
<meta charset="utf-8">
<script src="/lib/angular/angular.js"></script>
<script src="/lib/angular/angular-locale_<%= locale %>.js"></script>
<base href="/<%= locale %>/">
    . . .
</head>
```

The AngularJS `$location` service (and thus its routing system) can recognize the `<base>` tag, and handle all the routes as relative to the path specified in the href attribute.

Using a base tag that points to a locale folder has one more advantage as we can use relative URLs to download AngularJS templates (partials). If we decide to adopt build-time approach to localization we would generate translated partials in folders corresponding to a given locale. A properly configured `<base>` tag would assure that AngularJS downloads partials for a configured locale.

> Using the `<base>` tag on a page means that we need to use non-relative URLs for all static content that is not locale-dependent.

In the real-life deployment scenarios partials most probably will be pre-fetched at the beginning, instead of being downloaded on the fly so defining the `<base>` tag has less practical implications from the partials point of view. *Chapter 12, Packaging and Deploying AngularJS Web Applications* covers different deployment scenarios in great details.

Switching locales

In the current version of AngularJS all the dependent modules must be listed as dependencies of the main application module before an application is bootstrapped. The `ngLocale` module isn't an exception here, which means that it needs to be loaded into a browser, and declared as a dependency before AngularJS application can be started. As a consequence we need to select a module with local settings before an application starts. Moreover the selected module can't be swapped for another one without re-initializing AngularJS application.

> In the current version of AngularJS a locale needs to be selected upfront, before an application is initialized. The selected locale can't be switched on the fly, and requires that an application is re-initialized with another `ngLocale` module.

Given how the module system operates in the current version of AngularJS our best option for switching locale is to re-initialize an application by redirecting users to a URL with a new locale specified. A redirect means that the whole state in a browser will be lost. Fortunately, the AngularJS deep linking feature will take a user to the same place in an application after locale change.

To switch a locale by redirecting users we will have to prepare a string for a new URL first. We can do this easily using the API exposed by the `$location` service. For example, given the current URL: `http://host.com/en-us/admin/users/list` and a desired target URL `http://host.com/fr-ca/admin/users/list`.

We could write the following `switchLocaleUrl` function:

```
$scope.switchLocaleUrl = function(targetLocale) {
    return '/'+targetLocale+'/'+$location.url();
};
```

The `switchLocale` function just shown would calculate a URL taking users to a route equal to the current one, but in a specified `targetLocale`. This function could be used in the standard `<a>` tag to take users to a site with a new locale selected:

```
<a ng-href="switchLocaleUrl('fr-ca')" target="_self">Français</a>
```

Custom formatting for dates, numbers, and currencies

Some of the AngularJS filters can deal with locale-specific content by default. For example, as seen at the beginning of this chapter, the `date` filter can be supplied with a locale-dependent, named format, for example, `{{now | date:'fullDate'}}`. The exact mapping from the `fullDate` string to the actual format is defined in a file with locale-specific settings under the `$locale.DATETIME_FORMATS.fullDate` key. As an example, for the `fr-ca` locale the `fullDate` format is equivalent to: `EEEE d MMMM y`.

The default formats are usually exactly the ones we would expect for a given language and a country, but we might want to slightly adjust certain formats for some locales. This can be easily achieved by creating a decorator over a filter.

In AngularJS we can create a decorator over any existing service or filter. Such a decorator can wrap an existing service and "decorate" (extend) it with an additional functionality. AngularJS decorators are great example of the decorator pattern (http://en.wikipedia. org/wiki/Decorator_pattern).

For example, to change the `fullDate` format for the `fr-ca` locale we could write a wrapper around the `date` filter as follows:

```
angular.module('filterCustomization', [])
  .config(function ($provide) {
varcustomFormats = {
      'fr-ca': {
        'fullDate': 'y'
      }
    };

    $provide.decorator('dateFilter', function ($delegate, $locale) {
      return function (input, format) {
        return $delegate(input, customFormats[$locale.id][format]
          || format);
      };
    });
  })
```

Here we are taking an advantage of decorators in the AngularJS dependency injection system. By defining a new decorator (`$provide.decorator()`) we can wrap an existing service inside our custom one yet still keep access to the original service (`$delegate`). Apart from the new `$provide` service the rest of the code should be easy to follow. We are simply consulting a hash of overridden formats for a given locale (`customFormats`), and if an overridden format was specified we are using it to call the original data filter. Otherwise we are using a format supplied in a call the original `date` filter.

Our decorator replaces the `date` filter, since we've chosen to register it under the same name as the original one. The advantage of this approach is that we don't need to touch application's code to use the customized version of the filter.

We could elaborate this decorator further to choose a format in a situation when none was specified.

The other, brute force solution is to simply edit a file with locale-specific settings for a given locale. The drawback of this approach is that we need to remember to re-edit files, when upgrading from one version of AngularJS to another.

Summary

This chapter touched upon internationalization and localization problems specific to AngularJS applications. We saw that AngularJS provides the ngLocale module with locale-specific settings for dates, currencies and number formats. Those settings are derived from the closure library and influence behavior of some of the build-in filters.

The biggest part of localization efforts is often devoted to translating existing partials and messages embedded in JavaScript code. We've explored various approaches for making AngularJS partials work with translated data: filters, directives and the build-time solution. While the filter-based approach sounds like a good idea it comes with the performance-penalty that might be unacceptable for many projects. Directive-based approach solves the performance problem, but is not flexible enough for real life applications. This is why we've explored a recommended approach to translating strings in AngularJS partials build-time solution where translation is done before templates reach a browser.

We've concluded this chapter with number of i18n/i10n related patterns. We've started off by looking into options for initializing and switching locale. The current version of AngularJS requires that a locale is selected before the application's startup, and this is why we've focused on determining and initializing locale on the server-side, dynamically generating application's landing page. Switching locale on the fly is not an option with the version of AngularJS published as of time of this writing so our best call is to redirect users to a landing page to switch locales.

The other patterns described in this chapter dealt with customizing date, number and currencies format for data display. While AngularJS provides sensible defaults for locale-specific filters there are times where you might tweak things a little bit. A decorator around existing filters is a good approach to customize data output.

At this point we should have a fully functional, internationalized AngularJS web application. The next chapter will focus on making this application robust. More specifically, we are going to look into identifying and addressing any potential performance-related issues.

11
Writing Robust AngularJS Web Applications

Web applications' performance is one of the non-functional requirements that we need to juggle with other tasks and functional exigencies. Obviously we can't neglect performance, even if our application looks stunning and has all the required functionality, people might refuse to use it if it doesn't run smoothly.

There are several factors that affect overall performance of a finished web application: utilization of network, size of the DOM tree, number and complexity of CSS rules, JavaScript logic and algorithms, data structures used and many, many others. Not to mention that it all depends on a browser used and users' perception! Some of the performance-related concerns are universal and need to be addressed regardless of a technology used. Some others are AngularJS-specific and this chapter focuses on AngularJS particularities.

To understand AngularJS performance characteristics, we need to better understand its internals. This is why this chapter starts with a deep dive into AngularJS core machinery. What follows is an overview of performance-sensitive patterns alongside discussion of available options and trade-offs.

After reading this chapter you will:

- Learn how AngularJS rendering engine works under the hood. Getting familiar with AngularJS internals is essential to understand its performance characteristics.

- Understand theoretical performance-limits of AngularJS applications and be able to quickly decide if your particular project fits into set boundaries.

- Be able to identify and address CPU-utilization and memory-consumption bottlenecks in AngularJS applications. You will be well prepared to recognize performance-sensitive patterns before any code is written, as well as use performance-monitoring tools to spot problems in already existing code-base.

- Understand performance implications of using the `ng-repeat` directive with large data sets.

Understanding the inner workings of AngularJS

To understand performance characteristics of AngularJS applications, we need to poke under the hood of the framework. Getting familiar with the AngularJS machinery inner-working will allow us to easily identify situations and code patterns that have a major impact on applications' overall performance.

It is not a string-based template engine

Looking at simple code examples we might get an impression that AngularJS is yet-another client-side template engine. Indeed, just by looking at the following code:

```
Hello, {{name}}!
```

It is impossible to distinguish AngularJS code from a regular template system, say, Mustache (http://mustache.github.io/). The difference only becomes apparent if we add the `ng-model` directive:

```
<input ng-model="name">
Hello, {{name}}!
```

As soon as we do so, the DOM gets updated automatically in response to the user's input, without any further intervention from a developer. The two-way data binding might look like magic at first. Rest assured AngularJS uses only solid algorithms to bring the DOM tree to life! In the subsequent sections we are going to dissect those algorithms by examining how changes from DOM are propagated to the model and how model updates trigger DOM repaints.

Updating models in response to DOM events

AngularJS propagates changes from the DOM tree to the model through DOM event listeners registered by different directives. The code in event-listeners mutate the model by updating variables exposed on a $scope.

We can write a simplified equivalent of the ng-model directive (let's call it simple-model) that would illustrate essential bits involved in updating the model:

```
angular.module('internals', [])
  .directive('simpleModel', function ($parse) {
    return function (scope, element, attrs) {

        var modelGetter = $parse(attrs.simpleModel);
        var modelSetter = modelGetter.assign;

        element.bind('input', function(){
          var value = element.val();
          modelSetter(scope, value);
        });
    };
});
```

The key part of the simple-model directive consists of the input DOM event handler that listens to changes in an input element and updates the model based on the value entered by a user.

To set the actual model value we are using the $parse service. This service can be put in action to both evaluate AngularJS expressions against a scope and set a model's value on a scope. The $parse service, when called with an expression as its argument, will return a getter function. The returned getter function will have the assign property (a setter function) if the supplied AngularJS expression is assignable.

Propagating model changes to the DOM

We can use the $parse service to write a simplified version of the ng-bind directive that can render model values as DOM text nodes:

```
.directive('simpleBind', function ($parse) {
  return function (scope, element, attrs) {

    var modelGetter = $parse(attrs.simpleBind);
    element.text(modelGetter(scope));
  }
});
```

The `simple-bind` directive presented here takes an expression (provided as a DOM attribute), evaluates it against a `$scope`, and updates the text of a given DOM element.

Synchronizing DOM and model

With both directives ready we could try to use them in HTML as shown in the following code, and expect that new directives behave as the `ng-model` and `ng-bind` equivalents:

```
<div ng-init='name = "World"'>
    <input simple-model='name'>
    <span simple-bind='name'></span>
</div>
```

Unfortunately running the last example won't yield expected results! While the initial rendering will be correct, changes from the `<input>` field won't trigger updates in the `<span>` element.

We must clearly be missing something and a quick review of the `simple-bind` directive will help you realize that this directive covers only initial rendering of the model. The directive doesn't observe model changes and won't react on those changes. We can easily fix this by using the `$watch` method available on scopes' instances:

```
.directive('simpleBind', function ($parse) {
  return function (scope, element, attrs) {

    var modelGetter = $parse(attrs.simpleBind);
    scope.$watch(modelGetter, function(newVal, oldVal){
      element.text(modelGetter(scope));
    });
  }
});
```

The `$watch` method lets us monitor model mutations and execute functions in response to model changes. This method has a signature that could be, in its simplified form, described as follows:

```
scope.$watch(watchExpression, modelChangeCallback)
```

The `watchExpression` parameter can be either a function or AngularJS expression (indicating model value to observe). The `modelChangeCallback` parameter is a callback function that will get executed every time a value of the `watchExpression` changes. The callback itself has access to both new and old values of the `watchExpression`.

After getting familiar with the scope $watch mechanism we should realize that our simple-model directive would also benefit from model observing as a value in an input field and should be updated in response to model changes:

```
.directive('simpleModel', function ($parse) {
    return function (scope, element, attrs) {

        var modelGetter = $parse(attrs.simpleModel);
        var modelSetter = modelGetter.assign;

        //Model -> DOM updates
        scope.$watch(modelGetter, function(newVal, oldVal){
          element.val(newVal);
        });

        //DOM -> Model updates
        element.bind('input', function () {
            modelSetter(scope, element.val());
        });
    };
})
```

With the recent changes to our simple directives we've set up watches in order to observe model mutations. The code looks great and it is reasonable to expect that it should work correctly. Unfortunately those examples still won't work in a live application.

It turns out that we are missing one more fundamental piece of the whole puzzle: when and how AngularJS monitors model changes. We need to understand under which circumstances AngularJS will start evaluating all the watch expressions, checking for model changes.

Scope.$apply – a key to the AngularJS world

When AngularJS was first released to the public there were many "conspiracy theories" regarding its model-changes tracking algorithm. The most frequently repeated one was based on suspicion that it uses some kind of polling mechanism. Such a mechanism was supposedly kicking-in at certain intervals to check model values for changes and re-rendering the DOM if changes were found. All of this is false.

[AngularJS does not use any kind of polling mechanism to periodically check for model changes.]

The idea behind AngularJS model-changes tracking mechanism is based on the observation that at the end of the day, there is a finite (and rather small) number of situations where models can change. Those include:

- DOM events (user changing value of an input field, clicking on a button to invoke a JavaScript function and so on)
- XHR responses firing callbacks
- Browser's location changes
- Timers (setTimout, setInterval) firing the callbacks

Indeed, if none of the earlier events take place (user is not interacting with a page, no XHR calls have finished, no timers firing) there is no point in monitoring the model for changes. There is simply nothing going on for a given page, the model isn't changing, so there is no reason to re-render the DOM.

AngularJS starts its model-observing machinery if and only if it is explicitly told to do so. To bring this sophisticated mechanism to life we need to execute the $apply method on a scope object.

Going back to our simple-model directive example we could do it after each and every change to the input's value (so model changes are propagated after each keystroke. T his is how the ng-model directive behaves by default):

```javascript
.directive('simpleModel', function ($parse) {
  return function (scope, element, attrs) {

    var modelGetter = $parse(attrs.simpleModel);
    var modelSetter = modelGetter.assign;

    //Model -> DOM updates
    scope.$watch(modelGetter, function(newVal, oldVal){
      element.val(newVal);
    });

    //DOM -> Model updates
    element.bind('input', function () {
      scope.$apply(function () {
        modelSetter(scope, element.val());
      });
    });
  };
})
```

Or, we could change the default strategy and propagate model updates only after the user leaves the input field:

```
//DOM -> Model updates
element.bind('blur', function () {
    scope.$apply(function () {
    modelSetter(scope, element.val());
  });
});
```

Whatever the strategy chosen, the important point here is that model-changes tracking process need to be started explicitly. This might come as a surprise since by simply using built-in AngularJS directives we can see "magic" happening without calling the $apply method all over the place. But those calls are present in the built-in directives' code. It is just that standard directives and services ($http, $timeout, $location, and so on) take care of starting the whole model-changes tracking process for us.

 AngularJS starts the model-changes tracking machinery by calling the $apply method on a scope. This call is done inside standard services and directives in response to network activity, DOM events, JavaScript timers or browser location changes

Enter the $digest loop

In AngularJS terminology the process of detecting model changes is called $digest loop (or $digest cycle).The name comes from the $digest method available on Scope instances. This method is invoked as part of the $apply call and it will evaluate all the watches registered on all the scopes.

But why does the $digest loop exist in AngularJS? And how it does its job of determining what has changed in the model? AngularJS the $digest loop exists to address two related problems:

- Decide which parts of the model have changed and which DOM properties should be updated as a result. The goal here is to make this process as easy as possible for developers. We should just mutate model properties and have AngularJS directives automatically figure out parts of the document to be repainted.

- Eliminate unnecessary repaints to increase performance and avoid UI flickering. AngularJS achieves this by postponing DOM repaints till the very last possible moment when the model stabilizes (all the model values were calculated and ready to drive UI rendering).

To understand how AngularJS achieves its goals we need to remember that web browsers have a single UI thread. There are other threads running in a browser (for example, ones responsible for network-related operations) but only one thread is available to render DOM elements, listen to DOM events, and execute JavaScript code. Browsers constantly switch between the JavaScript execution context and the DOM rendering context.

AngularJS makes sure that all the model values are calculated and "stable" before giving control back to the DOM rendering context. This way UI is repainted in one single batch, instead of being constantly redrawn in response to individual model value changes. This results in faster execution (as there is less context switching) and better visual effect (as all the repaints are done once only). Repainting UI after each and every single model property change would give us slow and flickering UI.

Anatomy of a $watch

AngularJS uses **dirty checking** mechanism to determine if a given model value has changed. It works it out by comparing previously saved model values with the ones computed after one of the events that can result in model mutation occurs (DOM events, XHR events, and so on).

As a reminder, here is the general syntax to register a new watch:

```
$scope.$watch(watchExpression, modelChangeCallback)
```

When a new `$watch` is added on a scope AngularJS evaluates the `watchExpression` and internally saves the result of this evaluation. Upon entering the `$digest` loop the `watchExpression` will be executed once again, and a new value will be compared to the saved one. The `modelChangeCallback` will be executed only if the new value differs from the previous one. The new calculated value is also saved for further comparisons and the whole process can be repeated.

As developers we will be well aware of watches that are registered manually (in application controllers or custom directives). But we need to remember that any directive (both from the AngularJS core set of directives as well as from third party collections) can set up its own watches. Any interpolation expression (`{{expression}}`) will register a new watch on a scope as well.

Model stability

AngularJS considers that a model becomes stable (and we can move to UI rendering) if none of the watches detects any further changes. It is enough that one watch sees a change to mark the whole `$digest` loop as "dirty", and force AngularJS into another turn of the loop. It is the "one bad apple spoils the whole bunch" principle, and there are good reasons for it.

AngularJS will keep executing the $digest loop and re-evaluating all the watches on all scopes till there are no changes reported. Several turns of the $digest loop are necessary since watch callbacks can have a side effect. Simply put ting a given callback, executed as a result of a model change, can change the model value that was already computed and considered as stable.

Let's consider an example of a simple form with two date fields: Start and End. In such a form the end date should always come after the start date:

```
<div>
<form>
        Start date: <input ng-model="startDate">
        End date: <input ng-model="endDate">
</form>
</div>
```

To enforce in the model that endDate is always after the startDate we could register watches like:

```
function oneDayAhead(dateToIncrement) {
  return dateToIncrement.setDate(dateToIncrement.getDate() + 1);
};

$scope.$watch('startDate', function (newValue) {
  if (newValue <= $scope.starDate) {
$scope.endDate = oneDayAhead($scope.starDate);
  }
});
```

The watch registered in a controller makes two model values interdependent in a way that changes in one model variable can trigger changes in another. The callback on model change can have side effects that can potentially change a value that was already considered "stable".

A good understanding of the dirty-checking algorithm will make you realize that a given watchExpression is executed at least twice in each and every turn of the $digest loop. We can quickly confirm this by creating the following mark-up:

```
<input ng-model='name'>
{{getName()}}
```

With the getName() expression being a function defined on a scope as follows:

```
$scope.getName = function() {
  console.log('dirty-checking');
  return $scope.name;
}
```

If you run this example and inspect output of the console, you will notice that two log entries are written for each change in the `<input>` field.

 Any given `$digest` loop will have at least one turn, usually two. It means that each individual watch expression will be evaluated twice per `$digest` loop (before the browser leaves JavaScript execution context and moves to UI rendering).

Unstable models

There are cases where two turns inside the `$digest` loop are not enough to stabilize the model. Worse yet, it is possible to get into a situation where model never stabilizes! Let's consider a very simple example of the markup:

```
<span>Random value: {{random()}}</span>
```

Where the `random()` function is defined on a scope like:

```
$scope.random = Math.random;
```

Here a watch expression is equal to `Math.random()` and it will (most probably) evaluate to a different value on each turn of the `$digest` loop. This means that each turn will be marked as "dirty" and a new turn will be needed. The situation will keep repeating itself over and over again, until AngularJS decides that the model is unstable, and will break the `$digest` loop.

By default AngularJS will try to execute up to 10 turns before giving up, declaring the model as unstable and breaking the `$digest` loop.

Upon breaking the `$digest` loop AngularJS will report an error (using the `$exceptionHandler` service which, by default, logs errors on a console). The reported error will contain information about the last five unstable watches (with their new and old values). In majority of cases there will be only one unstable watch, making it easy to find a culprit.

After the `$digest` loop gets aborted, the JavaScript thread leaves "AngularJS world", and there will be nothing stopping a browser from moving to the rendering context. In this case, users will get their page rendered with the value computed by watchers in the last turn of the `$digest` loop.

A page will be rendered even if the configured limit of 10 turns per $digest loop is exceeded. The error is not easy to spot till you inspect a console so it might get unnoticed for a while. Still we should track down and resolve issues linked to unstable models.

$digest loop and a hierarchy of scopes

Each turn of the $digest loop recomputes all the watch expressions on all scopes, starting from the $rootScope. This might be counter intuitive at first, as one could claim that it would be enough to recompute the only expression on a given scope, and all of its children. Unfortunately, this could lead to UI being desynchronized with the model. The reason is that changes triggered in one of the child scopes can influence variables in a parent scope. Here is a simple example of an application with two scopes (one $rootScope and another one created by the ng-controller directive):

```
<body ng-app ng-init='user = {name: "Superhero"}'>
  Name in parent: {{user.name}}
  <div ng-controller="ChildCtrl">
    Name in child: {{user.name}}
    <input ng-model='user.name'>
  </div>
</body>
```

Changes to the model (user.name) are triggered from a child scope (one created by the ng-controller directive), but are changing properties of an object defined on the $rootScope.

Setups like this force AngularJS to evaluate all the watches, starting from the $rootScope, and continue down to child scopes (using depth-first traversal). If AngularJS had evaluated watches on a scope where changes were triggered (plus its children) it would have risked desynchronizing model values with the actual display. In the example discussed here, the Name in parent: {{user.name}} interpolation expression would not be evaluated and displayed correctly.

 In each and every turn of the $digest loop AngularJS needs to evaluate all the watches in all scopes. It does so starting from the $rootScope and traversing child scopes depth-first.

Putting it all together

Let's summarize what we know about AngularJS inner working by examining a simple example of an input field propagating changes live to DOM:

```
<input ng-model='name'>
{{name}}
```

The preceding code will result in two watches registered on a $scope, each one of them tracking the value of the name model variable. After the initial display, nothing happens on a page a browser will be sitting in an event loop, and waiting for any events. It is only when a user starts to type into an <input> field that the whole machinery is brought to life:

- A new DOM input event is fired. Browser enters the JavaScript execution context.

- A DOM event handler, registered by the input directive is executed. The handler updates the model value and calls scope.$apply method on a scope instance.

- JavaScript execution context enters the "AngularJS world" and the $digest loop is started. Upon the first turn of the $digest loop one of the watches (registered by the {{name}} interpolation directive) is declared as "dirty" and another turn of the loop is needed.

- Since a model change was detected a $watch callback is fired. It updates the text property of the DOM element where the interpolation expression is present.

- The second turn of the $digest loop is re-evaluating all the watches, but this time no further changes are detected. AngularJS can declare the model as "stable" and exit the $digest loop.

- JavaScript execution context can process any other, non-AngularJS JavaScript code. Most of the time there will be none, and a browser will be free to exit JavaScript execution context.

- The UI thread is free to move the rendering context, and a browser can re-paint the DOM node whose text property has changed.

- After rendering is done, a browser can come back to the waiting state in its event loop.

As you can see, there are a number of steps involved in propagating DOM changes to the model and back to the DOM.

Performance tuning – set expectations, measure, tune, and repeat

Performance tuning requires a disciplined approach where:

- Expectations regarding performance characteristics are clearly defined, including measurable performance counters, alongside conditions under which measures are taken.

- A current performance of a system is measured and cross-checked with expectations.

- If a system is not up to the expected standards, then performance bottlenecks need to be identified and fixed. After a fix is performed the whole process of measuring needs to be repeated to prove that a fix brings system performance to expected levels or identify further bottlenecks.

There are two very important lessons that we can draw from the process sketched earlier. First of all, we need to clearly set expectations and conditions under which performance characteristics are considered and measured. Secondly, the performance tuning is not a goal in itself, it is a process to bring the system to the point where it behaves as expected.

AngularJS, as any other well-engineered library, was constructed within a frame of certain boundary conditions, and those are best described by *Miško Hevery*, father of AngularJS (`http://stackoverflow.com/a/9693933/1418796`):

> *So it may seem that we are slow, since dirty checking is inefficient. This is where we need to look at real numbers rather than just have theoretical arguments, but first let's define some constraints.*

> *Humans are:*

> *slow – Anything faster than 50ms is imperceptible to humans and thus can be considered as "instant".*

> *limited – You can't really show more than about 2000 pieces of information to a human on a single page. Anything more than that is really bad UI, and humans can't process this anyway.*

> *So the real question is this: can you do 2000 comparisons in 50 ms even on slow browsers? That means that you have 25μs per comparison. I believe this is not an issue even on slow browsers these days.*

There is a caveat: the comparisons need to be simple to fit into 25μs. Unfortunately it is way too easy to add slow comparison into angular, so it is easy to build slow apps when you don't know what you are doing. But we hope to have an answer by providing an instrumentation module, which would show you which are the slow comparisons.

The boundary conditions set here give us very good hints about practical and theoretical limits of an application built with AngularJS, as well as set potential directions for performance tuning.

Luckily for us the "instrumentation module" mentioned by *Miško Hevery* exists and is called **Batarang,** and is available as a Chrome extension in the Chrome Web Store. In the following screenshot we can see the Batarang extension in action. Among other useful information Batarang can instrument watches declared on scopes and show:

- Execution time for the individual watches
- Relative time contributed by a given watch expression to the overall execution time of the entire `$digest` loop

Batarang allows us to easily pinpoint the slowest watch expressions, and measure our progress while taking the performance tuning steps.

Performance tuning of AngularJS applications

We would like to have applications that are "fast". But "fast" might mean different things to different people, and this is why we need to focus on measurable items that influence the overall performance. In this chapter, we are focusing on the in-browser performance and putting network-related problems aside (those are discussed in *Chapter 12, Packaging and Deploying AngularJS Web Applications*). If we narrow down performance concerns to what is happening in a browser, we need to look at the CPU utilization and memory consumption.

Optimizing CPU utilization

Apart from an application's logic there are number of AngularJS-specific operations that will eat up CPU cycles. The $digest loop requires our special attention. We need to make sure that individual $digest cycles are fast, and also arrange our code in a way that AngularJS enters the $digest loop as infrequently as possible.

Speeding up $digest loops

We need to strive to keep the $digest loop execution time under 50 ms so the human eye can't register its execution time. This is important since our application will be perceived as responding instantaneously to users' actions (DOM events) if the $digest loop is unnoticeable.

There are two primary directions we can explore in order to fly under the "50 ms per $digest cycle" radar:

- Make individual watches faster
- Limit the number of watches evaluated as part of an individual $digest cycle

Keeping watches slim and fast

If you recall the general syntax of a watch expression:

```
$scope.$watch(watchExpression, modelChangeCallback)
```

You will remember that each and every individual watch is composed of two distinct parts: watchExpression that is used to compare model values, and the modelChangeCallback that is executed when model mutation is detected. The watchExpression is executed far more frequently as compared to the callback, and this is why it is the watchExpression that requires our special attention.

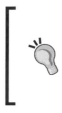
A given watchExpression is executed at least once (usually twice) in each and every turn of the $digest loop. It is possible to slow down the entire AngularJS application by introducing a watch expression that requires significant time to execute. We need to pay special attention to the watch-expression part of a watcher, and avoid introducing expensive computations in this part.

Ideally the watch-expression part of a watcher should be as simple as possible and execute as fast as possible. There are a number of anti-patterns that should be avoided in order to have watch-expression executing fast.

Firstly, we should minimize expensive computations in a watch-expression. Usually we use simple expressions in templates, which results in fast to execute watch-expressions, but there are two situations where it is easy to introduce non-trivial computations.

You should pay special attention to expressions that execute functions, for example:

```
{{myComplexComputation()}}
```

As those will result in the myComplexComputation() being part of the watch-expression! Another non-obvious consequence of using functions is that we can accidently leave some logging statements in them. It turns out that writing to console.log slows down a watcher considerably. Let's consider two functions:

```
$scope.getName = function () {
  return $scope.name;
};

$scope.getNameLog = function () {
  console.log('getting name');
  return $scope.name;
};
```

If you observe Batarang's performance tab for the markup shown as follows:

```
<span>{{getName()}}</span>
<span>{{getNameLog()}}</span>
```

You will notice a dramatic difference:

Watch Expressions

```
{{getNameLog()}}  | 31.3% | 97.00ms
```

```
{{getName()}}  | 0.323% | 1.000ms
```

 Always remove all the calls to the `consol.log` in your production code and use tools like **jshint** to assist you in this task. Never use logging statements in the middle of the profiling/performance tuning session as those statements will falsify the observed results.

Filters code is another place where we might unknowingly introduce expensive computations. Consider the following example:

```
{{myModel | myComplexFilter}}
```

A filter is nothing more than a function invoked using special syntax as part of AngularJS expression. Since it is part of a watch-expression, as such it will get executed at least once (twice most of the time) per each `$digest` loop. If logic executed in a filter is expensive it will slow down the entire `$digest` loop. Filters are particularly tricky since they can declare dependencies on services and invoke potentially expensive methods on services.

Each filter in the AngularJS expression is executed at least once (usually twice) for a given `$digest` loop. Monitor logic executed as part of the filtering method to make sure that it doesn't slow down your application.

Avoid DOM access in the watch-expression

There are times where you might be tempted to read DOM properties as part of the `watchExpression`. There are two problems with this approach.

Firstly, DOM properties access can be slow, very slow. The issue is that DOM properties are calculated live, synchronously, when a property is read. It is enough to watch a property whose computation is expensive to significantly slow down the entire `$digest` loop. For example, reading a property linked to elements position or dimensions will force a browser to recalculate the element's size and positioning, and this is an order of magnitude slower as compared to observing JavaScript properties.

Any DOM operation is slow and computed properties are extra slow. The real problem is that DOM is implemented in C++. It turns out that it is very expensive to call a C++ function from JS. So any DOM access is magnitudes slower than JavaScript object access.

The second problem is a conceptual one. The entire AngularJS philosophy is based on the fact that the source of truth is the model. It is the model that drives declarative UI. But by observing DOM properties, we are turning things upside-down! All of a sudden it is DOM that starts to drive the model that in turn, drives the UI. We are getting into a circular dependencies problem here.

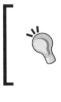

It might be tempting to watch for DOM property changes, especially when integrating third party JavaScript components into AngularJS application. Be aware that it might have a dramatic impact on the $digest loop performance. Avoid watching for DOM property changes or at least measure performance after introducing such a watch.

Limit the number of watches to be evaluated

If you've fine-tuned existing watches and removed all the bottlenecks, but your application still needs a performance boost, it is time to take more radical steps.

Remove unnecessary watches

AngularJS two-way data binding is so powerful and easy to play with that you might fall into a trap of abusing it in places where a static value would do.

In *Chapter 10, Building AngularJS Web Applications for an International Audience,* we were discussing one example of such a situation using data binding for translations. Translations data change very infrequently (if ever!). Yet, by adding AngularJS expressions for each translated string, we are adding a lot of calculations to each turn of the $digest loop.

When adding a new interpolation expression to templates, try to assess if it will really benefit from the two-way data binding. Maybe a value in a template could be generated on the server side, for example.

Think about your UI

Each watch registered on a scope represents a "moving part" on a page. If we remove all the unnecessary bindings (see earlier, things that are part of the $digest loop but are not changing, really) we are left with a "2000 moving parts per page" theoretical limit. In practice it is more complex than this, since we need to take speed of individual watches into account.

Still, 2000 is a good indicator. Is 2000 a sufficient number? This depends on who you ask, and the type of application being written, but we should really think of our users. Can they cope with 2000 "moving parts" at once? Are we giving them optimal user experience? Maybe UI of our application should be reevaluated to focus on presenting essential data and controls? One of the principles of user interface design the visibility principle says (http://en.wikipedia.org/wiki/Principles_of_user_interface_design) says:

> *The design should make all needed options and materials for a given task visible without distracting the user with extraneous or redundant information. Good designs don't overwhelm users with alternatives or confuse with unneeded information.*

By making UI lighter we can both speed up the $digest loop, and provide better user experience to people using an application. An option worth exploring!

Don't watch for invisible

AngularJS offers two directives that come handy when we need to conditionally show parts of the DOM: ng-show and ng-hide. As discussed in *Chapter 4, Displaying and Formatting Data*, those directives won't physically remove hidden elements from the DOM, but will hide elements by styling them appropriately (display: none). The bottom line is that "hidden" elements are still present in the DOM tree and any watches registered by those elements (or their children) will be evaluated in every $digest loop.

Let's skim through the following example and the corresponding Batarang's performance results:

```
<input ng-model='name'>
<div ng-show="false">
    <span>{{getNameLog()}}</span>
</div>
```

Here the `getNameLog()` is simply returning a name and uses `console.log` to simulate an "expensive" operation. If we start to type into the `<input>` field we will notice that the `getNameLog()` expression is evaluated on each keystroke. This happens even if results of the evaluation are never visible on a screen!

> Remember that expensive watches might not have any visual effects on a screen. If the hidden part of the display slows down your application consider using the `ng-switch` family of directives. Those directives physically remove invisible DOM elements from the DOM tree.

Call Scope.$digest instead of calling Scope.$apply when you know impacted scopes

In the first part of this chapter, we saw that AngularJS needs to traverse all the scopes in the whole application when executing its `$digest` loop. This is done to cater for the case where change triggered in one scope can mutate model in one of the parent scopes. But there are times where we know exactly which scopes are impacted by a given change, and we can use this knowledge to our advantage.

If we know exactly which scopes are impacted by model mutations we can call the `scope.$digest` method on the topmost impacted scope, instead of calling `scope.$apply`. The `scope.$digest` method will run a `$digest` loop on a limited subset of scopes. Only watches declared on a scope on which the method was called, plus child scopes, are going to be inspected for model changes. This can significantly reduce number of watch expressions to be evaluated and thus speed up the `$digest` loop.

As an example of a situation where we can narrow down impacted scopes, let's consider a `typeahead` (autocomplete) directive, shown as follows:

In this directive a pop up with autocomplete suggestion has its own scope holding all the proposals and a reference to a currently selected item (**California**). Users can navigate through the list of proposals using keyboard (up and down arrows) to change a selected item. When a keyboard event is detected we need to call `scope.$apply()` so AngularJS two-way data binding machinery kicks in, and an appropriate item is highlighted. But keyboard navigation can only influence a scope of the pop up so evaluating all the watches on all scopes in the entire application is clearly wasteful. We can act smarter and call the `$digest()` method on the pop up's scope.

Remove unused watches

You might face a situation where a registered watch is needed only for a fraction of the application's running time. AngularJS makes it possible to unregister obsolete watches like:

```
var watchUnregisterFn = $scope.$watch('name', function (newValue,
oldValue) {
  console.log("Watching 'name' variable");
  ...
});

//later on, when a watch is not needed any more:

watchUnregisterFn();
```

As you can see, a call to the `scope.$watch` method returns a function that can be used to unregister a given watch when it is no longer needed.

Entering the $digest loop less frequently

Usually the `$digest` loop is triggered from within AngularJS built-in directives and services, and we don't need to control it manually. Still, we should be aware of circumstances under which the `$digest` loop gets triggered. In general there are four types of events that are listened to by AngularJS directives and services, and result in the call to `scope.$apply()` method:

- **Navigation events**: Users clicking on links, using back and forward buttons, and so on.

- **Network events**: All the calls to the `$http` service (and resources created with `$resource`) will trigger a `$digest` loop when a response (either success or error) is ready.

- **DOM events**: All the AngularJS directives corresponding to DOM events (`ng-click`, `ng-mouseover`, and so on) will trigger a `$digest` loop when an event handler is firing.

- **JavaScript timers**: The `$timeout` service wraps the JavaScript `setTimeout` function and will trigger a `$digest` loop when a timer fires.

As you can see the `$digest` loop can run and evaluate all the watches quite often, especially where there are many DOM event handlers starting the loop. There are situations where we can't do much about it, but there are certain techniques we can use to minimize the frequency at which AngularJS enters the `$digest` loop.

Firstly we can try to minimize the number of network calls by arranging back-end's API in a way that an individual user action results in one single XHR call and one single response. Of course this is not always possible, but if you've got full control over your back-end, this might be a technique to consider. Not only would it limit number of network calls, but would also mean that AngularJS enters the `$digest` loop less frequently.

Next, we must pay special attention to the usage of timers, especially ones wrapped in the `$timeout` service. By default the `$timer` service will call `scope.$apply` each time a timer fires, and this can have farfetched consequences if we are not careful enough. To see what could go wrong, let's consider a simple clock directive displaying current time:

```
.directive('clock', function ($timeout, dateFilter) {
  return {
    restrict: 'E',
    link: function (scope, element, attrs) {

      function update() {
        // get current time, format it and update DOM text
```

```
        element.text(dateFilter(new Date(), 'hh:mm:ss'));
        //repeat in 1 second
      $timeout(update, 1000);

    }

    update();
  }
};
})
```

Such a directive, used with the `<clock></clock>`markup that would trigger the `$digest` loop every second. This is why we can pass an optional, third parameter to the `$timeout` service, which will indicate if `scope.$apply` should be called or not. The better way of writing the `update()` function is shown as follows:

```
function update() {
  element.text(dateFilter(new Date(), 'hh:mm:ss'));
  $timeout(update, 1000, false);
}
```

> We can avoid a `$digest` loop being triggered by the `$timeout` service if we pass `false` as the third argument when registering a timer.

Lastly, we can easily trigger a massive number of `$digest` loops by registering a significant number of certain DOM event handlers, especially ones related to mouse movements. For example, a very declarative, AngularJS-way of changing an element's class (say, to switch it to `active`), when a mouse is positioned over it, would be:

```
<div ng-class='{active: isActive}' ng-mouseenter ='isActive=true' ng-mouseleave='isActive=false'>Some content</div>
```

While the preceding code works and keeps CSS class names where they belong (HTML markup) it will trigger a `$digest` loop every time a mouse pointer travels over a given DOM element. This shouldn't generate many problems if used sparingly (on just a few DOM elements), but it might grind our application to a halt if this pattern is repeated for a large number of elements. If you start to observe performance issues linked to mouse events, consider rolling out your own, custom directive where you could do direct DOM manipulations in response to DOM events and model mutations.

Limit the number of turns per $digest loop

Models that are harder to stabilize will require more turns of a `$digest` loop. As a result all the watches will be re-evaluated multiple times. Typically a `$digest` loop requires two turns but it might quickly grow to the configured limit (10 by default) if a model never stabilizes.

Try to think of all the conditions that are necessary to stabilize a newly registered watch. Expressions that are highly unstable shouldn't be part of the watch expression but instead should be computed outside of a `$digest` loop.

Optimizing memory consumption

AngularJS uses a dirty-checking mechanism to decide if a given part of the model has changed, and if an action (updating DOM properties, changing other model values, and so on) should be taken as a consequence. An efficient values comparison algorithm is crucial for the proper functioning of the dirty-checking mechanism.

Avoid deep-watching whenever possible

By default AngularJS uses identity comparison (for objects) or values comparison (for primitive types) to detect changes in the model. Such comparisons are fast and straightforward but there are cases where we might want to compare objects on the property-by-property basis (so called deep-compare).

Let's consider a typical User object that has a number of different properties:

```
$scope.user = {
firstName: 'AngularJS',
  lastName: 'Superhero',
  age: 4,
  superpowers: 'unlimited',
  // many other properties go here…
};
```

Assuming that we would like to have the full name of this user in one single model variable, updated automatically whenever one of the first or last name changes, we could create a new watch on a `$scope`:

```
$scope.$watch('user', function (changedUser) {
  $scope.fullName =
    changedUser.firstName + ' ' + changedUser.lastName;
}, true);
```

We can supply a third true argument to the $watch method in order to indicate that AngularJS should use deep-comparison for objects. In this case the whole object (every property of it) is compared using the angular.equal function. In the **deep-watching** mode the comparison process will be slower. Not only does this AngularJS need to copy (angular.copy) and save the whole object for further comparisons. This is obviously wasteful from the memory consumption point of view as we are constantly copying and storing all the properties of a given object while being only interested in a subset of them.

Fortunately there are several alternatives to the deep-watching, and those can be easily applied if we are only concerned with a subset of object's properties. To start, we could simply watch results of the full name calculation:

```
$scope.$watch(function(scope) {
  return scope.user.firstName + ' ' + scope.user.lastName;
}, function (newFullName) {
  $scope.fullName = newFullName;
});
```

The advantage here is that only final results of the full name calculation are stored in memory for further comparisons. The downside is that the full name calculation takes place in each and every $digest loop turn, even if the user's properties don't change at all. By employing this technique we can save memory in expense of additional CPU cycles. As a side note, the same effect could be achieved by invoking a function from an AngularJS expression in a template:

```
{{fullName()}}
```

Where the fullName() function would be defined on a scope like:

```
$scope.fullName = function () {
  return $scope.user.firstName + ' ' + $scope.user.lastName;
};
```

 Deep-watching has a double performance penalty. Not only does AngularJS need to store a copy of an object in memory for further comparisons but the actual equality check is slower as well. Try to use alternatives presented here if you are only interested in a subset of properties for a given object.

Performance tuning is a delicate balancing act. This is very well visible in the earlier examples where we need to often trade memory bytes for CPU cycles. An optimal solution to be applied in your application will depend on performance bottlenecks identified.

Consider the size of expressions being watched

Even if we manage to avoid deep-watches we should still try to think about an exact value being watched and compared by AngularJS. This is not always obvious, especially with watches registered by AngularJS while processing templates.

See the following example of a longer text with one AngularJS expression inside:

```
<p>This is very long text that refers to one {{variable}} defined on a
scope. This text can be really, really long and occupy a lot of space
in memory. It is so long since... </p>
```

You would probably expect that AngularJS, while processing this template, will create a watch where the `watch` expression is equal to `variable`. Unfortunately, this is not the case; the whole text enclosed by `<p>` tags will be used. This means that the whole, potentially long text will be copied and stored in memory. We can limit the size of this expression by introducing a `<span>` tag to delimit part of the text that should be data-bound:

```
<p>This is very long text that refers to one <span ng-
bind='variable'></span> defined on a scope. This text can be really,
really long and occupy a lot of space in memory. It is so long since...
</p>
```

After this simple change AngularJS will register a watcher where the watch expression consists of the `variable` only.

The ng-repeat directive

The `ng-repeat` directive would probably win a contest for the most useful directive, if one could be organized. It has enormous power coupled with very simple syntax. Unfortunately, `ng-repeat` is also one of the most performance-sensitive directives. There are two reasons for this. Firstly it needs to do nontrivial inspection of a collection in each turn of the `$digest` loop. Then, when changes are detected, impacted DOM elements need to be reshuffled which may result in many DOM operations.

Collection watching in ng-repeat

The `ng-repeat` directive needs to keep track of changes to the collection it iterates over. To operate properly the directive needs to be able to identify elements that were added to a collection, moved within a collection or removed entirely. It does so by executing a nontrivial algorithm as part of each `$digest` loop. Without going into the details of this algorithm, its performance is linked to the size of a collection.

Many bindings made easy

The `ng-repeat` directive, when used on data sets of substantial size, can quickly result in many watches being registered on scopes.

An easy calculation is in order here. Let's consider a simple table with five columns. Each column will probably have at least one binding. This means that one row in a table will produce five bindings. If we assume that theoretical limits of AngularJS are around 2000 bindings we can't expect tables of over 400 items to perform reasonably. Of course more columns (or more bindings per column) will lower the number of items that can be reasonably managed and displayed.

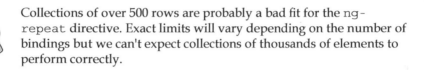

> Collections of over 500 rows are probably a bad fit for the `ng-repeat` directive. Exact limits will vary depending on the number of bindings but we can't expect collections of thousands of elements to perform correctly.

Unfortunately there is not much we can do about the `ng-repeat` directive with large data sets. We should strive to pre-filter and trim a collection before leaving it in the hands of `ng-repeat`. All tricks are good here: filtering, pagination, and so on.

If you are working in a domain where you really need to display thousands of rows the built-in `ng-repeat` directive might not be a tool of your choice. In this case you should be ready to roll out your own directive. Such a directive shouldn't create two-way data bindings for individual items, but rather render DOM elements based on the content of a collection. This will avoid creating enormous amounts of bindings.

Summary

This chapter provided in-depth coverage of AngularJS internals. We need to get a good grasp of AngularJS inner-working in order to understand its performance characteristics and theoretical limits.

All performance-related improvements must start with scrupulous measurements so as to identify and understand existing bottlenecks. Starting the performance-tuning process without hard data is like shooting in the dark. Fortunately, there is an excellent Chrome extension, Batarang, that lets us inspect a running application.

We should pay special attention to the AngularJS `$digest` loop execution time as it can determine users' perception of the entire application. Allow the `$digest` loop to run for more than 50ms-100ms, and users will start perceiving our application as unresponsive. This is why we've spent so much time in this chapter discussing how the `$digest` loop operates and what we can do to speed it up.

Running time of a `$digest` loop is proportional to number of watches and their execution time. We can speed up the `$digest` loop both by limiting number of watches or making them run faster. We can also enter the loop less frequently.

Memory consumption is another aspect of the overall performance that should be monitored. In AngularJS-specific code precious memory bytes can be consumed by deep-watches. We should avoid them as much as possible, not only when creating watches manually (`scope.$watch`), but we should also make sure that we don't create them accidently in templates.

The `ng-repeat` directive is especially performance-sensitive, both in terms of CPU utilization and memory consumption. It might easily create a performance hotspot if applied to a collection of several hundred items. To make, most of the `ng-repeat` directive you need to keep source collections small by pre-filtering them. If you need to display collections of several hundreds of elements you might consider writing your own directive that would be fine-tuned for your particular use-case.

The next chapter is going to illustrate how to prepare a fine-tuned application for the production deployment. It will also discuss network-related performance patterns.

12
Packaging and Deploying AngularJS Web Applications

After all the laborious coding, testing, and performance tuning there comes the time for production deployment. But let's not rush things, there are still a number of little details to be taken care of before our application is ready for the prime-time!

Firstly, we need to make sure that our application makes reasonable use of network resources. We can achieve this by limiting the number of HTTP requests as well as the size of data downloaded with each individual request. Preloading and minification of static resources are the two common techniques of reducing network traffic, and we will see how to apply those techniques in the context of AngularJS applications.

The landing page of any web application gives the first impression of what to expect next. If the very first experience is negative, users might get discouraged and abandon an application we've worked so hard on. This is why it is so important to optimize the initial page of our application. This chapter discusses various adjustments we can make to make the first page experience as smooth as possible.

The last section discusses AngularJS support on different browsers with a special focus on Internet Explorer.

In this chapter you will learn:

- How to minimize network utilization for downloading static resources by minifying and merging JavaScript code as well as preloading partial templates
- How to optimize the landing page
- Which browsers are supported by AngularJS and which particular steps are necessary to make it run on Internet Explorer without glitches

Improving network-related performance

As web developers we should offer our users functional applications with an intuitive user interface. Users should have a snappy experience even before an application starts. To do so we can limit HTTP traffic and reduce application's loading time by downloading less data in each request and limiting the number of HTTP requests.

Minifying static resources

One way of minimizing download times over a network is to reduce the number of bytes that are sent between the web server and the browser. Nowadays minification of JavaScript, CSS, and HTML code is one of the standard practices in web development. Minification reduces size of data that needs to be downloaded into a browser. Additionally it makes the source code much harder to read and adds minimal protection from the unwelcomed eyes.

While you can safely continue using all the CSS and HTML minification techniques you know and love, AngularJS-specific JavaScript code needs some attention before it can be processed by standard tools.

How does AngularJS infer dependencies?

AngularJS heavily relies on the **Dependency Injection** (DI) pattern throughout the framework. In our own AngularJS application code we can easily express dependencies on registered services and have them injected into our code.

AngularJS can infer the dependencies of a given function, fetch them from the `$injector` service, and provide them as arguments to our functions. The AngularJS DI engine introspects dependencies for a function using a surprisingly simple technique. To see how it works let's take an example from one of the controllers in our sample SCRUM application:

```
angular.module('projects', ['resources.projects'])
  .controller('ProjectsViewCtrl', function ($scope, $location) {
    //controller's code
  });
```

A function for the `ProjectsViewCtrl` parameter declares dependencies on two services: `$scope` and `$location`. AngularJS parses out those dependencies by converting function definition to a string and using a regular expression to match the function's argument names. We can see this technique using the following minimal example:

```
var ctrlFn = function($scope, $location) {};
console.log(ctrlFn.toString());
```

This technique upon execution, will log the body of the `function` method as a string:

```
"function ($scope, $location) {}"
```

With the declaration of the `function` method captured as a string, it is enough to do some simple regular expression matching to parse out the names of declared arguments, and thus find out names of required dependencies.

Now, let's consider what happens with function definitions during the JavaScript minification process. The exact details will vary from one processor to another but most minifiers will rename function arguments so the code will look similar to the following code:

```
angular.module('projects', ['resources.projects'])
  .controller('ProjectsViewCtrl', function (e, f) {
    //minified controller's code referencing new argument names
  });
```

Obviously AngularJS can't discover dependencies from minified functions, as `e` and `f` are not valid service names.

Writing minification-safe JavaScript code

Standard JavaScript minification processes the `destroy` parameter information that is needed by AngularJS to infer dependencies. Since this information is lost from the signature of `function`, we need to provide hints using different constructs.

AngularJS offers different ways of providing dependency hints for the minified code, but we would like to encourage you to use array-style annotations as shown in the following example:

```
angular.module('projects', ['resources.projects'])
  .controller('ProjectsViewCtrl', ['$scope', '$location', function
($scope, $location) {
    //controller's code
  }]);
```

This code when minified, would look as follows:

```
angular.module('projects', ['resources.projects'])
  .controller('ProjectsViewCtrl', ['$scope', '$location', function (e,
f) {
    //controller's code
  }]);
```

Even if `function` arguments were changed, the minification process can't touch elements of the array, and AngularJS has enough information to find all the dependencies for a given function.

 If you want your code to be minification-safe, replace all functions (declaring at least one dependency) with an array where initial elements of an array correspond to the function's argument names and the last element of an array contains the function itself.

The array-style Dependency Injection annotation syntax might look odd at times, so let's skim over several examples taken from the SCRUM sample application. Subsequent sections of this chapter show examples for the most common use cases.

 All the code written for the sample SCRUM application contains array-style DI annotations. You can refer to the code hosted on GitHub to find examples of those annotations used in different situations.

Modules

The `config` and `run` functions on a module level can be injected with dependencies. Here is an example of defining configuration time dependencies in the minification-safe way:

```
angular.module('app')
  .config(['$routeProvider', '$locationProvider', function
($routeProvider, $locationProvider) {
  $locationProvider.html5Mode(true);
  $routeProvider.otherwise({redirectTo:'/projectsinfo'});
}]);
```

Functions to be executed in run blocks can be annotated in the following fashion:

```
angular.module('app')
  .run(['security', function(security) {
    security.requestCurrentUser();
}]);
```

Providers

AngularJS offers several ways of registering providers (recipes for object instances). Factories are probably the most common way of defining new singletons as follows:

```
angular.module('services.breadcrumbs', [])
  .factory('breadcrumbs', ['$rootScope', '$location',
function($rootScope, $location){
    . . .
}]);
```

The ability to define decorators around services allows us to easily enrich existing code with additional functionality. The syntax to define decorators is not very intuitive, especially when coupled with array-style DI annotations. To make you more comfortable with this syntax, here is an example of a decorator with DI annotations:

```
angular.module('services.exceptionHandler')
  .config(['$provide', function($provide) {
    $provide.decorator('$exceptionHandler', ['$delegate',
'exceptionHandlerFactory', function ($delegate,
exceptionHandlerFactory) {
      return exceptionHandlerFactory($delegate);
  }]);
}]);
```

Directives

Defining directives in a minification-safe way doesn't differ much from defining other providers. For example, the `field` directive described in *Chapter 9, Building Advanced Directives* would be defined as follows:

```
.directive('field', ['$compile', '$http', '$templateCache',
'$interpolate', function($compile, $http, $templateCache,
$interpolate) {
  . . .
  return {
    restrict:'E',
    priority: 100,
    terminal: true
    ...
  };
}]);
```

Defining controllers for directives needs a bit of attention as the syntax might be surprising at first. Here is an example of the `accordion` directive (also discussed in *Chapter 9, Building Advanced Directives*) that defines a controller as follows:

```
.directive('accordion', function () {
  return {
    restrict:'E',
    controller:['$scope', function ($scope) {
    // This array keeps track of the accordion groups
    this.groups = [];

      . . .
    }],
    link: function(scope, element, attrs) {
      element.addClass('accordion');
      . . .
    }
  };
})
```

The pitfalls of array-style DI annotations

While array-style DI annotations make the AngularJS-specific code minification safe, they do so at the price of code duplication. Indeed, we need to list arguments of the function twice: in the function definition and in the array. As with any code duplication, this one can be problematic, especially when refactoring existing code.

It is relatively easy to forget a new argument and omit it in the annotation array, or mix the order of arguments in two places as shown in the following example:

```
angular.module('app')
  .config(['$locationProvider', '$routeProvider', function
($routeProvider, $locationProvider) {
    $locationProvider.html5Mode(true);
    $routeProvider.otherwise({redirectTo:'/projectsinfo'});
}]);
```

Writing DI-annotations requires concentration, as errors resulting from incorrect annotating are hard to track down.

 You can try to alleviate the pain connected with writing DI annotations by using build-time tools that would post-process your code and add annotations automatically. Such tools are not trivial to write (as JavaScript code analysis is required) and are not widespread yet. Still, if your build system is Grunt.js based, you can give the ngmin (https://github.com/btford/ngmin) Grunt.js task (grunt-ngmin) a try.

Preloading templates

With AngularJS we've got many opportunities to divide HTML mark up into smaller, reusable, partial templates. AngularJS allows us to save partials into individual files and download them on the fly when needed. While having many small files with individual partials is good from the development, and from the code organization point of view, it might negatively impact performance.

Consider a typical route definition, which is as follows:

```
angular.module('routing_basics', [])
  .config(function($routeProvider) {
    $routeProvider
      .when('/admin/users/list', {templateUrl: 'tpls/users/list.
html'})
      . . .
  })
```

If we save route's partial in a separate file (tpls/users/list.html), AngularJS will have to download this file before navigating to a route. Obviously downloading a template over the network means additional time that needs to be spent before the UI can be rendered. By spending this time for network communication, we are losing the opportunity of having a snappy, responsive UI.

Route definitions are only one example of a construct that can point to template partials. Templates can be also referenced from the ng-include directive as well as from the templateUrl property of a custom directive definition.

Preloading of partials can significantly reduce network traffic and increase responsiveness of our UIs. AngularJS offers two slightly different ways of preloading template partials before their first usage: the <script> directive and the $templateCache service.

AngularJS is smart enough to cache (in the $templateCache service) all the partials it has requested. Simply put, AngularJS will check the content of the $templateCache service before fetching a template over the network. As a result it will never request the same partial twice over the network. By priming the $templateCache service we can make sure that all the partials are ready upon the application's startup and are never downloaded over the network.

Using the <script> directive to preload templates

AngularJS has a very handy <script> tag directive that can be used to pre-load individual templates into the $templateCache service. Typically one would embed these partials to be preloaded in the initial page (index.html or similar) loaded in a browser. Taking an example of the previously discussed route, we could embed a partial as follows:

```
<script type="text/ng-template" id="tpls/users/list.html">

  <table class="table table-bordered table-condensed">
    <thead>
      <tr>
        <th>E-mail</th>
        <th>Last name</th>
        <th>First name</th>
      </tr>
    </thead>
    <tbody>
    ...
    </tbody>
  </table>

</script>
```

To pre-load a partial template we need to enclose its content within the <script> tag with the AngularJS-specific type: text/ng-template. The URL of a partial template must be specified as the value of the id attribute.

> Any <script> tag containing a partial template needs to be placed as a child of the DOM element that contains the ng-app directive. The <script> tags placed outside the DOM subtree managed by AngularJS won't be recognized, and as a result, their templates will not be preloaded but instead AngularJS will attempt to download them over the network upon their first usage.

It would be very cumbersome to maintain all the partial templates embedded inside `index.html` (or similar initial file). During development we would still prefer to keep each template as a separate file. In this case the final `index.html` file should be generated as part of the build process.

Filling in the $templateCache service

Preloading partial templates with the `<script>` directive works OK for small number of templates, but can get out of hand for larger projects. The main issue is that we need to post process the `index.html` file as part of the build. This might become problematic as this file usually contains a substantial amount of hand-written code. Mixing generated and hand-written code in one file is not ideal, and it would be better to put all the templates to preload in a separate, dedicated file. The other problem with the `<script>` directive is that it can't be used to pre-load templates for directives in the unit test environment. Fortunately, there is a remedy for both problems.

We can prepopulate `$templateCache` content as part of application's startup. Each entry in the `$templateCache` service has:a key equal to the template's URL and a value equal to the content of a template (converted and stored as a JavaScript string).

For example, given a template with the following content:

```
<div class='hello'>Hello, {{world}}!</div>
```

And the URL `tpls/hello.tpl.html`, we could fill in the `$templateCache` service as follows:

```
angular.module('app', []).run(function($templateCache){
  $templateCache.put('tpls/hello.tpl.html', '<div
class=\'hello\'>Hello, {{world}}!</div>');
});
```

Adding templates to the cache "by hand" is very inconvenient, as we need to take care of escaping quotes (as shown in the example with the `class` attribute). Once again, the solution here is to use a build-time task that would iterate over templates in your project and generate JavaScript code responsible for filling in `$templateCache`. This is the approach taken by the sample SCRUM application – a dedicated build task generates a module (`templates`) with a `run` block responsible for filling in the `$templateCache`. The `templates` module is then added as a dependency to the application module, alongside with other functional modules as follows:

```
angular.module('app', ['login', 'dashboard', 'projects', 'admin',
'services.breadcrumbs', 'services.i18nNotifications', 'services.
httpRequestTracker', 'directives.crud' 'templates']);
```

 Preloading partial templates into $templateCache is a common practice in the AngularJS community and there is a dedicated Grunt. js task to automate this process: grunt-html2js (https://github. com/karlgoldstein/grunt-html2js). This Grunt.js task was inspired by the build process of the sample SCRUM application described in this book.

In reality, the build system of the sample SCRUM application creates a separate AngularJS module for each and every template. In this case, a template URL is used as a module name as follows:

```
angular.module("header.tpl.html", [])
  .run(["$templateCache", function($templateCache) {
  $templateCache.put("header.tpl.html",
    "<div class=\"navbar\" ng-controller=\"HeaderCtrl\">" +
    . . .
    "</div>");
}]);

angular.module("login/form.tpl.html", [])
  .run(["$templateCache", function($templateCache) {
  $templateCache.put("login/form.tpl.html",
    "<div modal=\"showLoginForm\" close=\"cancelLogin()\">" +
    . . .
    "</div>" +
    "");
}]);
```

All the individual template modules are later put as dependencies of the templates module, so an application can simply depend upon this one module only to include all the templates as follows:

```
angular.module('templates', ['header.tpl.html', 'login/form.tpl.html',
  ...]);
```

Having one AngularJS module for each partial template is very convenient for unit testing, we can precisely control which templates are loaded into the `$templateCache` service for a given test. This assures that individual tests are as isolated as possible.

Combining different preloading techniques

Template preloading, as many other performance-tuning techniques, is a balancing act. By putting templates into the `$templateCache` service, we are minimizing network traffic and increasing UI responsiveness at the expense of memory consumption. Indeed, each entry in the `$templateCache` service consumes additional bytes, their number being proportional to the template's size. This might be problematic in really huge applications (and by this we mean ones with several hundreds of partial templates), especially ones divided into multiple logical sections. Depending on an application and its usage patterns, it might happen that a given user won't visit the majority of pages and thus many partial templates would be preloaded for nothing.

Fortunately, we don't have to apply the all-or-nothing logic to partial templates preloading. We can combine different strategies, for example, preload the most used templates with the initial application load, and then load additional templates on demand. We can also prefetch templates and put them into the `$templateCache` service after application startup. For example, when a user enters a certain section of an application we could preload all the templates for this section.

Optimizing the landing page

Optimizing performance of the initial landing page of any web application is crucial. After all this is the first page that users are going see and get the first impression of our application.

With single-page web applications, it is a bit tricky to get the first page load and display "right". There is usually a substantial amount of the network communication involved, and many scripts need to be downloaded before the JavaScript-powered, rendering engine can start its job. This section covers certain AngularJS-specific techniques that can be used to improve the user's perception of the initial page load and display.

Avoid displaying templates in their unprocessed form

An AngularJS-powered web page needs to download both AngularJS code and application scripts before templates can be processed and rendered. This means that users can momentarily see AngularJS templates in their raw, unprocessed form. Taking the classical "Hello World!" example and assuming that JavaScript takes a long time to download, users would be presented with the following page until scripts are downloaded and ready:

After all the scripts are downloaded the AngularJS application will be kickstarted and the interpolation expression ({{name}}) will be processed to display value defined on a scope. The whole process is less than ideal: not only might people might be surprised seeing strange looking expressions displayed on a page, but they also might notice UI flickering when expressions are replaced with their interpolated values. AngularJS has two directives that help battling those negative UI effects: ng-cloak and ng-bind.

Hiding portions of the DOM with ng-cloak

The ng-cloak directive lets you hide (display:none) parts of the DOM tree until AngularJS is ready to process the whole page and make it live. You can hide any part of the DOM tree by placing the ng-cloak directive on chosen DOM elements as follows:

```
<div ng-controller="HelloCtrl" ng-cloak>
    <h1>Hello, {{name}}!</h1>
</div>
```

If the first page of your application consists of parts, which are mostly dynamic, you may decide to hide content of the whole page by placing the ng-cloak directive on the <body> element. If, on the other hand, the first page is a mixture of dynamic and static content, placing ng-cloak on elements enclosing dynamic parts is a better strategy, as at least users will see static content while AngularJS is being loaded and bootstrapped.

The `ng-cloak` directive works with CSS rules to hide elements containing dynamic content, and show them again when AngularJS is ready, and compile the DOM tree. To hide DOM elements, there is a CSS rule that matches the `ng-cloak` HTML attribute, which is as follows:

```
[ng\:cloak], [ng-cloak], [data-ng-cloak], [x-ng-cloak], .ng-cloak,
.x-ng-cloak {
  display: none;
}
```

Those CSS rules are created dynamically in the main AngularJS script so you don't have to define them by hand.

When AngularJS is loaded and kickstarted it will go over the DOM tree compiling and linking all the directives. The `ng-cloak` directive is both a regular HTML attribute and a directive, that when executed will remove the `ng-cloak` attribute from a DOM element. As a result CSS rules matching the `ng-cloak` attribute won't be applied and a DOM element will be shown.

Hiding individual expressions with ng-bind

The `ng-cloak` directive is a good option for hiding large portions of the DOM, until AngularJS is ready to do its job. While it removes unpleasant UI effects it doesn't change that fact that our users won't see any content until dynamic scripts are fully functional.

Ideally we would like to prerender the first page on the server side and blend it with dynamic JavaScript functionality when AngularJS is ready. Different people are experimenting with various server-side rendering techniques, but as of the time of writing, there is no official AngularJS support for server-side rendering. Still, if the first page of your application consists of mainly static content, you can use the `ng-bind` directive in place of interpolation expressions.

Provided that you've got mostly-static HTML with a couple of interpolation directives use the following code:

```
<div ng-controller="HelloCtrl">
    Hello, {{name}}!
</div>
```

You could replace {{name}} with the `ng-bind` attribute equivalent as follows:

```
<div ng-controller="HelloCtrl">
    Hello, <span ng-bind="name"></span>!
</div>
```

The advantage here is that AngularJS expressions with their curly braces, do not appear in the HTML and as such are never shown to the users in their raw, unprocessed form. Custom attributes (ng-bind) aren't recognized by the browser and are simply ignored till AngularJS has a chance of processing them. By using this technique we could even provide a default value for the expression as part of the initial HTML as follows:

```
<div ng-controller="HelloCtrl">
    Hello, <span ng-bind="name">Your name</span>!
</div>
```

The default value (Your name) will be rendered by a browser before AngularJS has a chance to process the ng-bind directive.

> The technique employing the ng-bind directive, as described here, should be only used on a landing page of an application. In subsequent pages we can safely use interpolation expressions, since AngularJS will be loaded and ready to handle them.

Including AngularJS and application scripts

This section of the book, devoted to optimizing the landing page, wouldn't be complete without touching upon script loading. The topic is even more important if we consider the rising popularity of asynchronous script loaders.

Referencing scripts

Pushing <script> tags to the very bottom of the landing page is generally considered as a good practice. But this pattern, as any other, should be evaluated and only applied if suitable. If the <script> tags are placed at the end of a page, downloading and parsing of JavaScript files won't block other downloads and HTML rendering. This pattern makes a lot of sense in pages with a substantial amount of static content sprinkled with occasional JavaScript code. But for highly dynamic, JavaScript-generated web applications this pattern has a debatable value.

> If a landing page contains a maximum of static content, with very few dynamic parts, put the <script> tags at the very bottom of a page and use the ng-bind directive to hide bindings, while a page is being loaded and processed. Otherwise move the <script> tags to the <head> tag and use the ng-cloak directive.

AngularJS and Asynchronous Module Definition

Asynchronous Module Definition (AMD) specification, popularized by `Require.`
`js` and similar JavaScript libraries, aims to create a set of rules to be followed by reusable JavaScript modules that can be loaded asynchronously. AMD modules can be loaded on demand, taking inter-module dependencies into account. Alternatively, AMD module definitions can be used by an offline-build script to prepare a combined version of all the modules needed for the proper application functioning.

AngularJS has its own module system. While both AngularJS and the AMD specification use the word "module", the same word is used to mean two different things, which are as follows:

- AngularJS modules define how different JavaScript classes and objects should be combined together during application runtime. AngularJS modules don't enforce any script loading strategy. On the contrary, AngularJS expects that all modules are loaded into a browser before an application can be bootstrapped

- AMD modules are mostly concerned with scripts loading. The specification allows you to break down your application into several smaller scripts and load only the needed parts asynchronously, on-the-fly, when needed.

AngularJS modules and AMD modules address different problems and, as such, shouldn't be confused.

In the current version (1.1.x), AngularJS expects that all the scripts making up an application are loaded into a browser before an application is kickstarted. In this setup there is no room for asynchronous, on-demand modules containing application code. It is simply not possible to register new modules nor providers (services, controllers, directives, and so on) after AngularJS application was initialized.

In the current version of AngularJS asynchronous loading of AMD modules can be only used to load JavaScript libraries and application code upfront, before the application is initialized. Loading of additional application code on-the-fly, when needed, is not currently supported.

Lack of on-demand loading of AngularJS modules might sound like a big limitation, but once again, we need to evaluate it in the right context. The AMD modules were created to address several concerns, which are as follows:

- Loading scripts asynchronously, so that a browser is not blocked and can load several different resource types in parallel.

- Loading JavaScript code on demand, as users navigate through an application. This effectively removes the need of loading application code upfront.

- Using module definitions to figure out inter-module dependencies and package-required modules for the production deployment.

You can use AMD modules to load AngularJS library, all the third-party dependencies, and the application's code before bootstrapping your application. The benefit here is that you can load all the scripts asynchronously and avoid blocking processing of the `<script>` tags. This might have a positive effect on the performance of your application (or not!) depending on the number of libraries to be loaded.

While working with AMD modules you can no longer use the `ng-app` directive to bootstrap AngularJS application. The reason is that AngularJS will start to process the DOM tree on the document-ready event. At this point asynchronous modules might not yet be loaded in a browser and AngularJS would try to bootstrap an application before all the required JavaScript files are downloaded. To cover this use case AngularJS provides a manual, JavaScript-based way of bootstrapping an application: `angular.bootstrap`.

 If you decide to use AMD modules in AngularJS application you need to drop the `ng-app` directive and use the `angular.bootstrap` method from JavaScript instead. This way you can control the timing of AngularJS kickstarting the application.

We should also look into the topic of on-demand script loading. This optimization technique trades initial download, startup time, and memory consumption for the increased network traffic. Downloading on-the-fly assumes that JavaScript files making up our application are "big enough" to pay for the additional network time. But usually code written with AngularJS is really, really small as compared to code written with alternative frameworks. This small code base minified and gzipped might result in a really small artifact to download and store in the browser's memory.

The creators of AMD modules recognize that loading of many small files asynchronously will result in a number of XHR calls. The performance penalty incurred by the increased network traffic might be too high and you would be better off loading all the scripts, combined together. This is why there are AMD tools that can analyze inter-module dependencies and package files for deployment. But a well-crafted build script can combine JavaScript files as well. This is particularly easy in AngularJS web applications as AngularJS modules are designed in a way that individual modules can be loaded into a browser in a random order.

Given that the current AngularJS doesn't support on-the-fly loading of application's code, cumbersome setup steps and debatable performance gains we would advise against using asynchronous loaders (Require.js and similar) in AngularJS 1.1.x applications.

Supported browsers

The AngularJS source code is rigorously tested on a **continuous integration** (CI) server. Each code change in the framework triggers a comprehensive battery of unit tests. No code can make it into the framework code base, unless it is accompanied by a corresponding unit test. This strict approach to unit testing assures stability of the framework and its long-term, smooth evolution.

The CI server executes at the time of writing, over 2000 individual tests on different browsers: latest versions of Chrome, Firefox, Safari, and Opera, as well as Internet Explorer version 8, 9, and 10. The number of tests and a list of browsers used for testing should give a good idea of the framework's maturity and solidity. AngularJS is guaranteed to work on the browsers listed here. It is very likely that it also works on other modern browsers not enumerated here (mobile browsers come to mind).

Working with Internet Explorer

It shouldn't come as a surprise that there are certain particularities when it comes to Internet Explorer support. While IE9 and IE10 should work out-of-the-box, supporting IE8 needs special attention.

Normally one would bootstrap an AngularJS application by using the `ng-app="application_name"` directive. Unfortunately, it is not enough for IE8 and we need to add another attribute: `id="ng-app"`.

IE8 won't recognize custom HTML tags if additional steps are not taken. For example, we can't include templates similar to the following one, until we teach IE8 to recognize the `<ng-include>` custom tag:

```
<ng-include="'myInclude.tpl.html'"></ng-include>
```

We can do so by creating custom DOM elements first, as shown in the following code snippet:

```
<head>
  <!--[if lte IE 8]>
    <script>
      document.createElement('ng-include');
```

```
        document.createElement('ng-view');
          . . .
   <![endif]-->
</head>
```

 Custom elements must be created in a script located in the `<head>` section of the page. This is to assure that it runs before the parser sees the new element type.

Of course we can side step aside the whole problem of custom HTML tags by using the attribute-version of the `ng-include` directive as follows:

```
<div ng-include="'myInclude.tpl.html'"></div>
```

Supporting IE7 is even more problematic. To start with, you will need to take care of all the steps required for IE8. But IE7 is not part of the integration build and tests, so there is no guarantee that all the AngularJS functionality will be supported on this browser. On top of this, IE7 lacks many of the APIs commonly present in modern browsers. The best example is JSON API that isn't implemented in IE7, and thus requires a polyfill (`http://bestiejs.github.io/json3/`).

IE6 is not supported.

 AngularJS documentation has a comprehensive section describing all the steps necessary to support IE 8 and IE 7: `http://docs.angularjs.org/guide/ie`.

Summary

This chapter revolved around deployment-related concerns. We started off by discussing various network-related optimization techniques. In general, we can reduce the time a browser is spending on network-related tasks by pushing fewer bytes over the wire and limiting the number of individual requests.

Minification of HTML, CSS, and JavaScript files is a common technique used to trim down the number of bytes to be downloaded by a browser. The specification of the AngularJS Dependency Injection machinery forces us to write our JavaScript code in a minification-safe way. In practice it means that we should use array-style annotations for all the functions that declare dependencies to be resolved by the AngularJS DI subsystem.

We can combine and preload individual, partial templates to limit the number of XHR requests issues by a browser. In this chapter, we saw two different techniques of preloading templates: using the `<script>` directive and the `$templateCache` service.

AngularJS is a framework for creating dynamic pages in a browser and as such heavily relies on JavaScript. Client-side page generation of HTML can only take place after all the required JavaScript libraries are loaded into a browser and ready to use. The undesirable side effect of this approach is that users might see a half-baked screen, while the initial page is being loaded and processed. AngularJS provides two directives that are of great help in removing unpleasant UI effects: `ng-cloak` and `ng-bind`. The `ng-cloak` directive can hide larger portions of the DOM tree, and is mostly useful for applications where the landing page is highly dynamic and there is not much static content to display. In contrast, the `ng-bind` directive works best for the landing pages with mostly static content.

While optimizing user experience for the landing page we should also think about loading order of various page elements. Putting references to JavaScript files at the very bottom of a page is normally considered a good practice, but it might be of little practical value in highly dynamic, JavaScript-driven web applications. Still, if your landing page is mostly static and has substantial amount of HTML, pushing the `<script>` tags to the end of a page might be a good idea. For the pages that are mostly dynamic, loading scripts in the `<head>` tag will often yield better results, especially in conjunction with the `ng-cloak` directive.

This chapter briefly touched upon the asynchronous script loaders. While the AMD pattern is very popular these days, its value is somehow diminished in AngularJS application. The bitter truth is that at the time of this writing, AngularJS didn't play well with asynchronous script loaders, especially when it comes to downloading applications code. Given limited benefits and the cumbersome setup, we would recommend setting up AngularJS applications without AMD modules.

If you have to deploy your applications to a large public, you should very much care about supporting different browsers. The good news is that AngularJS itself works flawlessly on all the major browsers. Internet Explorer support requires a bit of additional setup and all the necessary steps were discussed toward the end of this chapter.

Index

configuration object primer
  about 77
  cache property 77
  headers property 77
  method property 77
  params property 77
  timeout property 77
  transformRequest property 77
  transformResponse property 77
  url property 77
configuration phase, modules 33
constructor-level
  and instance-level methods 97, 98
  behavior, adding to resource objects 99, 100
  custom methods 98, 99
constructor-level
  and instance-level methods 97
content delivery network (CDN) 11
continuous integration (CI) server 333
controller based pagination directive
  creating 258
controller field 219
controller property 256
controllers
  about 56
  testing 67-70
cookie snooping
  preventing 194, 195
CORS 81-83
CPU utilization
  $digest loops, speeding up 303
  DOM access in watch-expression, avoiding
    305, 306
  optimizing 303
  unnecessary watches, removing 306
  unused watches, removing 309
  watch expression, syntax 303-305
Cross-origin resource sharing. *See* **CORS**
cross-site request forgery
  preventing 198
cross-site scripting attacks
  HTML content in AngularJS expressions,
    securing 195
  HTML, sanitizing 196
  preventing 195
  unsafe HTML bindings, allowing 196
currency filter 276

currentUser property 199
custom validation directive
  creating 230, 231
  directive controller 231
  implementing 235
  tests, writing 233, 234

D

Daily workflow 71
data conversion 79
dataSource expression 146, 147
data transformations
  in filters 136
date filter 275, 286
datepicker input directive 239
debugging 74
declarative template view 22, 24, 25
deep-watching mode 313
deferred object 207
dependency injection (DI)
  about 8, 27, 28, 259, 318
  benefits 28, 29
describe function 64
details
  multiple rows, displaying 118, 119
  one row, displaying 117, 118
DI annotations
  pitfalls 322
directive() 218
directive controllers
  about 256, 257
  accordion directive, implementing 263
  accordion directive suite, creating 261
  accordion-group directive, implementing
    263, 264
  and link functions 258
  compilation process 259, 260
  controller based pagination directive,
    creating 258
  dependency injection 259
  in accordion, using 262, 263
  optional, creating 231
  other controllers, access to 260
  parents, searching 232
  priority property, using 256
  requiring 231

Mustache
  URL 290
MVC pattern
  about 12
  Birds eye view 13
  scopes 15
  view 21, 22

N

name field 219
native browser validation
  disabling 157
navigation events 310
network events 310
network-related performance
  improving 318
ngBind
  model values, rendering with 111
ng-bind directive
  about 111, 195
  individual expressions,
      handling with 329, 330
ng-bind-html directive 112, 196, 197
ng-bind-html-unsafe directive 112, 196
ngClass 119
ng-class directive 156
ngClassEven directive 119
ngClassOdd directive 119
ngClick
  using, to handle form submission 162
ng-click directive 186
ng-cloak directive 329
ng-controller directive 13, 15, 178
ngFormController
  about 153
  name attribute, using 154
ng-hide family 113
ng-include directive 114, 174
ng-init attribute 13
ngLocale module 275, 282, 284
ngModel 110
ngModelController
  $error 232
  $formatters 232
  $parsers 232

$setValidity(validationErrorKey, isValid)
      232
  $valid 232
  about 151, 232
  input field validity, tracking 153
  transformation pipeline 152
ng-model directive 291, 294
ngModel directive 141
ngOptions directive
  array data sources, using 146, 147
  dynamic options, providing 146
  examples 146
  object data sources, using 147
ng-repeat directive 116
  about 114-116, 222, 256, 314, 315
  bindings, simplifying 315
  collection, watching 314
ngRepeat directive 115
ngRepeat patterns 117
ngSanitize module 112, 196, 197
ng-show family 113
ngSubmit
  using, to handle form submission 162
ng-switch directive 113
ng-transclude directive 248
non-GET request 192
NotificationsService service 30
novalidate attribute 157
novalidateForm attribute 157
number filter 276

O

OAuth2
  URL 193
object data sources
  using 147
Object.observe 41
objects
  collaborating 27
onLoginDialogClose() method 201
onSelectPage() function 230
openLoginDialog() helper 200, 201
optionBinding expression 146, 148
orderBy filter 125, 129
  sorting with 129-131

W

watched expressions
  size 314
watches
  deep watching, avoiding 312, 313
  number, evaluating 306
  unnecessary watches, removing 306
  unused watches, removing 309
watchExpression 292-303
web application 289
widget
  implementing 228, 229
worldsPercentage function 17

X

XHRrequests
  types 77
XMLHttpRequest (XHR) 75
XSRF. *See* **cross-site request forgery**
XSRF-TOKEN 198
XSS. *See* **cross-site request forgery**
X-XSRF-TOKEN 198

Thank you for buying
Mastering Web Application
Development with AngularJS

About Packt Publishing

Packt, pronounced 'packed', published its first book "*Mastering phpMyAdmin for Effective MySQL Management*" in April 2004 and subsequently continued to specialize in publishing highly focused books on specific technologies and solutions.

Our books and publications share the experiences of your fellow IT professionals in adapting and customizing today's systems, applications, and frameworks. Our solution based books give you the knowledge and power to customize the software and technologies you're using to get the job done. Packt books are more specific and less general than the IT books you have seen in the past. Our unique business model allows us to bring you more focused information, giving you more of what you need to know, and less of what you don't.

Packt is a modern, yet unique publishing company, which focuses on producing quality, cutting-edge books for communities of developers, administrators, and newbies alike. For more information, please visit our website: www.packtpub.com.

About Packt Open Source

In 2010, Packt launched two new brands, Packt Open Source and Packt Enterprise, in order to continue its focus on specialization. This book is part of the Packt Open Source brand, home to books published on software built around Open Source licences, and offering information to anybody from advanced developers to budding web designers. The Open Source brand also runs Packt's Open Source Royalty Scheme, by which Packt gives a royalty to each Open Source project about whose software a book is sold.

Writing for Packt

We welcome all inquiries from people who are interested in authoring. Book proposals should be sent to author@packtpub.com. If your book idea is still at an early stage and you would like to discuss it first before writing a formal book proposal, contact us; one of our commissioning editors will get in touch with you.

We're not just looking for published authors; if you have strong technical skills but no writing experience, our experienced editors can help you develop a writing career, or simply get some additional reward for your expertise.

Instant AngularJS Starter

ISBN: 978-1-78216-676-4   Paperback: 66 pages

A concise guide to start building dynamic web applications with AngularJS, one of the Web's most innovative JavaScript frameworks

1. Learn something new in an Instant! A short, fast, focused guide delivering immediate results.

2. Take a broad look at the capabilities of AngularJS, with in-depth analysis of its key features

3. See how to build a structured MVC-style application that will scale gracefully in real-world applications

4. Examine how popular features are implemented in AngularJS, such as

Backbone.js Cookbook

ISBN: 978-1-78216-272-8   Paperback: 306 pages

Over 80 recipes for creating outstanding web applications with Backbone.js, leveraging MVC and REST architecture principles

1. Easy-to-follow recipes to build dynamic web applications

2. Learn how to integrate with various frontend and mobile frameworks

3. Synchronize data with a RESTful backend and HTML5 local storage

4. Learn how to optimize and test Backbone applications

Please check **www.PacktPub.com** for information on our titles

Backbone.js Testing

ISBN: 978-1-78216-524-8   Paperback: 168 pages

Plan, architect, and develop tests for Backbone.js applications using modern testing principles and practices

1. Create comprehensive test infrastructures

2. Understand and utilize modern frontend testing techniques and libraries

3. Use mocks, spies, and fakes to effortlessly test and observe complex Backbone.js application behavior

4. Automate tests to run from the command line, shell, or practically anywhere

Ext JS 4 Web Application Development Cookbook

ISBN: 978-1-84951-686-0   Paperback: 488 pages

Over 110 easy-to-follow recipes backed up with real-life examples, walking you through basic Ext JS features to advanced application design using Sencha's Ext JS

1. Learn how to build Rich Internet Applications with the latest version of the Ext JS framework in a cookbook style

2. From creating forms to theming your interface, you will learn the building blocks for developing the perfect web application

3. Easy to follow recipes step through practical and detailed examples which are all fully backed up with code, illustrations, and tips

Please check **www.PacktPub.com** for information on our titles

Made in the USA
Lexington, KY
28 February 2014